Creative Photoshop CS4

Digital Illustration and Art Techniques

Derek Lea

ELSEVIER

AMSTERDAM • BOSTON • HEIDELBERG • LONDON • NEW YORK • OXFORD • PARIS
SAN DIEGO • SAN FRANCISCO • SINGAPORE • SYDNEY • TOKYO
Focal Press is an imprint of Elsevier

Focal Press

Focal Press is an imprint of Elsevier
30 Corporate Drive, Suite 400, Burlington, MA 01803, USA
Linacre House, Jordan Hill, Oxford OX2 8DP, UK

Library of Congress Cataloging-in-Publication Data
Application submitted

British Library Cataloguing-in-Publication Data
A catalogue record for this book is available from the British Library.

ISBN: 978-0-240-52134-3

For information on all Focal Press publications
visit our website at www.elsevierdirect.com

09 10 11   12 5 4 3 2 1

Printed in Canada

Contents

For my daughters, Charlotte and Isabella

Foreword

Back in the early 1990s, people in the former Eastern Bloc countries were just getting used to their new freedoms. I was at university, and one of my lecturers commented that after so many years of state-controlled media, television was their window on the world. It's something that's stuck with me, and I think that if television can be a window on the world, then perhaps Photoshop is a window on the imagination.

Round about the same time, in the early 1990s, the first versions of the program were being developed very much with photo editing in mind. I remember getting my first Macintosh and installing an old version of doubtful legality. (Hey, I was just a student!) Having scanned in some photos of a fellow journalism student, and cropping his head into a triangle shape, I began duplicating it across the document and applying different combinations of sharpen, blur, and posterize filters to each version of his now sorry-looking face.

I knew what I created wasn't at all good but others were impressed for roughly 15 minutes, which made me feel like I'd been a bit of an Andy Warhol—for just about that long.

Fast forward 5 or 6 years and while I still couldn't create anything from my own imagination using Photoshop, or even crayon for that matter, I had discovered a man who could. Derek Lea was producing illustrations for us on *Computer Arts* magazine, the likes of which we'd never seen. A colleague of mine at the time suggested that not only should we ask Derek to create an image for us, but what if we asked him to produce a step-by-step article, complete with screenshots, showing how his piece was developed. I called Derek up, he accepted, and I promised him a beer the next time I was in Toronto.

We didn't realize it at the time but we had unleashed a new force in the world of art and illustration. Derek was showing our readers how they could use Photoshop creatively and artistically. Pretty soon other magazines, both within our own group and rivals, picked up on Derek's talent. He's gained illustration clients around the world, written books, and won awards.

His edge is that he won't stand still, and this new edition of his book brings the proof. Despite the magic of Photoshop, digitally retouched images often leave viewers cold, and to combat this, many creatives bring natural media elements into their artwork. For a number of years Derek has been enthusiastically mixing media like watercolors and inks, papers, paint on wood—not to mention found objects—and photographs. The skills involved in combining real-world richness with the flexibility of Photoshop are at your disposal in the new section in this edition.

Some of the commissions I've sent Derek over the years appear in these pages, where you can follow how they were made. Once again it's been an honor to write this foreword. As for my own Photoshop skills, I figured I'd quit while I was ahead back in the 1990s. Derek Lea is your man when it comes to image creation—I stick to the words.

Garrick Webster
Writer and magazine editor
(Former editor of *Computer Arts*, *3D World*, and
Cre@te Online)

Introduction

Photoshop and me

When I first discovered Photoshop, it was 1993. I started a new job as a designer at a clothing company. It was a really horrible job, but at least they bought me a new scanner. In those days a lot of scanners came bundled with Photoshop. The first thing I did when I opened the scanner box was to take the Photoshop 2.5 disks and put them in my jacket pocket. When I got home that night, I installed Photoshop on my Mac IIci at home, and my life began to change. I know it sounds ridiculous, but in hindsight, that was a pivotal moment for me.

I had been working in Adobe Illustrator for a few years by then, but Photoshop seemed like a bottomless pit of creative possibilities. There was so much I could do that at times I didn't even know where to start. I began spending hours and hours every night just experimenting. As a result of this endless experimentation, I gained enough knowledge and experience to successfully land myself a position as a professional retoucher at a photography studio. This meant that I could spend all day, every day, working in Photoshop.

The problem with hiring artists to do retouching work is that although they may be good at it, they get bored. I was no exception. Yes, I was getting good at making cheap jewelry look expensive, and making static cars look like they were in motion, but the novelty of those achievements wore off quickly. Frustrated and bored with my work, yet still in love with Photoshop, I began to deviate from working with photography in the classic sense. On my own time, I started to experiment with different methods to create actual artwork within Photoshop. I began entering contests and then winning awards. The next thing I knew, I had art directors calling with commissions and just like that I became an illustrator. Illustrating digitally allowed me to work all day, every day, within Photoshop. But this time, I wasn't limited to retouching photographs anymore.

Another pivotal point came when my work was noticed by the world's best-selling creative magazine: *Computer Arts*. I was featured in *Computer Arts* and developed a working relationship with them that continues to this day. They started asking me to not only illustrate but to write for them as well. Working with *Computer Arts* really lit a fire under me creatively. The commissions from them constantly demanded new things and challenged me both creatively and technically. I cannot stress the importance of my work with them enough, as my contributions to *Computer Arts* eventually provided the starting point for much of the content you'll find within this book.

Why does the world need another Photoshop book?

As a Photoshop neophyte in the early 1990s, I was always hungry for resource materials. I would scour the local bookstores looking to be informed and inspired. What I noticed then was that Photoshop books, more or less, fell into one of two categories.

There were books that contained beautiful collections of digital art. These books would inspire me with their rich and thought-provoking images, but they lacked detailed instruction on how to achieve those results. Apart from artistic inspiration, these books really didn't offer much to a guy who wanted to learn how.

The other option was books of a more instructional nature. Generally offering lots of information, instruction, helpful hints, and tips, I found these books always lacking in the inspiration department. Granted, I found some useful information in these books, but more often than not, I had to read the chapters on faith alone. Basically, I would hope that afterward, I could do something remarkable on my own with the knowledge they contained, because the imagery within those books never really impressed me.

What you hold in your hands is the book I always wanted. My aim is to inspire you as well as inform you. I have spent a great deal of time perfecting a variety of artistic styles and working practices in Photoshop. And I have also spent a great deal of time producing images that I hope will inspire you to learn. This book is for those of you who not only appreciate art but also want to know in explicit detail how to create it on your own. There seems to be an infinite amount of Photoshop books out there, and many of them are excellent. However, I still haven't found that perfect book that inspires as much as it instructs. After all these years I came to the conclusion that the book I was after didn't exist, so I decided to write it myself. If you are reading this right now, chances are you've been looking for the same thing too.

How to use this book

This book is a series of projects. Each chapter opens with an inspirational image, and the step-by-step instructions required to re-create that image immediately follow. You'll find all of the resource files needed to create each image available for download at www.creativephotoshopthebook.com. This book is written in a nonlinear manner, meaning that you do not have to start at the beginning and progressively work your way toward the end. Each chapter is independent of the others, so you can start wherever you like and move around randomly from one chapter to the next. Pick a chapter with an image that inspires you and follow it through to fruition; it's as simple as that.

This book includes variety not only in style and subject matter but also in technique and working methods. You'll find a vast array of tools, features, and options as you work your way through. Fundamental and essential working methods will appear repeatedly, but each chapter definitely has something unique to offer in terms of both technique and artistic style.

A guitar teacher once told me that the best way to teach someone to play is to get him or her working on something they like straightaway. Forget showing them all of the chords or notes when it makes no sense to them yet, just get them to do something they're interested in. That is the approach I have taken here. You'll get your feet wet while producing something worthwhile, and at varying stages in the process you'll begin to understand the value of what you've done. When knowledge begins to fall into place as you work, and it most certainly will, the proverbial light comes on. At that point, you'll really begin to see the potential of what you've learned. So don't limit yourself to simply finishing the chapters in this book. Try to think of ways that you can take what you've learned from each chapter and use it to create original artwork of your own.

Basic Photoshop knowledge

Creative Photoshop is not a beginner's guide, nor is it exclusively for experts. It falls into that mysterious category in-between often referred to as intermediate. The idea of what an intermediate user does or does not know will often vary depending upon whom you're talking to. I have written this book assuming that you, as the reader, know your way around Photoshop and understand the basics. I am assuming that you have an idea of what the tools do, what layers are, the difference between vectors and pixels, etc.

Numerous functions and tools within Photoshop will be explored in depth, via the step-by-step instructions in the following chapters; however, you'll need to know the basics to follow along with ease. For those of you who possess more ambition than Photoshop know-how, I can certainly relate. As a beginner, I would've picked up this book too. My advice to those who are just starting out is to get familiar with the Photoshop Help menu. Any time you get stuck, you can do a specific search. The results will explain anything you need to know about using a tool or function in Photoshop. Once you find what you're after, you can continue following along where you left off.

Expert tips

In addition to step-by-step instruction and inspirational imagery, you'll find hundreds of expert tips scattered throughout this book. Some of the tips pertain to the instructions on a particular page, but many are additional hints and pieces of advice which will prove useful for almost anything you set out to do within Photoshop. Feel free to flip around the book and examine different tips, just as you would randomly flip from chapter to chapter. Tips are divided into six categories, represented by different icons as follows.

Shortcuts

These time-saving tips will shave hours off of your time spent working. Whether it is a keyboard command or a quicker way of doing something, these tips will allow you to focus on creating, rather than spending all of your time executing certain tasks the long way.

Info

These tips contain useful tidbits and extra information that may not be addressed in the step-by-step instructions within each chapter. Or additional, more detailed, information is provided to accompany a specific stage in the process.

Download files

These tips will point you toward the specific files required to follow along. All project files are available for download in the project files section of the Creative Photoshop Web site.

Caution

Be extremely careful when you see this tip. You are being warned of potential pitfalls and must carefully pay attention to prevent things from going horribly wrong.

CS4

This tip draws your attention to functions, features, and/or tools that are available only within Photoshop CS4.

Creative tips

Creative tips provide valuable hints and advice regarding the artistic process of creating within Photoshop. Everything from unconventional tool usage within Photoshop itself to hints on how to extract resource materials from the physical world surrounding you is included here.

Become part of the Creative Photoshop community

Your exploration into the artistic side of working with Photoshop does not end with this book. Visit the Creative Photoshop Web site and explore the user forum. Share knowledge with, and ask questions of other readers. Be sure to post your finished images within the user forum for everyone else to see. Submit the works you've created by following the chapters here, or post your own work, showcasing your new creative Photoshop skills. Also, don't forget to investigate the cover challenge on the Web site, discussed in the final chapter of this book.

Join the Creative Photoshop community at **www.creativephotoshopthebook.com**.

Acknowledgments

First and foremost, a massive thank you goes out to my wife Janet. She has always encouraged and supported me. Even when I decided that writing a book would be no problem with a brand new baby in the house. And speaking of babies, a big hug and thank you goes out to our wonderful daughter Charlotte. Her mission thus far seems to be teaching the old man that there is much more to life than work. She is succeeding. Another big hug goes out to Charlotte's little sister Isabella. She is the wonderful new addition to the family that coincided with the CS4 edition of this book.

Thanks to my mother for always being supportive in my pursuit of art. She always made sure that I received art supplies every year at Christmas. I hope she plans to continue this tradition with her granddaughters in the years to come.

Thanks to Garrick Webster for writing the foreword to this book, and also for being the person responsible for turning me into a writer all those years ago. I'm glad that I know exactly who to blame for all of this. Thanks to Philip Cheesbrough for changing my life by introducing my art to the entire world; seriously Phil, it may seem insignificant to you but this was a life changer.

A very special thanks to all of the editors I've worked with over the years: Dan Oliver, Andrea Thompson, Paul Newman, Gillian Carson, Vicki Atkinson, Dom Hall, Joseph Russ, Alex Summersby, Shaun Weston, Tom Mugridge, and anyone else that I may have forgotten to name here. Also, a huge thanks goes out to all of the art directors who have been, and in many cases, continue to be a pleasure to work with: Roddy Llewellyn, Esther Lamb, Johann Chan, Matt Harvey, Martha Weaver, Dyan Parro, Domenic Macri, Jeff Kibler, Mike Mansfield, Erik Spooner, Michael Di Ioia, and the dozens of others that I am surely forgetting to mention here.

A special thanks goes out to Rob Wright at the *Toronto Star* newspaper. He was the first person to ever commission my work regularly, and although he claims that he was only exploiting me at the time, this was integral to me becoming a successful illustrator. He just won't admit that he had anything to do with it.

Thanks to Ron and Ann Katz at Kamdar Studios in Toronto. They provided a position for me at their studio that was admittedly demanding, but integral to me learning everything about Photoshop that I know now. Nicest people I ever worked for. Of all the jobs I had, it was the only one that I didn't end up hating.

Thanks to all of my friends and family who have donated their modeling services over the years.

Thank you to Orlando Marques for agreeing to photograph the model that you see on the cover. Thanks to Josie Lee for agreeing to be that model. And thanks to Carla Marques for her excellent work on Josie's hair and makeup. You were all a pleasure to work with, and thank you for donating your services to such a worthy cause.

A very special thanks goes out to Steve Caplin. Every once in a while you come across a truly selfless person, and that is Steve. His enthusiasm for this project and willingness to offer advice were invaluable. Everyone should check out his book *How to Cheat in Photoshop*; it is the perfect companion to this one.

Acknowledgments

A massive thanks goes out to Mike Shaw, senior quality engineer at Adobe. He agreed to go through this manuscript yet again in microscopic detail, which was a daunting task to say the least. His meticulous work was helpful in so many ways that there literally isn't enough room to go into it here. Thanks again Mike.

Also, I'd like to thank Valerie Geary, Emma Baxter, Marie Hooper, Carlin Reagan, and everyone else at Elsevier/Focal Press. You are an exceptional group of people, and every step of this process has been a pleasure because of you. I am looking forward to the next edition.

Thanks to Sean Palmerston at Sonic Unyon Records for arranging permission to use the Nein's press photo. Thanks to my longtime friend Mark DiPietro of Teenage USA Recordings for allowing me to reproduce the Weekend's press photo. Also thanks to Paul O'Connor from www.paulandpaul. co.uk for allowing me to use his lovely model photo as a rcsource.

And finally, a huge thank you goes out to all of you who read my books, tutorials, articles, and like my artwork. Thanks for all of your e-mail messages; I get so many from all you that I cannot possibly reply to all of them. Please don't think that your feedback is unappreciated if I do not reply to you; that is not the case. There just aren't enough hours in each day for me to reply to everyone.

PART ONE

Drawing and Painting

Chapter 1

Painting in Photoshop

The simulation of natural media is always a tricky prospect when working digitally. There are endless filters and niche applications out there that promise convincing results. However, quick fixes and prefab effects often are disappointing. When you are painting digitally, the old saying "If you want something done right, do it yourself" comes to mind, and this is exactly what you'll learn to do in this chapter. Photoshop may not be the first application that you think of when you're setting out to paint. However, a closer look at what Photoshop has to offer in terms of paint tools will reveal that everything you need is there. The tools and features at your disposal are a bottomless pit of options and flexibility. There is a little something in there to suit any user or simulate almost any artistic style.

Equally as valuable when it comes to painting are all of the image compositing tools at your disposal. A successful painted result relies not only on actual brush strokes but also on the way the image is carefully constructed within Photoshop. In this chapter, rather than predictably going through every single appropriate tool and feature like a list, you will focus more on establishing a logical method of working as well as explore the techniques involved in building up a realistic-looking painted file.

You'll need a very basic understanding of the Layers palette and Photoshop's paint tools. You don't need to know anything about image editing tools or selection tools or anything like that. We are simply discussing the act of painting digitally in a methodical way.

What you'll learn in this chapter

Creative Techniques and Working Methods

Think of Photoshop as your digital studio

When it comes to working, Photoshop nicely addresses the issue of translating your traditional tools from within the tactile realm into their digital counterparts. The Swatches palette can be thought of as your artist's palette, allowing you to store all of the colors you're going to use. The Tool Preset picker is a fantastic place to store your brushes as you create them, allowing you to instantly switch back and forth between your own custom tools.

   When you decide to use Photoshop as your digital paint tool, you'll never run out of paint or canvas, you'll never misplace your favorite tool, and you'll never have to worry about cleaning your brushes at the end of the day. As you work your way through this chapter, not only will you learn to paint methodically, but you'll also gain an understanding of the organizational potential within Photoshop.

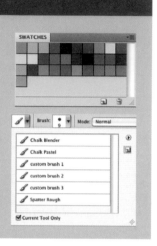

Photoshop Tools, Features, and Functions

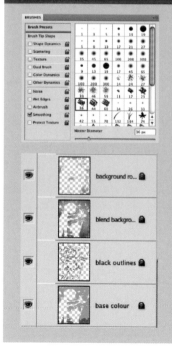

The Brushes palette

The Brushes palette is an excellent resource for crafting convincing and customized brush looks. Whether you want to simply tweak a preset brush tip or create something entirely new with which to paint, everything you need is there.

Painting on layers

Layers are invaluable tools when painting too, as they allow you to separate applications of paint, giving you the flexibility to edit specific painted regions and colors without affecting the rest of your image. In addition to editing advantages, layers also allow you to easily and gently build up brush strokes within your file, resulting in a beautiful and authentic appearance.

1 Open up the sketch.jpg file. Starting with a sketch is an essential part of the process when painting in the tactile realm, and working in Photoshop is no exception. The main difference here is that in this case the sketch is scanned rather than being drawn directly onto the canvas. Once you've opened up the sketch, select the Brush tool. In the Brushes palette, enable the Smoothing option at the left. We're going to work with this option enabled for the entire chapter because smoothing guarantees that your brush strokes contain nice, smooth curves. And that is an essential quality when you want your painting to look convincing.

Default brushes

Although Photoshop is equipped with a plethora of excellent brush libraries, we're going to focus on some simple default brushes capable of producing exceptional results.

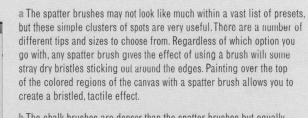

a The spatter brushes may not look like much within a vast list of presets, but these simple clusters of spots are very useful. There are a number of different tips and sizes to choose from. Regardless of which option you go with, any spatter brush gives the effect of using a brush with some stray dry bristles sticking out around the edges. Painting over the top of the colored regions of the canvas with a spatter brush allows you to create a bristled, tactile effect.

b The chalk brushes are denser than the spatter brushes but equally as useful. Strokes created with chalk brushes do not have any stray bristles sticking out the sides, but they do provide a nice rough effect at the beginning and at the ending of each stroke. They are ideal for establishing basic, yet convincing, colored regions within your painting.

c The Dual Brush option is an excellent tool that allows you to combine two different brushes within a single tip. Why do we point out this single feature amid a sea of others? Well, using the Dual Brush option allows you to quickly and easily combine two brush tips to create a new one. We'll explore this feature in detail using custom brush tips later in the chapter.

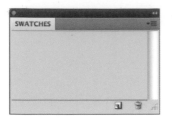

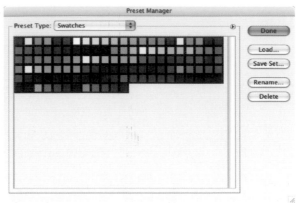

Project files

All of the files needed to follow along with this chapter and create the featured image are available for download on the accompanying Web site in the project files section. Visit www.creativephotoshopthebook.com.

Saving swatches

When you hit upon a combination of swatches you like, it is possible to save them for use at a later date. Simply choose the Save Swatches option from the Swatches Palette menu. This option allows you to name and then save your swatches as a library file. Save this file anywhere you like. You can always reload your saved swatches by choosing the Load Swatches option from the Swatches Palette menu and navigating to your saved preset file. If you place your library file in the presets/swatches folder within the Photoshop program folder, the library will appear within the list at the bottom of the Swatches Palette menu the next time you launch Photoshop.

2 Now, the next thing we're going to do is establish the Swatches palette as our paint palette and fill it with our own set of colors unique to this painting. By doing this, we can return to the Swatches palette and select one of our custom colors at any point later on. Choose Edit > Preset Manager from the menu. Choose Swatches from the Preset Type menu. The Preset Manager can also be accessed via the Swatches Palette menu. If you access it via the Swatches Palette menu, the Preset Type is automatically set to Swatches. When the swatches appear, click on the first swatch and then Shift-click on the last swatch. This will target all of the swatches. When all of the swatches are targeted, click on the Delete button. After they're all deleted, click on the Done button to exit the Preset Manager, and you'll notice that the Swatches palette has been emptied.

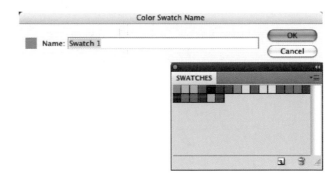

3 When the Swatches palette is empty, click on the Foreground Color swatch in the toolbox to access the picker. Select a new foreground color from the picker and click OK. Move the mouse over the empty area of the Swatches palette. You'll see it temporarily switch to a paint bucket. When you see the paint bucket, click to add the new color to the Swatches palette. Name your new swatch when prompted and then click OK. After naming, the new color is added to the Swatches palette. Use this method to add a variety of colors to the Swatches palette. This method is an excellent way to exercise a little forethought, establishing a predefined color scheme to work within before you begin painting.

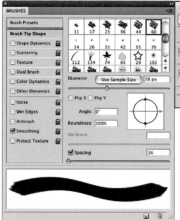

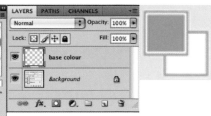

4 After selecting the Brush tool, choose the largest Chalk Brush preset from the Brushes palette. In the Brush Tip Shape section of the Brushes palette, increase the diameter of the brush. You want a large brush here because, first, we want to cover most of the background with color, giving us a new base color other than white. Leave the spacing option enabled but reduce the amount to 1 so that there is no stepping or spaced brush marks present within your strokes. Choose a foreground color from the Swatches palette and click the Create a New Layer button in the Layers palette.

PART TWO: The background and figure outlines

5 Target your new layer in the Layers palette and begin to paint a series of strokes on the new layer. Focus on areas that are the background, as indicated in the sketch. Just start painting some strokes; don't cover the line work of the sketch on the underlying layer; and allow a little white to show through between strokes here and there. Also, increase and decrease the brush diameter in the Brushes palette to accommodate different regions on the canvas. For open areas of the background, use a brush of very large diameter; for tighter regions, such as between the small figure's fingers, use a brush of much smaller diameter.

Brush angles

The chalk family of Brush presets is a perfect example of presets that are ideally suited to right-handed people. Generally, right-handed people paint from bottom left to top right, or from top right to bottom left. The angle of the Chalk Tip presets ensures that right-handed painters working in the typical manner get the majority of the available brush width from each stroke. If you're left handed, try rotating the angle in the Brushes palette. You can specify any angle you like, and this angle will likely vary from preset to preset. Try starting somewhere between 37° and 45° and experiment from there. Besides rotating the angle, you can enable the Flip X option instead. This option flips the brush tip horizontally, creating a mirror image of the brush tip.

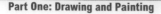

Canvas rotation

In addition to altering the angle of the brush as you paint, Photoshop CS4 provides you with the ability to rotate the canvas. This feature helps to lend an intuitive feel to the process as you work. First, ensure that in the Performance section of the Photoshop preferences, you have enabled OpenGL drawing by checking the appropriate checkbox. Then simply select the Rotate Canvas tool from either the toolbar or the Application bar. After that, all that you need to do is click and drag on the canvas to rotate it. Also note that you can enter a numeric value for your angle or reset the view instantly in the Tool Options bar when this tool is selected.

6 Choose a different color from either the picker or one of your own custom swatches and paint the background area at the bottom of the canvas. When you're finished, choose a black foreground color and create a new layer in the Layers palette. Target the new layer and use the brush to begin tracing the black outlines of the underlying sketch on this new layer. Reduce the opacity of your brush in the Tool Options bar to 50% so that there is a translucent effect as you paint small strokes over the top of each other.

Locking layers

As your file gets bigger, it will become easier and easier to accidentally paint on the wrong layer. To prevent accidentally painting over the wrong layers, simply lock the layers that aren't in use in the Layers palette. Choose the Lock All option just to be safe, and remember you can always go back to an old layer and edit it; you just need to unlock it first.

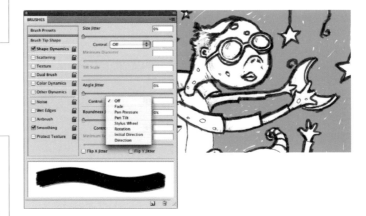

7 Click on the Brush Tip Shape option from the left in the Brushes palette. Use this area often to vary the angle of the brush as you paint. You'll need to tweak the angle frequently when painting around areas such as the heads of these creatures. If you don't adjust the angle at times, there will be areas where the strokes appear too thin compared to others. Click on Shape Dynamics in the Brushes palette to enable Shape Dynamics and then on the Angle Jitter Control menu to view the options.

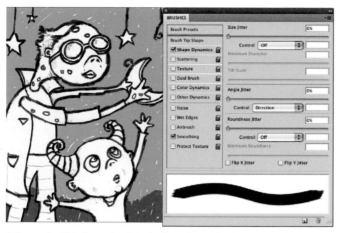

8 Choose the Direction option from the Control menu, but leave the angle jitter amount set to 0. This setting causes your brush to base the angle of the brush tip on the directions of your stroke as you paint them. Because we still want a somewhat smooth edge to the strokes, the amount is set to 0. The more you increase the amount, the rougher the edges of the strokes will appear. By simply enabling the Shape Dynamic function, you can save yourself the trouble of having to constantly adjust the angle as you paint. Finish painting the black outline.

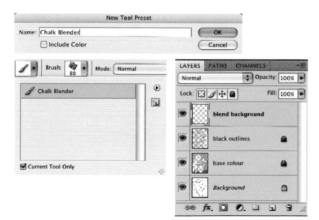

9 Reduce the opacity of your brush to 25% and then open the Tool Preset picker at the far left of the Tool Options bar. Click on the Create New Tool Preset button. When you are prompted, name the tool "Chalk Blender." Disable the Include Color option and click OK. This brush is now added to the preset picker, with all of the Brushes palette options and dynamic functions intact. You can access it directly from the preset picker from now on. Create a new layer in the Layers palette and ensure that it is targeted.

Current tool only

In the Tool Preset picker, you will see an option for the current tool only. Enable this option for the duration of this chapter. Enabling this option will show only presets for the Brush tool rather than the saved presets for all of Photoshop's tools. Because we're only using the Brush tool from here on in, there is no need to view other tool presets.

Canvas rotation shortcuts

You can quickly access the Canvas Rotation tool by pressing the "r" key. After rotating, press the "esc" key to return the canvas rotation to its original state. Also, you can simply hold down the "r" key while you're painting, which will allow you to temporarily access the Canvas Rotation tool. You can click and drag to rotate and then, when finished, release the "r" key to return to the Brush tool.

Brush presets versus tool presets

When you save one of your current brushes as a tool preset, not only are all of your Brushes palette options saved within the preset, but all of your Tool Options bar items are also included. If you wish to save a Brush preset without the Tool Options bar items being included, do so via the Brushes palette menu. Choose New Brush preset from the Brushes Palette menu to save your current brush, adding it to the list of presets in the Brushes palette, independent of the Tool Options bar items.

Using a stylus

You can indeed paint with a mouse, but it can be a laborious task at times. It is certainly not the most intuitive way to paint. If you plan on doing much painting in Photoshop, it is definitely worth investing in a pressure-sensitive tablet and a stylus. Drawing with a pen is much more intuitive and easier than drawing with a mouse. Also, there are a number of dynamic brush functions that work with pressure sensitivity, tip angle, and stylus rotation. So yes, you can complete this chapter and learn about painting by using a mouse. But if you really want control when you paint, a stylus is a worthwhile investment.

10 Use your current brush, set to 25% opacity, to blend the background fill colors together on the new layer; this is precisely why we named the preset "Chalk Blender." Start by painting strokes over the areas where light and dark colors meet. Paint dark strokes over light areas, and vice versa. Go back and forth painting like this until colors begin to blend together. Change the direction of your brush strokes often as well as the size of your brush tip. Also, if using an opacity of 25% does not give you a blend effect that is as smooth as you'd like, try reducing it when necessary.

11 Now add different colors from the Swatches palette into the background here and there, using the same brush on the current layer. Try initially adding them using a higher brush opacity setting, and then blending them into the background using lower opacity settings. A quick way to work is to Alt(PC)/Option(Mac)-click on areas of the canvas to sample color rather than always returning to the Swatches palette. This technique is especially useful when blending as you can sample "in-between" colors. Using this method, if you happen to sample a foreground color that you like, feel free to add it to the Swatches palette so that you can access it later.

12 In the Brush presets section of the Brushes palette, select the spatter 59 pixels Brush Tip preset. Now, in the Brush Tip Shape section of the Brushes palette, adjust the angle of the brush tip until you've achieved the roughest looking stroke possible. In the Tool Options bar, set the opacity of the brush to 35% and the flow value to 15%. Save this new brush as a tool preset and name it Spatter Rough.

13 Create a new layer and use your newly created tool preset to paint over areas of the canvas on this layer. Increase or decrease the opacity as required and use colors from the canvas or the Swatches palette. The goal here is to paint with the new brush over areas that look very smooth. Because of the brush tip and very low flow setting, the resulting strokes will add a rougher, more textured feeling to the areas you paint. Using large brush strokes and bold colors will pronounce the rough effect. Use this effect sparingly as it can tend to overpower an illustration.

Flow

While opacity controls how transparent or solid your strokes will appear on your layer, it is the flow setting that controls how much paint is deposited within a brush stroke as you paint. Reducing the flow drastically, as we've done here, will make the brush stroke look dryer because less paint is deposited. Increasing the flow will cause the bristles that make up the brush stroke to be less pronounced, as the stroke is heavier with paint and the space between the bristles will fill in.

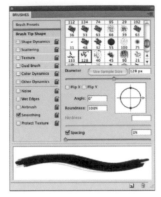

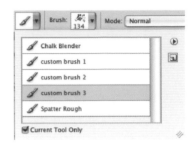

14 Open up the brush1.jpg file. Choose Edit > Define Brush preset from the menu. Name your brush and return to the working file. Choose your new custom brush tip from the end of the list in the Brush Presets section of the Brushes palette. In the Brush Tip Shape section of the Brushes palette, set the spacing to 1. In the Tool Options bar, set the opacity to 50% and the flow to 15%. Save this brush as a new tool preset. Use this same method to open up brush2.jpg and brush3.jpg and save them as new tool presets, using the same spacing, opacity, and flow settings.

Dual brushes

Now we'll explore the Dual Brush function in the Brushes palette, creating entirely new brushes from combinations of custom brush tips.

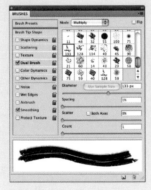

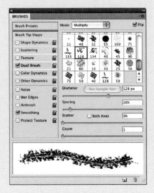

1 Choose your first custom brush from the Tool Preset picker. Then, in the Brushes palette, click on the Dual Brush label at the left side of the palette to enable the Dual Brush function and access the settings.

2 Choose your second custom brush tip from the Tool Preset picker. Enable the Random Brush Flip option at the upper right corner and set the mode to multiply. Increase the spacing to about 20%; you'll notice that it looks like a chalk pastel stroke in the preview.

3 Leave the opacity and flow at their current settings in the Tool Options bar and then add this new dual brush to the Tool Preset picker. Because it looks like a chalk pastel, go ahead and name it something appropriate.

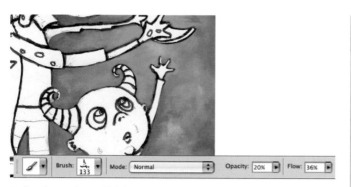

15 Now that you have added three new custom brushes and a new dual brush to the Tool Preset picker, use them to paint some rough strokes on this layer. Just because the presets contain embedded settings for opacity and flow, that doesn't mean that you can't change them each time you use them. Use a variety of colors, brush sizes, opacity, and flow settings to introduce some very real and tactile feeling brush strokes on the current layer. Again, ensure that you do not overdo it as these new brushes, which produce such distinct strokes, can visually overpower the softly blended background quite easily.

Defining brushes

When we created custom brushes from images previously, the images were black and white only. However, you can use a color or grayscale image as well. The advantage to using black and white is that you can get a good idea of how your resulting stroke will look from the image used to define the brush. Black areas will deposit paint and white areas will not. A grayscale brush tip will deposit paint according to the density of black it contains. Color images are converted to grayscale when you define brush tips from them.

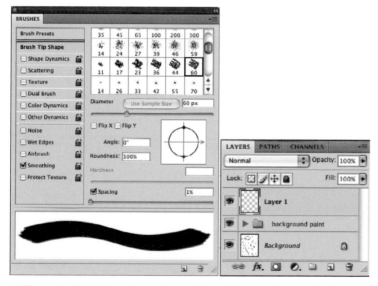

16 When you're finished, target the top layer and then Shift-click on the layer directly above the background layer in the Layers palette. This will target all of your paint layers. Choose Layer > New > Group From Layers from the menu to add them to a group. Because we're going to start painting the other image components, this grouping of layers will help us keep things separate and organized. Create a new layer for the base color of the figures. In the Brushes palette, choose one of the default chalk brush tip presets. Ensure that Smoothing is enabled, and in the Brush Tip Shape section of the palette, reduce the spacing amount to 1.

PART THREE: Painting the figures

17 In the Tool Options bar, set the opacity of the brush to 100% and the flow to 50%. Add this brush to the Tool Preset picker and name it "base color," as we'll be using it to create a flat, colored base for the figures and the stars. Use this brush to add flat color on the new layer in all empty regions of the figures and the stars. Choose colors from the background via the Eyedropper or select them from the Swatches palette. Increase or decrease the size of the brush tip as necessary.

 ### Brush size

When you have a brush selected, a quick way to increase or decrease the brush size incrementally is to use the square bracket keys on the keyboard. Press the "]" key to increase the diameter, or press the "[" key to decrease the diameter. This method is great for adjusting size on the fly.

 ### Importing brushes

The brushes used to create this chapter's painting are in the same archive as the rest of the project files. You can load the brushes by choosing the Load Tool Presets option from the Tool Preset picker's Palette menu. Navigate to the aforementioned file and these brushes will become available in the Tool preset picker.

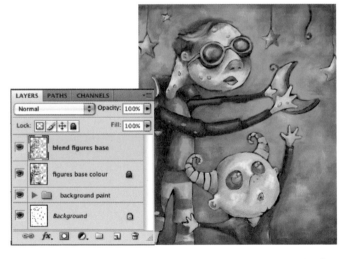

18 Create a new layer and select the Chalk Blender preset that you created earlier from the Tool Preset picker. As you did earlier with the background, blend the colors beneath this layer together with the Chalk Blender preset on your new layer. Hold down Alt(PC)/Option(Mac) to quickly sample colors from the canvas and then paint with your newly sampled colors in the appropriate areas until sharp areas of color begin to blend together on this layer. Feel free to alter brush size and opacity as required. Also, feel free to add new areas of color on this layer to indicate highlights and shadows.

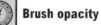

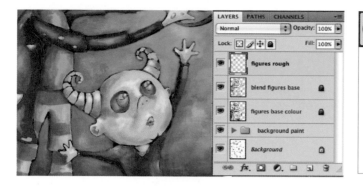

Brush opacity

When you are working with the Brush tool, a quick way to alter the brush opacity is to simply use the number keys on the keyboard as you paint. Just type the opacity value you're after, and it will automatically change in the Tool Options bar.

19 When you are finished adding colors and creating a blending effect on this layer, create a new layer and target it in the Layers palette. Select your Spatter Brush preset from the Tool Preset picker. Now use the spatter brush to paint some light, yet rougher brush strokes over your recently blended areas on the new layer. Use colors sampled from the canvas or from the ever-growing amount of custom swatches in the Swatches palette. Vary the brush size and opacity as needed. You probably want to leave the flow setting fairly low so that the bristles remain pronounced in each stroke.

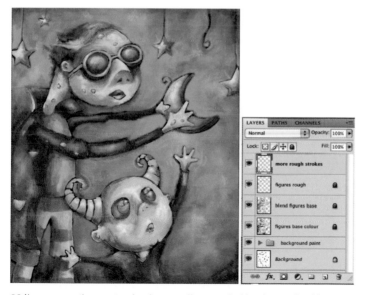

20 Now use your three custom brushes as well as your dual brush to really add a sense of roughness to the figures and the stars by painting with them on the current layer. Vary size, color, and opacity as needed. Also, if you feel like experimenting, yet are worried about making a mistake on your current layer, go ahead and create another layer to work on. This way, if you like the effect, you can keep the layer. If you don't like it, you can always delete the layer or even reduce the opacity to lessen the effect.

PART FOUR: Realistic canvas texture

21 Now, the painting techniques that you've used so far are certainly successful in creating a realistic painterly effect. However, when painting digitally, no matter how convincing your brush strokes are, it is the smooth and perfect surface that ruins the authenticity you've tried so hard to achieve. In order to remedy this, it is often helpful to involve something genuine. Open up the painting.jpg file. This file is a desktop scan, in grayscale, of a section of an oil-painted canvas. We're going to add this to our painted file to make use of the canvas texture and the cracked paint effect.

 Saving tool presets

To save all of the tool presets that you've created from existing brushes as well as custom brushes you've defined from image files, launch the Preset Manager. Choose Tools from the Preset Type menu and click on one of your own brush tools. Hold down the Shift key and click on the remaining brush tools you created. When they are all selected, click on the Save Set button to save them as a separate file on your hard drive. Loading the preset file later on is as simple as clicking the Load button and navigating to your saved preset file.

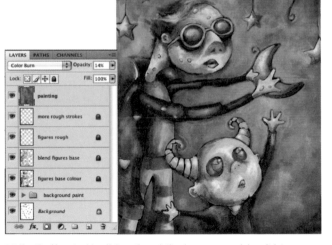

22 Use the Move tool to click on the painting.jpg canvas and drag it into your working file as a new layer while holding down the Shift key. Holding down the Shift key ensures that it lands in your file in the proper position. Ensure that the new grayscale paint layer is at the top of the Layers palette and change the blending mode of the layer to color burn. Reduce the opacity of the layer to 14%, and you'll see that a surface texture effect is beginning to take shape as the colors on the underlying layers become darker and more saturated.

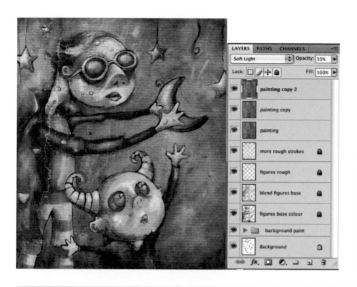

23 Now duplicate your painting layer by dragging it onto the Create a New Layer button at the bottom of the Layers palette. Change the blending mode of your duplicate layer to vivid light and increase the opacity to 35%. Finally, duplicate your current painting copy layer and then change the blending mode of the recently duplicated layer to soft light to intensify the surface texture effect within the image.

Examining your technique

Now that you're finished, let's take a closer look at some of the things that make this the ideal process for painting digitally.

a When you customize your own brushes, and especially when you create your own brush tips from images, saving your tool presets is a very good idea because it ensures that they are always available to you. And saving them as a preset library file ensures that you can access them at any point later on, within this or any other Photoshop file.

b Building up your own custom swatches in the Swatches palette is the digital equivalent of a handheld painter's palette. Your colors will always be available to you here. Choose the Save Swatches option from the Swatches Palette menu to save them as a file on your hard drive. You can load them or replace an existing set of swatches by choosing either option from the Swatches Palette menu and navigating to your saved file. Swatches can also be saved or loaded in the Preset Manager.

c Keeping different elements and different stages in the process separated on a series of layers allows you enough flexibility to revisit things later and alter them. You can target individual layers and edit or mask their contents. Also, you can insert adjustment layers between layers to affect only certain portions of the composition.

d Using a real-world surface texture is an excellent way to add another level of authenticity to your painting. The simple grayscale scan used here on a series of layers helps to remedy the ultrasmooth digital canvas surface, making it more realistic in the end.

A more realistic approach

This method of painting is certainly not limited to the subject matter or rough style that was covered previously in this chapter. You can apply this method to the subject of your choice and paint in any style that comes naturally. Here I decided to give traditional portraiture a try. Rather than starting with a sketch, I placed a photograph on an underlying layer and used it as a guide while I was working. Unlike the sketch, it proved to be too distracting if it was visible the entire time. So I simply enabled the visibility of the photo periodically to stay on track. Another thing to consider when you're after a more realistic approach is the fact that you'll need to spend a lot more time blending colors together to make smooth, seamless transitions.

Virtual life drawing

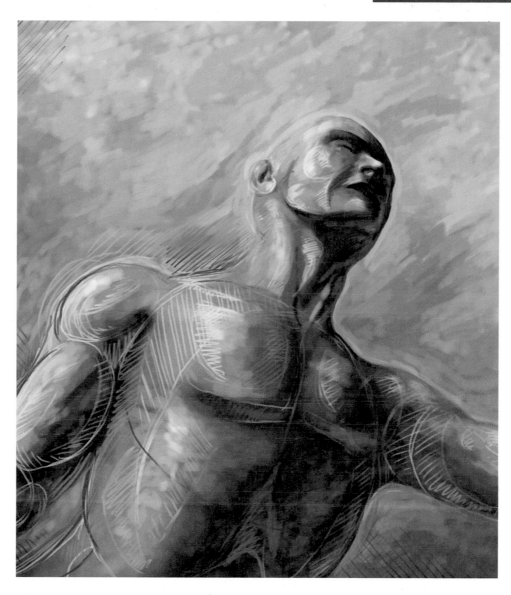

Rather than sitting in a studio with charcoal, paper, and an actual model, why not replicate the process on your laptop or PC? I launched Poser and rendered a male figure using the pose shown here and a couple of colored lights. I then rendered the file and opened it in Photoshop. This acted as my base layer. Then, I employed the techniques explained on the previous pages across a series of layers to create this impressionistic figure painting.

Chapter 2

Creating Characters with Shape Layers

When it comes to creating flat, sharp, and colorful characters in Photoshop, it is always advantageous to involve the use of vectors. Vectors are mathematical objects that define shapes or curves. Unlike pixels, vectors are resolution independent. This means that they can be scaled to any size, edited, or transformed an infinite amount of times without any deterioration of clarity or loss of detail. In Photoshop, vector art can be integrated into your image files in the form of paths, vector masks, or shape layers.

Different vector tools and functions are suited to a variety of tasks in Photoshop. In our case, the creation of whimsical character faces is ideally suited to working with shape layers. A shape layer can be created with the Pen tool or any of the shape tools. What causes one of these tools to create a shape layer, rather than a path, is the designation that you choose in the Tool Options bar. Shape layers allow you to build up stacks of resolution-independent shapes that are absolutely perfect for tasks like creating faces. The available preset shapes are excellent building blocks for features and the Pen tool affords you the flexibility to create any custom shape you desire.

Once you create a number of shape layers, the flexibility doesn't end there. When you select more than one shape on a layer, you'll notice that there are a number of options available for creating compound shapes. You can add, subtract, intersect, and exclude shapes as well as perform a plethora of alignment options to get your complicated features placed exactly where you want them on the face.

Like traditional layers, shape layers can also be linked or grouped so that multiple elements across a series of layers can be moved, rotated, or scaled together at the same time. No matter what style of face you're creating, when it comes to flexibility and versatility, shape layers are the absolute key to success.

DIFFICULTY 2.0/5 You'll need a basic understanding of how to draw and edit Bezier curves. A slight familiarity with shape or path area operations will make things easier. Knowledge of the basic differences between tools like the Path Selection tool and the Direct Selection tool will be beneficial.

What you'll learn in this chapter

Creative Techniques and Working Methods

Creating from virtually nothing

Building a character like those shown here is the result of piecing together the right ingredients and knowing just how to edit select components to make them unique. The predefined shapes we'll use are basic. The shapes we'll create with the Pen tool are nothing extravagant. However, the method of construction and the ability to visualize the result are important. As you work your way through the chapter, the logic will fall into place and you'll get a feel for how simple regions of sharp color, on a series of layers, can act together to create an expressive character with a unique personality.

Cut your work in half

Obviously, details like eyes or antennas are things that appear more than once on the face. Just because there are two eyes or two antennas, it doesn't mean that you must carefully construct each instance. You'll learn how to logically group the shape layers that make up each feature, duplicate them, and flip or alter specific details to make these features look as if they belong together on the face or head.

Photoshop Tools, Features, and Functions

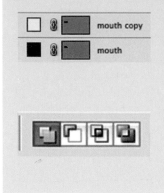

Duplicate shape layers

Shape layers are wonderful and flexible resources. However, it is important not to underestimate the potential that lies within existing shape layers. In this chapter, you'll learn how to duplicate shape layers and edit them with a clear intent to make something entirely new out of them. Using them as building blocks for new shapes can provide you with a starting point that already has part of the work done for you.

Area operations

Whether you want to combine two shape components together or use one shape to punch a hole in another, shape area operations are an essential part of the procedure. The results will be neater and more versatile when you use basic shapes and area operations together rather than trying to draw the resulting shape on your own.

1 The first thing you need to do is open up the background.jpg file. This brightly colored painting provides an ideal backdrop for the bright, whimsical characters we're about to create in this chapter. All of your shape layers will be added to this file to create a plethora of strange creatures. To get started, select the Pen tool. Then, in the Tool Options bar, ensure that the Shape Layers function is enabled. Do this by clicking on the button at the left. Press "d" on the keyboard to set your foreground color to black and zoom in closer on a section of the background.

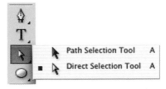 **Project files**

All of the files needed to follow along with this chapter and create the featured image are available for download on the accompanying Web site in the project files section. Visit www.creativephotoshopthebook.com.

Path Selection Tool   A

Direct Selection Tool   A

2 Click and drag with the Pen tool to create a curved point. Move the mouse, then click and drag again to create another curved point joined to the previous point by a line segment. Repeat this method, making your way back to the original point. Click and drag on the original starting point to close the shape. Once the shape is closed, select the Direct Selection tool. Use the Direct Selection tool to click on the individual points that make up your curved shape. When you click on a point, the Bezier handles that define that point will become visible.

3 Click and drag the Bezier handles to reshape the curves and move the points with the Direct Selection tool until you have achieved the desired shape. When you're finished, select the Pen tool again and click on the Foreground Color swatch in the toolbar to launch the picker. Choose a blue color from the picker to change the foreground color to blue. Ensure that the Create New Shape Area option is selected in the Tool Options bar, and then use the previous method to create a smaller blue shape on a new layer. Edit the points and curves with the Direct Selection tool using the previous method.

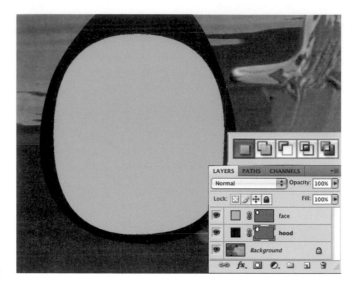

Affect which shape layer?

You've probably noticed by now that before you create a shape layer, I instruct you to set the foreground color in the toolbar first, specifying a fill color for your new layer before you create it. However, you've probably noticed that there is a Color swatch in the Tool Options bar that allows you to specify the fill color of a shape layer too. Before you choose a different color from the swatch in the Tool Options bar, you need to pay attention to a small Chain-Link button to the left of it. When enabled, this option affects the properties of the current layer, the layer you already created. So when this option is enabled, changing the color in the Tool Options bar will affect your already existing layer. If you disable this option, your current shape layer will remain unaffected when you choose a new color. But any new shape layer you create will use the new color selected in the Tool Options bar.

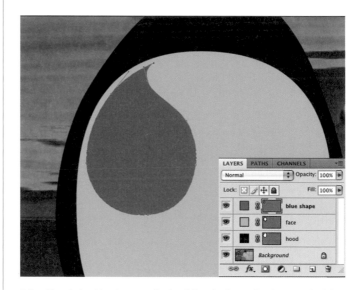

4 Specify a darker blue foreground color. Select the Pen tool and ensure that it is set to create a new shape layer in the Tool Options bar. This time, when starting your shape, just click once instead of clicking and dragging, then move the mouse and click and drag. This will create an initial sharp or corner point, and your second point will define the curvature of the line. Click and drag to add more curved points and then, when returning to your starting point, just click. By clicking once on the starting point, you ensure that this point remains sharp, not curved.

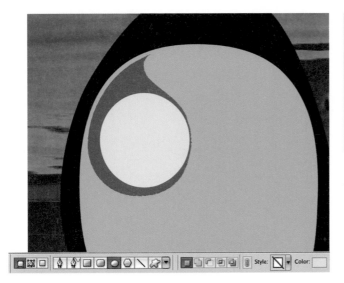

5 In the Tool Options bar, select the Ellipse tool and then disable the Chain-Link button by clicking on it, so that the new color we choose from the swatch in the Tool Options bar is not applied to the currently targeted shape layer. Click the Color swatch in the Tool Options bar and select a dirty yellow color from the picker. Ensure that the Create New Shape Layer option is enabled and then click and drag while holding down the Shift key to create a perfectly circular shape layer. You can reposition the entire shape layer with the Move tool.

Which tool do I use?

Using the Move tool will allow you to move an entire shape layer around on the canvas. However, if you want to move your shapes around within your layer, you'll need to use the Path Selection tool. Simply click on the shape you wish to move and drag it with the Path Selection tool. This is especially useful when your shape layer contains more than one shape and you wish to move shapes independently of each other.

6 Drag the shape layer onto the Create a New Layer button in the Layers palette to duplicate it. Target the original layer (the one beneath the copy) in the Layers palette. Choose Edit > Free-Transform from the menu and drag the corner points of the box outward to increase the size, and alter the shape of the shape layer. Press the Enter key to apply the transformation. In the Tool Options bar, enable the Chain-Link button to affect the current layer. Then specify a black fill color via the swatch in the Tool Options bar.

7 Target the top layer in the Layers palette so that your next layer will be created above it. Again, use the Ellipse tool to draw a smaller circle in his eye area. Ensure that the Create New Shape Layer option is enabled as you create the circle. Next, change the fill color of the new layer to red via the Color swatch in the Tool Options bar. With this new layer targeted, choose the stroke effect from the Layer Styles menu at the bottom of the Layers palette. Add a darker red stroke to the outside of the circle.

Finish, group, duplicate, and flip

Complete the eye area and add a cheek detail. Then flip the artwork to the other side of his face.

1 Use the same methods to create two new shape layers: one containing a black pupil shape and another containing a purple cheek shape. Target all of the eye and cheek shape layers in the Layers palette. Type Control(PC)Command(Mac)-g to group them.

2 Select the Move tool and ensure that your group is targeted. Hold down the Alt(PC)/Option(Mac) and the Shift key as you drag the artwork to the right side of his face creating a duplicate of the group, aligned horizontally.

3 Choose Edit>Transform>Flip Horizontal from the menu to horizontally flip your duplicated group. Expand the duplicated group in the Layers palette and target the red iris layer. Shift-drag to the right on the canvas with the Move tool. Repeat this process with the duplicated pupil shape layer. This will remedy his cross-eyed appearance.

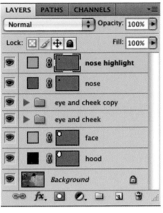

8 Collapse the group in the Layers palette. Use the Eyedropper tool to click on the dark blue area around his eye, sampling it as the current foreground color. Use the Pen tool to create a new shape layer in the middle of his face. Carefully draw a nose shape with the Pen tool. Take your time, clicking oncc to create sharp points, clicking and dragging to create curved points. Edit the shape with the Direct Selection tool wherever necessary. Next, select the Ellipse tool and draw a lighter blue ellipse over his nose on a new shape layer.

Subtracting and combining shapes

Now we'll explore how multiple shapes can be used together within a single shape layer, producing a nice nostril highlight at the same time.

1 Select the Ellipse tool, and select the Create New Shape Layer function in the Tool Options bar. Crcate a light blue ellipse on the canvas, over his nostril, as a new shape layer. Use the Path Selection tool to reposition it if necessary.

2 Use the Path Selection tool to drag the shape to the right and down a little while holding down the Alt(PC)/Option(Mac) key, duplicating it. With the duplicate shape selected, click on the Subtract from Shape Area button in the Tool Options bar.

3 Click the Combine button to create a single shape resulting from the subtract operation. Alt(PC)/Option(Mac)-drag this shape to the right with the Path Selection tool. Choose Edit>Transform Path>Flip Horizontal from the menu. Press Enter and adjust the positioning of the flipped duplicate shape if necessary.

9 Set the foreground color to black. Select the Pen tool and ensure that the Create New Shape Area option is enabled. Draw a closed shape to indicate his mouth. Click and drag to create a series of curved points and use the Direct Selection tool to edit your points and curves until the mouth shape is looking just right. Duplicate the mouth shape layer in the Layers palette so that there are now two of them. Target the duplicate mouth layer and press the Link button in the Tool Options bar so that when you change the color, this layer will be affected.

 ### Switching to a selection tool

When you are working with the Pen tool, you can temporarily switch to the Direct Selection tool by holding down the Control(PC)/Command(Mac) key. When you are working with a shape tool, holding down the Control(PC)Command(Mac) key will temporarily switch your tool to the Path Selection tool. Releasing the Control(PC)Command(Mac) key will revert back to your original tool.

10 Click the Color swatch in the Tool Options bar. When the picker opens, move the mouse out over the yellow part of the eye on the canvas and then click to select this yellow as the fill color for this shape layer. Click OK and select the Pen tool. Choose the Intersect Shape Areas option in the Tool Options bar and then draw a closed shape that contains two fangs that overlap the mouth area. As you draw, you'll see the layer content disappear and then only reappear in areas where the new shape overlaps the existing shape within the current shape layer.

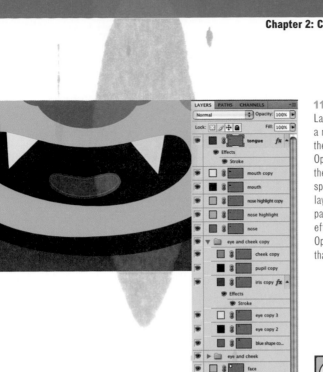

11 Use the Pen tool with the Create New Shape Layer option enabled to draw a tongue shape on a new shape layer that sits within his mouth on the canvas. Click the Color swatch in the Tool Options bar and when the picker opens, click on the red area of one of his eyes in the image to specify that as the fill color for your new shape layer. Expand one of your groups in the Layers palette. Find one of the layers with the stroke effect applied to it. Hold down the Alt(PC)/ Option(Mac) key and then drag the effect from that layer onto your new layer, copying it.

Combining shape components

The shape area functions in the Tool Options bar provide nearly everything you need to create diverse and unique composite shapes. However, there may be instances where you wish the visible results were indicative of one actual shape or perhaps you wish to perform different shape area functions on the resulting shape. In these cases, simply click on the Combine button in the Tool Options bar to change the group of shape components into a single, editable shape. Be cautious when combining because once you combine the shape components, they are no longer editable as separate components. If you keep the components separate you still have the option of altering the physical qualities of the shape as well as changing any shape area functions applied to your individual shapes.

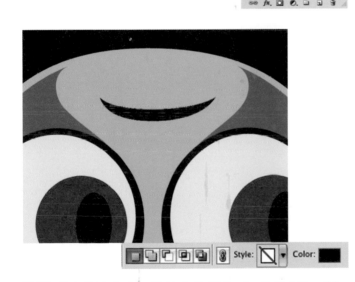

12 If the Chain-Link button is enabled in the Tool Options bar, disable it. Then click on the Color swatch in the Tool Options bar and select black from the picker. If you do this while the Chain-Link button is enabled, it will change the color of your tongue shape layer. Disabling it ensures that only a new shape layer will contain black. Also, ensure that you set the style setting back to none; otherwise, the next layer you create will have the previous layer's stroke style applied to it. Use the Pen tool with the Create New Shape Layer option enabled to draw a forehead wrinkle shape.

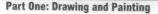

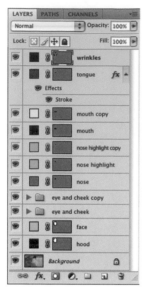

13 Now select the Add to Shape Area function and draw some more closed shape components to indicate wrinkles on his forehead and the left side of his face. Use the Path Selection tool to select one of the wrinkle shape components that you created at the left. Then, hold down the Shift key and click on the other wrinkle shape components at the left to select them as well. While holding down the Alt(PC)/Option(Mac) key, click on the selected shape components and drag them to the other side of the face, copying them.

 Custom shapes

When you have spent some time creating a shape of your own with the Pen tool or by editing a preset shape, you may wish to save it for use later on. To do this, simply select the shape with the Path Selection tool and choose Edit>Define Custom Shape from the menu. This will allow you to name the shape and save it. The next time you select the Custom Shape tool, your custom shape will appear in the list of presets available in the Tool Options bar.

14 Now, to flip your duplicated wrinkles over, choose Edit>Transform Path>Flip Horizontal from the menu so that they look like they belong on the right side of the face. Reposition them if necessary with the Path Selection tool. Your top layer is currently targeted in the Layers palette. Hold down the Shift key and click on the shape layer directly above the background layer. This targets the new layer, the top layer, and all layers and groups in-between. Now choose Layer>New>Group From Layers from the menu to add all of the targeted contents to a single group.

PART TWO: The second character

15 It is likely that by now you are becoming familiar with the process of creating new shape layers. So let's put that familiarity to work again. Navigate to another area of the canvas. Use the Pen tool, set to Create New Shape Layer to draw the shape of an alien's head. Don't worry about the fill color of your layer at this point. Next, select the Add to Shape Area option in the Tool Options bar. Draw an ear at the left of his head. Then use the Path Selection tool to Alt(PC)/Option(Mac) + Shift-drag his ear to the other side of the head, copying it.

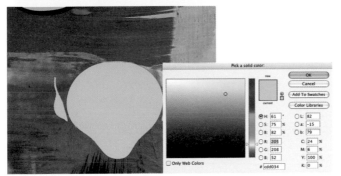

16 Flip the copied shape component horizontally via the same methods you've previously used for flipping other shape components. Use the Path Selection tool to position it exactly where you want it on the layer. Now, double-click your shape layer thumbnail in the Layers palette. This will launch the picker. Choose a new, light green fill color for your layer and click OK. You can change the fill color of any shape layer at any point by double-clicking the layer thumbnail. As you can see now, there are numerous ways to specify and edit the fill colors of your shape layers.

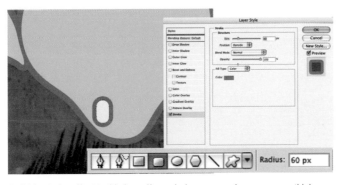

17 Add a stroke effect to this layer. Use a darker green color, a generous thickness, and position it outside so that it surrounds the exterior of the shape components. Select the rounded rectangle shape tool in the Tool Options bar. Set the radius very high. Then click and drag to create a tooth shape on a new shape layer. Change the fill color of the layer to light yellow. This layer automatically has the previous stroke effect applied to it. Double-click the effect in the Layers palette to edit it, reducing the size of the stroke.

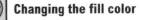

Changing the fill color

Another way to quickly change the fill color of a shape layer is to start by targeting a shape layer in the Layers palette. Next, choose a foreground color from the picker. Then type Alt(PC)/Option(Mac)-Delete on the keyboard to fill the layer with the new foreground color.

18 Use the Path Selection tool to select your tooth shape component and Alt(PC)/Option(Mac)-drag it to the right to copy it within the shape layer. Repeat the process again until there are three teeth on this layer. Target all three shape components and then click on the Align Vertical Centers button in the Tool Options bar to align the shape components. Use the Pen tool to create an antenna shape on the left side of the head, on a new, different colored shape layer. Ensure the Link button is disabled in the Tool Options bar, and set the style back to none in the style picker.

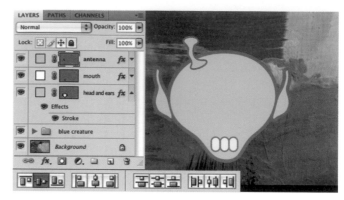

Build half of the face
Put your new shape layer skills to good use as you create all of the details for the left side of the face on a series of shape layers.

1 Use the methods employed so far to create a new, red, elliptical shape layer. Choose Edit>Free>Transform Path from the menu. Drag the corner points to resize, then click and drag outside of the box to rotate. Press Enter to apply the transformation.

2 Use this method to create a smaller, orange ellipse shape layer on top of the red one. Then repeat the process again, creating a smaller, black ellipse shape layer. Create a white ellipse shape layer over top of the black ellipse and reduce the layer opacity.

3 Use the Pen tool, the Ellipse tool, and the skills you've learned so far to create the rest of his face details on a series of new shape layers until the left side of his face is complete. Target all of these layers, including the antenna layer, and add them to a new group.

19 Ensure that your group is targeted in the Layers palette and select the Move tool. Hold down the Alt(PC)/Option(Mac) and Shift keys as you click on the canvas and drag to the right, duplicating the group and ensuring that it stays aligned vertically with the previous group. Then choose Edit>Transform>Flip Horizontal from the menu to flip the group. Use the Move tool or the arrow keys on the keyboard to adjust the positioning on the canvas if necessary. Target all of the layers and groups that make up the alien character in the Layers palette and add them to a new group.

PART THREE: The third character

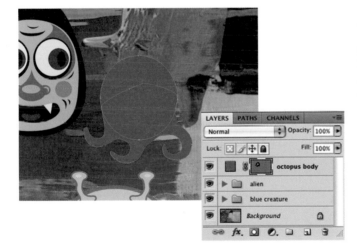

Transforming and flipping artwork

You don't always have to go to the Edit menu each time you wish to perform a transformation or flip a layer, shape component, or group. Simply type Control/Command-t to activate the Free-Transform command. You'll see the bounding box appear, allowing you to transform your object, layer, or group. While the bounding box is present, right-click(PC)/Control-click(Mac) within the box to access a pop-up menu. Alongside other options, you'll be able to flip your artwork by choosing the appropriate option from the menu. As always, pressing Enter will apply the transformation.

20 Now that you've created two distinctly different characters out of shape layers, storing each in a group of its own, create one more for the sake of diversity. Use the Pen tool to click and drag, creating a closed object that resembles tentacles on a new shape layer. Specify a green fill color and then switch to the Ellipse tool. Ensure that the Add to Shape Area function is enabled in the Tool Options bar. Click and drag to create a large ellipse that overlaps the top of the tentacles shape on the same layer, creating a strange octopus body.

21 Again, as you've done with the previous two characters, create a series of new shape layers to add the character's essential features and details to the file. All of the methods are the same as before. Even the mouth, although it has more teeth, can be created by using the same methods that you used to create the blue creature's mouth earlier on. When you're finished, target all of the shape layers that make up the octopus in the Layers palette and add them to a new group.

 Examine the downloaded files

At this point in the chapter, you should have the three main characters completed and organized into groups. Everything you need to know to effectively create the characters has been outlined on the previous pages. However, if you still find yourself confused by a small detail or are scratching your head over something, have a look at the sample files included in the archive you downloaded. The files are named sample-1.psd, sample-2.psd, and sample-3.psd. Each file contains a single character group and you can inspect the shape layers and components in detail within these files.

22 Now, just because your finished creatures are neatly organized into groups in the Layers palette, it doesn't mean that you can't add more shape layers within a group or edit existing ones. Here, new shape layers were added to the octopus group as well as the alien group. Spots were added to the tentacles of the octopus on a new shape layer and to the alien's forehead using the same method. Each new layer was placed in the appropriate group, ensuring that the Layers palette remained organized.

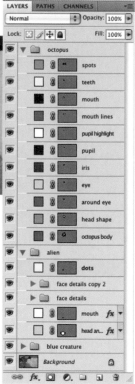

PART FOUR: Duplicates and variations

23 Duplicate the octopus group. Use Free-Transform to rotate, resize, and move it to another location on the canvas. Double-click individual layers within the group and change their fill colors. Delete the shape layers that make up his mouth by dragging them into the trash in the Layers palette. Then add a new shape layer that contains a small black ellipse to the group, creating a new mouth with a different facial expression. Use this method to create a number of different octopus groups on the canvas. Alter colors and shape layers as you see fit.

24 Continue to make duplicates of your groups, moving them to different areas of the canvas, and using Free-Transform to rotate and resize your groups. Move them up and down within the Layers palette so that some characters are overlapping others. Try varying blending modes of your duplicate groups here and there. Also experiment with reduced opacity to make some of them less prominent.

25 Duplicate the blue creature group. Move it to another location and use Free-Transform to resize and rotate the group. Repeat this process over and over, adding a number of blue creatures to the scene. Inside some of your groups, disable the visibility of some of the layers or delete them so that only select portions of the characters' faces remain visible. Like you did previously with the octopus, move duplicate groups up and down within the Layers palette altering the blending modes and opacity settings of entire groups as you go.

 Hiding versus deleting

When you are creating duplicate character groups and wish to remove layers from the group, disable them rather than delete them. You can disable the visibility of any layers you wish to hide, and when you transform an entire group, these hidden layers will be transformed alongside the rest. This is a better option than deleting as it gives you the option of making the layers visible again if you change your mind later on.

26 Use these methods to introduce a variety of copied alien groups into the image as well. Alter blending modes, opacity, and try disabling the visibility of some layers. Try combining some of your duplicates into groups as well. Here, this creature was created by adding a blue creature group and an octopus group into a new group. The blue creature was positioned on top of the octopus and the fill color of the octopus layer was changed to match that of the blue creature. Then, the blending mode of the new group was changed to luminosity.

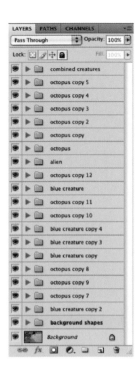

27 Now that you're finished with the character groups, apply the same methods you've used so far to create some shape layers out of basic shape combinations. Use the Subtract and Add to Shape Area options freely. Also, have some fun with different blending modes, color fills, and layer opacity settings. Drag all of the new shape layers beneath the character groups in the Layers palette, so that the new shape layers are used to enhance the painted background rather than overlapping the creatures. Place the new shape layers in a group of their own, just to keep the Layers palette organized.

Examining your shape layer masterpiece

Now that you're finished creating the image, let's take a final look at some of the exceptional features and techniques involved.

a By duplicating a group of features, you're not only cutting your work in half, but you are effectively creating an identical set of features for the other side of the face.

b One great thing about shape layers is that you can change the fill color at any point, so duplicate groups can look diverse rather than monotonous.

c Replacing something as simple as the shape layers that make up the mouth in a duplicate group can completely change the emotion of your character.

d When you're spreading duplicate groups around the canvas, disabling the visibility of base layers within a group can result in ghostly, floating creatures rather than identical duplicates.

e Experimenting with blending modes allows you to use your characters in subtle ways. In this case, the creature enhances the background using only its luminosity.

Get creative with subject matter

Here is another image that was created using the same methods. It is quite similar stylistically, but the subject is a little different. There is a lot you can do when you begin experimenting with shape layers, groups, blending modes, and underlying textures. Subject matter can be anything you like; you're only limited by your imagination.

Try to deviate from basic shapes

In order to create truly unique characters, you'll need to get away from basic preset shapes and master the process of drawing with the Pen tool. It takes a bit of practice, but as you can see here, the results are worth it. It may take a while before you're creating detailed slugs like the creature shown here, but mastering the Pen tool will help you achieve other tasks in Photoshop with ease. Path drawing skills also prove valuable outside of Photoshop and are of great assistance when you're working within a vector art program like Adobe Illustrator.

Chapter 3

Graffiti Spray Paint Art

To create realistic graffiti art, you no longer have to hit the streets with a backpack full of spray cans, looking for that secluded area where you won't get caught. You don't need to place yourself at the mercy of the elements, and you don't need to break the law. All that you need these days is a digital photo, a scanned drawing of your plan, and a little Photoshop know-how.

Photoshop offers all of the tools necessary to add innovative digital graffiti to any photographed scene. Brushes, selections, and layer blending modes are essential Photoshop tools to get the job done. In this chapter, the standout features are the Brush tool's Airbrush option and flow settings. Above all other features, these are key ingredients in producing convincing graffiti art. These two features give the Brush tool its authentic spray paint feel and allow you to produce convincing spray paint results.

However, in order to make things feel real, you'll also need to incorporate some real-world imperfections. While producing real spray paint art, you get annoying drips littering your masterpiece when you apply too much paint to a single area at once. And although this imperfection is something you'd try to avoid in the real world, here, in the digital realm, this imperfection is required to lend authenticity to your art.

For the authentic spray paint look, you'll need to incorporate the real thing. In this particular case, I've incorporated some basic paint drips, done traditionally, into the digital composition, giving it an authentic feel. And rather than creating a digital backdrop for the graffiti art, it is painted directly on top of a photo of a bare wall, using layer blending modes to make it look as if it really belongs there. So remember, when creating realistic graffiti in Photoshop, it is not just paint techniques that you'll need to employ but innovative image composition methods as well.

DIFFICULTY 2.0/5 A basic understanding of the Brush tool and Layers palette will make this chapter easier for you. Experience in painting with a mouse will be your greatest asset here, as the most difficult part will be actually producing the strokes that you intend to make. It takes practice. If you're a pressure-sensitive tablet user, the process will be less cumbersome, as painting with a mouse can feel unintuitive at times.

What you'll learn in this chapter

Creative Techniques and Working Methods

Combining digital with tactile

Something as small as the inclusion of actual paint drips can have an immense effect on how authentic the work seems at the end of it all. It is very important to exercise a little forethought when you set out to do something like this. Knowing that I was going to be spraying paint digitally, and knowing that I could get that paint to build up naturally, I knew that I wanted it to drip. Now, there is no gravity in Photoshop, so creating dripping paint would have to be done in the real world or carefully faked digitally. Although this is a common theme that pops up again and again throughout this book, it is very important to mentally prepare yourself for the task at hand.

Pre-Photoshop preparation

Simply put, think about what you're going to do ahead of time. Get everything together and then launch Photoshop. As you work your way through this chapter and get to the dripping paint part, it will become clear that spraying these drips on paper ahead of time was the best and most efficient method to create a realistic effect. You'll develop an understanding of the importance of preparation as well as how very small details can be the deciding factor in whether or not your artwork appears genuine.

Photoshop Tools, Features, and Functions

Airbrush capabilities

This feature does not get enabled often. But for this chapter, we wouldn't be able to live without it. It allows the brush to deposit paint the way a spray can would. There is an endless stream when you hold the button down and the movement of the mouse directly affects how much paint is deposited in a given area.

Opacity and flow

Using these two Brush tool options together allows you to customize how paint is deposited by your virtual airbrush. The numbers you enter in these fields will have an immense effect on how natural your sprayed strokes appear.

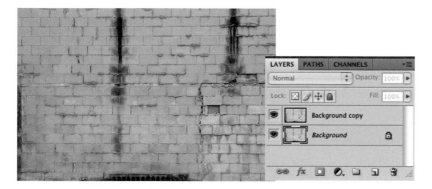

1 Open up the wall.jpg file. This will act as your background for the image and this file will become the bottom layer of our multilayered working file. The first thing you notice about the wall is that the darker details are not pronounced enough. Perhaps the original photograph was a little overexposed. To remedy this, drag the background layer onto the Create a New Layer button at the bottom of the Layers palette to duplicate it. Target the duplicate layer and change the blending mode of the layer to linear burn. Reduce the opacity of the layer to 67% so that the burn effect isn't overpowering.

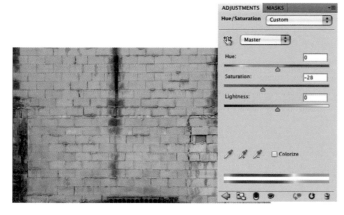

2 In order to make the painting stand out even more, let's reduce the amount of color in this already very neutral-feeling background. Click on the Create New Fill or Adjustment Layer button at the bottom of the Layers palette to access the pop-up menu of Adjustment and Fill Layer options. Choose Hue/Saturation from the list to create a new hue/saturation adjustment layer. Another method for creating a hue/saturation adjustment layer is to click on the Hue/Saturation button in the Adjustments panel. The method you choose to create the hue/saturation adjustment layer doesn't matter. In either case, reduce the saturation by around 28 in the Adjustments panel to remove color from the underlying layers. Click OK.

Project files

All of the files needed to follow along with this chapter and create the featured image are available for download on the accompanying Web site in the project files section. Visit www.creativephotoshopthebook.com.

PART TWO: Black outlines

3 Open up the drawing.jpg file. Choose Image>Adjustments>Invert from the menu to convert the artwork to a negative. Type Control(PC)/Command(Mac)-a to select all and then type Control(PC)/Command(Mac)-c to copy the selected image. Return to your working file and navigate to the Channels palette. In the Channels palette, click on the Create New Channel button at the bottom of the Channels palette to create an empty alpha channel. Target your new alpha channel and type Control(PC)/Command(Mac)-v to paste the copied art into your new channel.

 Go your own way

The black-and-white art here is a very sharp and finely tuned piece of artwork. However, what makes every graffiti artist unique is his or her style of drawing. Feel free to carefully draw your own black-and-white artwork and substitute it for the one used here. There is no part of the process more appropriate to expressing your individual style than the black-and-white art stage. You can create any subject you like, but try to make it a nice, sharp piece in solid black and solid white. This will help to keep the channel clean, resulting in a nice, clearly defined selection border.

4 Ensure that the new channel remains targeted and then click on the Load Channel as Selection button at the bottom of the Channels palette. Return to the Layers palette and click on the Create a New Layer button to create a layer at the top of the stack within the palette. Press the "d" key to set your foreground color to black. Then, ensure that your new layer is targeted and type Alt(PC)/Option(Mac)-Delete on the keyboard to fill the current selection with black on the new layer. Type Control(PC)/Command(Mac)-d to deactivate the selection.

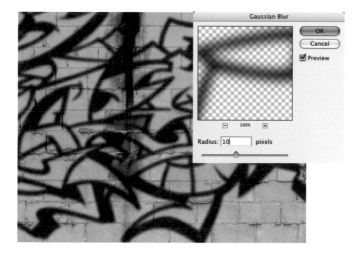

Inverting images

Because you are pasting black art on a white background into an alpha channel, it needs to be inverted first, so that the art is white and the background is black. A quick way of inverting your art is to type Control(PC)/Command(Mac)-I on the keyboard. Or, you can leave your art in its positive state and double-click your alpha channel in the Channels palette. Then, from within the Channel options, change things so that color indicates selected areas rather than masked areas before you paste your copied art into it.

5 Use the Move tool to position the layer contents a little higher on the canvas. Change the layer blending mode to multiply and then reduce the opacity of the layer to 75%, providing a hint of transparency. With your black outline layer targeted, choose Filter>Blur>Gaussian Blur from the menu. Enter a radius setting that softens the edges of your black line work. Softening the edges, combined with the layer blending mode of multiply, is what will give the art on this layer the appearance of being sprayed onto the wall. Be careful not to soften the edges too much, you still want your artwork to look like something.

PART THREE: Paint drips and buildup

6 Now, as mentioned in the introduction, sometimes you need to resort to the real thing to achieve authenticity in your digital art. Here, a series of black paint drips were painted on a white piece of paper. Holding the can in one place while spraying allows you to build up enough paint in that spot so that it begins to run. Black and white were used because these paint drips, after being scanned, are destined to be used to create custom selections within a series of alpha channels.

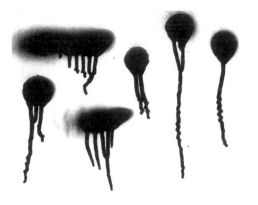 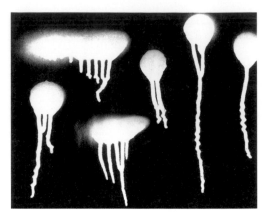

7 Go ahead and paint your own drips if you like. If you're doing it on your own, be certain that the paint is completely dry before you scan it. Spray paint is difficult to remove from any surface—that's what makes it so appealing for outdoor art. If you'd rather focus on Photoshop instead of making a mess, the dirty work here has already been done for you. Open up the drips.jpg file. This is a desktop scan of a group of spray paint drips. Invert the file and then use the Lasso tool to draw a rough selection that contains one entire drip.

Adding a paint drip

Paste a copied paint drip into your alpha channel using the visible composite channel to aid with proper positioning.

1 Copy the selected drip and return to your working file. Create a new channel, ensuring that color indicates masked areas (the default setting). Target your new channel and enable the visibility of your CMYK composite channel in the Channels palette.

2 Now that you have your new channel targeted and your composite channel visible, paste the copied art into your new channel. Choose Edit>Free-Transform from the menu. Shift-drag a corner of the bounding box inward to reduce the selection contents.

3 Click and drag outside of the bounding box to rotate the contents as necessary. Click and drag within the bounding box to position your drip over a corner area of your black outline art. Press Enter to apply the transformation.

8 Use this method to copy selected drips from the drips.jpg file and paste them into your alpha channel. Keep the visibility of the composite channel enabled to help you position your drips properly and use Free-Transform to adjust size, rotation, and placement. When you have a number of drips in your channel that sit nicely over appropriate areas of the image, load the channel as a selection.

Placing drips

When placing a drip area within the image, try to think of where it would occur realistically. You know that drips traditionally occur because too much paint is applied in a single area at one time. So try to look at areas of the art where a spray can is likely to spend a lot of time. Corners are a perfect place. Actually, anywhere where two lines meet means that the spray can will deposit more paint in that area. Working along these lines will aid in achieving a realistic result. However, don't let the rules of the real world deter you from adding a drip where you think it will look good. Although we're using the laws of nature as our guide here, they certainly don't bind us.

9 After generating the selection, click on the CMYK composite channel at the top of the Channels palette to target it. Next, click on the eye icon to the left of your alpha channel to disable the visibility of that channel, causing the red overlay to disappear. Return to the Layers palette and ensure that the layer containing your black outline art is targeted. Fill the current selection with black on this layer and deselect. If you haven't changed your foreground color, it should still be set to black. In this case, all that you need to do to fill the selection is to type Alt(PC)/Option(Mac)-Delete. Then type Control(PC)/Command(Mac)-d to deactivate the selection.

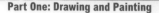
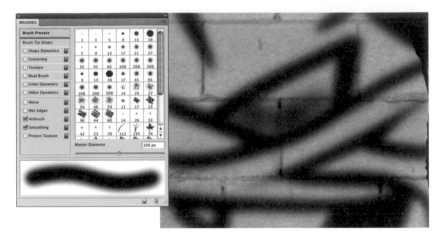

10 Select the Brush tool. In the Brushes palette, choose one of the soft, round brush tip presets. Disable shape dynamics because we do not want the actual thickness of the stroke to change. Enable the Airbrush option as well as the Smoothing option. Leave the brush opacity set to 100% but reduce the flow to 30% in the Tool Options bar. Try painting a few strokes at various areas on the black layer that surround the outline art. The longer you stay in one place with the mouse button down, the more the paint will build up in that area.

Saving your tool preset

When you've hit upon a combination of brush settings you like, you can save the brush in the current state as a preset, to access it again directly at any point later on. Just open the Tool Preset picker at the far left of the Tool Options bar. Once the picker is open, just click on the Create New Tool Preset button to add your current tool to the list of presets. From that point on, your brush will reside within the preset picker for immediate access.

11 Reducing the flow forces the brush to behave like true spray paint because paint is deposited in your stroke at a slower rate. Move the mouse quickly while holding down the button to paint a light stroke or move slowly to paint a darker stroke. The faster you move the mouse, the less paint will be deposited in the stroke because the flow cannot keep up with you—just like real-world spray painting. Try creating a stroke very quickly while holding down the mouse button. Then stay completely still at the end of the stroke while continuing to hold down the mouse button. This will cause paint to build up in the area where you are hovering—just like it would if you were using a real spray can.

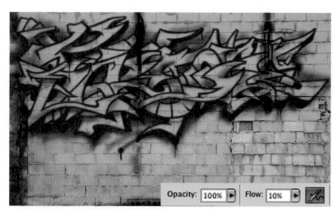 

Opacity: 100% ▶ Flow: 10% ▶

12 Use this method to add some primarily lighter strokes around the edges and over top of the black outlines, giving it an authentic look. Also try increasing the brush size and reducing the flow so that it looks as if the spray can was held further away while you were painting on the wall. Continue painting on this layer until you think the black spray paint effect is complete. Also, if you feel that you need some more drips on this layer, use the methods employed previously to add drips. Create a new layer and drag it beneath the black outline layer in the Layers palette.

PART FOUR: Color and highlights

Adding color

1 Click on the Foreground Color swatch in the toolbox and choose a pink color from the picker. Reduce your brush diameter slightly in the Brushes palette. Begin to paint some strokes within areas defined by black outlines on the new layer.

2 Paint like you did previously, using a very low flow setting and numerous strokes of varying speed and thickness. Now select a purple color from the picker and continue to paint some purple strokes within the same regions of the artwork on the current layer.

3 Use this method to add a variety of colors into the shape areas on the current layer, defined by the black outline layer. Remember to vary flow settings, brush diameter, and the speed at which you paint your strokes to achieve the authentic spray paint effect.

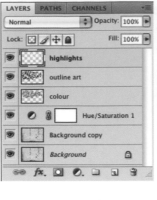

13 Create a new layer and drag it to the top of the Layers palette. With the new layer targeted, and the Brush tool still selected, press "d" on the keyboard to reset the foreground and background colors to their default settings of black and white. Then type "x" to reverse them. Reduce the master diameter of your brush tip considerably in the Brushes palette and if you've reduced the flow setting, increase it to 30% once again. Use the current brush settings to paint a series of white strokes on this new layer to create highlights on the shapes inside the black outlines.

 Opacity and flow

Rather than always returning to the Tool Options bar to adjust opacity and flow settings when using the Brush tool, a couple of useful keyboard shortcuts will improve your efficiency while working. Quickly pressing a number key on the keyboard will set your brush opacity, using a multiple of ten. Or, if you want something precision, simply type the two numbers of your desired opacity. Holding down Shift while pressing a number key will allow you to adjust the flow instead of the opacity. If you have the Airbrush option enabled, things are reversed. When the Airbrush is enabled, simply pressing a number key changes the flow and holding down the Shift key while you press a number key changes the opacity.

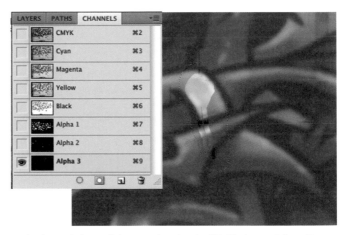

14 Continue painting until there are deposits of solid white here and there. Also, increase the diameter of the brush and reduce the flow. Then paint some strokes with these brush settings to create a softer, more gradual highlight effect within the shapes. When you're finished painting, return once again to your inverted drips. jpg file. Use the Lasso to draw a rough selection around a cluster of drips and copy it. Return to the working file, create another alpha channel, and target it in the Channels palette. Enable visibility of the composite channel again and then paste into your new alpha channel.

15 As before, use Free-Transform to rotate, resize, and position the drip. Position it so that it overlaps an area of opaque white and then press Return to apply the transformation. Repeat this process to add a few drips to the alpha channel and then generate a selection from it. Target the composite channel and disable the visibility of your new alpha channel. With the current selection active, return to the Layers palette. Target the layer with the white highlights painted onto it. Specify a white foreground color and fill the active selection with it. Deactivate the selection.

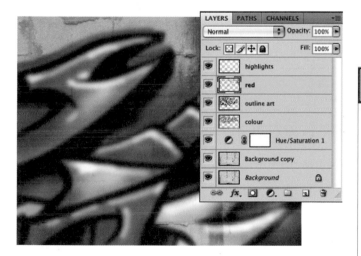

 Varying paint colors

Unlike traditional painting, we can change our minds regarding color after the fact when creating graffiti art in Photoshop. Because different colors exist on different layers you can target any individual layer and alter the color via Image>Adjustments>Hue/Saturation. Also, you can target a layer in the Layers palette, enable the transparency lock, and then fill the targeted layer with any color you choose. This will allow you to instantly change the painted areas of the layer while preserving the transparent areas.

16 Create a new layer and drag it beneath the white highlight layer in the Layers palette. Greatly reduce the size of your brush so the stroke thickness is similar to that of your thin white highlight strokes. Set the flow to 35% and begin to paint some red highlights outside the black outline on the new layer. Be certain to paint over some areas enough times so that there are a few solid red blobs of paint on this layer. Also, increase the brush diameter and reduce the flow setting. With these brush settings, paint some larger, softer strokes here and there on the current layer.

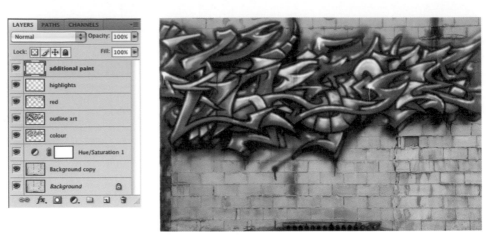

17 And now for what is becoming a familiar operation, again, return to the drips image file. Paste some selected drips into a new alpha channel. Generate a selection from the channel and fill the selected areas with the same red foreground color on the current layer. Deactivate the selection. Feel free at this point to embellish the image by painting some finer strokes of vibrant color on top of the existing layers on a new layer. Use the now familiar methods you've employed all along to finesse your graffiti art.

Dissecting your graffiti art

Let's recap which methods and techniques are vital when it comes to creating convincing acts of virtual vandalism.

a Working with the flow setting allowed us to create brush strokes with a paint density that reacted to the speed of the mouse movement. Moving quickly deposited less paint, allowing us to see the detail of the wall through the paint in a number of areas.

b Although we imported a perfectly sharp black-and-white drawing as our outline art, a simple application of the Gaussian Blur filter produced a soft, convincing spray paint effect here.

c By incorporating paint drips via channel-based selections, we were able to force gravity to take its toll on the artwork, adding to the feeling of authenticity. Even while using the Airbrush option, no matter how long you hold the mouse button down in Photoshop, the paint simply will not drip as it piles up.

d By moving the brush quickly and then holding it in one place with the mouse button pressed, you can simulate what really happens when you do this with a can of actual spray paint. It is light where the motion was quick and heavy where the tool was stagnant.

This graffiti is portable

You can now take what you've created here and apply it to any background. First target only the layers that make up the painted graffiti in the image. Group them and then simply drag the group into another image window. After you've dragged the paint group into an appropriate scene, simply use Free-Transform to adjust the size and position until it looks authentic.

Chapter 4

Creating Stencil Art

Stencil graffiti is a form of urban art that offers quick and easy reproduction. Traditionally, a stencil is made from paper, cardboard, or plastic. Usually the stencil is held tight against a wall or another surface and paint is sprayed onto it. Removing the stencil after painting reveals an instant application of the stencil art on the desired surface. Ideally, the paint will only touch the surface in areas where holes are present in the stencil. However, part of the signature appearance of stencil graffiti is the overspray effect that occurs around the edges.

In this chapter, we're going to create a virtual stencil from an existing work of black-and-white art. The ideal way to do this is to edit the art and then define it as a Custom Brush preset. However, rather than painting with the New Brush preset, as we did in Chapter 1, we'll be using it as a stamp. All that you need to do to add a virtual stencil to an existing scene is choose the Custom preset and click once. Photoshop's custom brush capabilities allow you to put a virtual graffiti stamp on any digitally photographed scene with a single mouse click.

This chapter involves simple use of the Brushes palette. Angle and diameter are about as complicated as it gets. Aside from working with brushes, you'll do some very basic work with selections, layers, masks, and blending modes.

What you'll learn in this chapter

Creative Techniques and Working Methods

Distressing the brush

What makes your stencil art effect convincing is what you do to your artwork before you define it as a brush. In this chapter, you'll learn to distress the brush art, as if it were scratched and affected by the elements. Your overspray needs to look convincing, and for both realistic distress and convincing overspray, you'll learn to incorporate desktop scans of the real thing. Applying stencil art in Photoshop is indeed as simple as a single click of the mouse, but ensuring that it looks realistic is the direct result of the care you take in preparing your custom brush artwork.

Size, color, and position

In addition to authentic-looking brushes, placement and position of the stencil itself is crucial. You really need to think about your underlying image. You'll need to decide which color to use and where to put the stencil in the image. With a little practice, you'll develop an understanding for what looks real and what doesn't. Simple analysis will aid you in determining rotation via brush angle and the size relationship of your stencil against the background.

Photoshop Tools, Features, and Functions

Custom brush tips

You'll master the process of creating a customized brush tip. Bearing in mind that black areas deposit paint and white areas do not, you'll learn to create distressed and authentic tips that are ideal for stencil effects. You'll also gain an understanding of what size to work at while creating your custom brush.

Lighten

When building up a distressed effect on your brush, you'll learn the value of the lighten blending mode as you place the artwork on top of a black brush tip. Do this by choosing textural images that express distress in white areas against black, and combining those images with this blending mode.

PART ONE: Creating a distressed brush

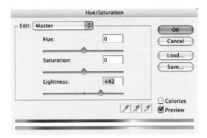

1 Open up the mask.jpg file. This file provides the subject matter for our initial piece of stencil art. Generally, stencil graffiti art provides social commentary or incorporates an activist theme, so a gas mask is certainly an appropriate subject matter here. The first thing we need to do is lighten the density of the black so that even when our brush is eventually used at 100%, the resulting stamp is still not entirely opaque. Choose Image>Adjustments>Hue/Saturation from the menu and increase the lightness by about 42.

2 Now open up the spatter.jpg file. Select the Move tool and then, while holding down the Shift key, click anywhere on the canvas and drag the image into your mask.jpg file. This will add the spatter.jpg image to the mask file as a new layer. This layered file will be the working file for your stencil art from this point on. Reduce the opacity of the new layer so that you can see the mask image beneath it. Use the Polygonal Lasso tool to draw a rough selection that surrounds the gas mask, yet includes a bit of white background as well.

Project files

All of the files needed to follow along with this chapter and create the featured image are available for download on the accompanying Web site in the project files section. Visit www.creativephotoshopthebook.com.

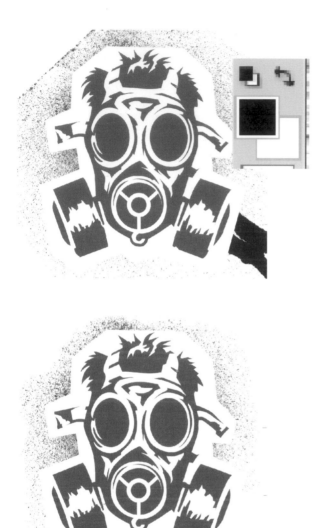

3 With your spatter layer targeted and your current selection active, choose Layer>Layer Mask>Hide Selection from the menu. After masking, increase the opacity of the layer to 80%. Ensure that the layer's mask is targeted in the Layers palette and select the Brush tool. Choose a large, soft, round Brush preset. Set the foreground color to black by first pressing the "d" key, and then press the "x" key. Pressing the "d" key sets the foreground and background colors to their masking defaults, which is white in the foreground and black in the background. Pressing the "x" key inverts the colors so that the foreground color is black and the background color is white.

 Make your mark

Although there is artwork provided on the CD as the subject matter for your stencil art, you can feel free to create your own. Traditionally, stenciling, as a guerilla art form, has been all about expressing yourself and your opinions. So, if you feel that there is something you'd like to say, and you can translate that concept into bold black-and-white artwork, feel free to use it here instead of the files provided. The process remains the same and will work with a variety of subjects.

4 Leave the brush opacity set to 100% and then paint over the areas within the mask to hide them. Paint over the dark drips in the lower right; also paint over any sharp edges where the spatter abruptly ends, like the upper left, the upper right, and around the edges of the canvas. Now that you've added the spatter layer and masked it accordingly, you can see that the artwork is already beginning to look as if a stencil and a spray can be applied to it.

5 Open up the scratches.jpg file. Again, use the Move tool to drag the image into your working file as a new layer. Hold down the Shift key as you drag to ensure proper positioning when the scratches file reaches the destination. In the Layers palette, change the blending mode of your new scratches layer to lighten. This ensures that only the areas on the current layer that are lighter than areas on the underlying layer appear, creating a scratched paint effect on your black stencil art. Next, target your background layer and select the Magic Wand tool.

Add light and dark areas

Adding light and dark areas within your stencil art helps to create a genuine weathered look when you apply it to your surface destination.

1 Ensure that the Target All Layers and Contiguous options are disabled in the Tool Options bar. Leave the tolerance set to 32 and click on a non-white area of the background layer. Click on the Create a New Layer button in the Layers palette.

2 Drag the layer to the top within the Layers palette and select the Brush tool. Press "d" to set the foreground color to black and then paint within the selection here and there on the new layer. Alter brush opacity and diameter as you paint.

3 Press the "x" key to switch the foreground color to white. Create a new layer and then paint some faint white areas within the active selection on this layer. Increase the diameter of your brush and use a very low opacity setting.

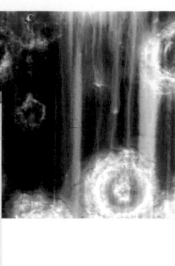

6 Open up the rusty.jpg file. This is a grayscale detail photo of a rusted metal surface. It is not the subject matter that is appealing in this case, but rather the contrast and interesting divisions between light and dark. Type Control(PC)/Command(Mac)-I on the keyboard to invert the image. Then use the Move tool to drag it into the working file as a new layer. Ensure that you hold down the Shift key as you drag to maintain correct positioning.

 **Recognizing potential**

This rust texture application is an excellent example of the less than obvious usage of certain images. When you originally look at the digital photo of the rusted box, you see an intriguing texture, but it is important to look at it with different blending mode applications and Layer stacking options in mind as well. Try to visualize the lighten and darken usage opportunities of basic texture shots. Examine dark and light areas, and think about how they would affect different types of underlying artwork. Experiment with different scans and photos of texture using different blending modes. You're bound to hit upon some interesting effects that would not have been immediately apparent when viewing the images in their normal state.

7 Change the blending mode of the layer to lighten so that only the light areas of the texture appear against the dark areas of the underlying artwork. To intensify the rusty texture effect, drag the layer onto the Create a New Layer button at the bottom of the Layers palette to duplicate it. Use the Move tool to drag the duplicated layer's texture to the right a little, so that it overlaps the texture on the underlying layer. This is a great way to increase the textured effect. Use the same procedure to duplicate your scratches layer and move it too.

PART TWO: Creating a second distressed brush

8 Open up the skull.jpg file. We'll use this image to create a second piece of stencil art that is less of a social comment and more of a lowbrow urban art icon. To begin, use the same hue/saturation adjustment method you used for your gas mask art to lighten it. Now, ensure that you are working in Standard Screen mode so that you can view both the skull file and the gas mask working file at the same time. If your windows are currently tabbed, choose Window>Arrange>Float All in Windows from the menu or choose the Float All in Windows option from the Arrange Documents menu in the Application bar. Use the Move tool while holding down the Shift key to drag the first scratches layer from the gas mask file's Layers palette onto the skull file's canvas area.

 Creating custom brushes

The most important thing to remember when building a file to use as a Brush preset is that brush tips operate using the principles of grayscale. Simply put, this means that wherever you have a solid black area, 100% paint will be applied when you use this image as your Brush preset. Inversely, areas of white will deposit no paint at all, and areas of grayscale will fall into place in-between, dependent upon the amount of black in those particular areas.

9 After adding the scratches layer to the skull file, repeat the process of selecting the dark areas of the background layer with the Magic Wand. Use the same method and tool options that you used earlier in the gas mask file. Then, on a series of layers, paint some lighten and darken areas with the Brush tool. Again use the same methods, tools, and tool options as before. Deactivate your selection and then Shift-drag the rust texture layer from the gas mask file into your new file. Reposition the layer as required within the skull file.

PART THREE: Defining your stencil brushes

10 Open up the spatter.jpg file again and Shift-drag it into the skull working file with the Move tool to add it as a new layer. Reduce the opacity of the new layer to see the art beneath. As you did previously with the gas mask file, use the Polygonal Lasso to create a rough selection border and then add a layer mask that hides the contents of the selection. Use a large, soft, round brush with a black foreground color to paint over the hard edges on that layer within the mask to remove them. When you're finished editing the mask, target the layer instead of the mask, and change the layer opacity to 80%.

Make it big

Another useful thing to remember when creating a custom brush is that it is always a good idea to start with an image that is larger than any brush you'll want to use later on. That way, your Brush preset is always larger than what you require and you can always reduce your preset size without affecting the sharpness of the tip. However, increasing the size of your brush beyond its original size will result in poor quality and possibly visible pixels when you use your brush as a stamp later on. Photoshop will allow you to define a Brush preset as large as 2500 pixels wide by 2500 pixels high.

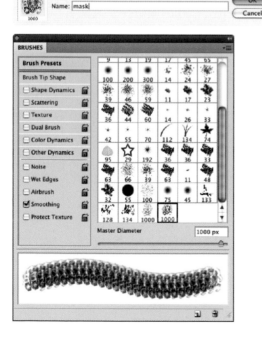

11 Next, choose Edit>Define Brush preset from the menu. When prompted, name your brush "skull" and click OK. Save and close your skull file. Return to your gas mask file and define this image as a Brush preset too, by using the same Edit menu command. Name this preset "mask" and click OK. Save and close this file as well. Now, go ahead and open up any background image you like, and select the Brush tool. If you want to replicate what is being done here, open the background.jpg from the CD. In the Brushes palette, choose the new Skull or Mask option from within the list of available presets.

PART FOUR: Applying stencils

12 Look for a place within your image that is ideal for an application of this new stencil. Think about the color of spray paint you'd use, and then click on the Foreground Color swatch to access the picker. Select your desired color from the picker. Because the file we used to define the Brush preset was 1000 pixels wide and 1000 pixels high, there is a good chance you'll want to reduce the diameter in the Brushes palette. After you've sized your brush accordingly and chosen a foreground color, click once in the desired location within your image to apply the stencil art.

 Adjusting the angle

In the Brushes palette, there is a small circle and a cross hair diagram that allow you to adjust the angle and roundness of your brush tip. Do not alter the roundness as it is not an appropriate adjustment when creating stencil art. However, go ahead and drag the arrow in the diagram to adjust the angle; you can see the result of the adjustments immediately in the stroke preview below. You can also enter a numeric value; however, dragging has a more intuitive feel to it.

13 Certainly, you can stamp your stencil directly onto your images and the results will be just fine. However, if you want to keep your files editable, it is always a good idea to work on separate layers. So, create a new layer and ensure that it is targeted. Go ahead and apply numerous instances of one Brush preset. Alter the angle, color, and the size as you see fit.

PART FIVE: Repeating the process

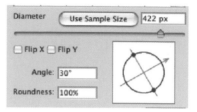

14 Now, go ahead and add instances of your other Brush preset. First, choose a color from the picker each time. Then select your preset in the Brushes palette. Adjust the size and angle each time and then simply click once on your new layer to add another instance of your stencil art. Repeat this process until you're satisfied with the result. Once you've added your custom brushes to the list of presets, you can use them in any file you like.

Examine the finished art

Let's take a look at both of our Brush presets and note what is effective when it comes to producing convincing stencil art.

a Overspray can't be avoided in the process of real-world stenciling, so it is important that it is included here. Using a scan of the real thing certainly helps to create an authentic appearance.

b Adding scratches lends authenticity to the results. Untouched and perfectly even paint coverage is rarely evident in real-world stencil art; the elements and environmental factors definitely take their toll over time.

c Rotating your brush tip is a nice option when it comes to simulating realism. Rarely will you see a real-world stencil applied to a surface at a perfect right angle. Guerilla artists just don't have time for that sort of thing.

d Remember, because your stencil art is a Brush preset, you can use any color you like. If your background is dark, you can use a light color, or if your background is light, then you can use a dark color. All of the color combinations within the picker are available. This vast range just isn't available when you're working with spray cans in the real world.

Planning multicolored stencil art

If you plan ahead, you can create a number of custom brush tips that will work together to create a multicolored stencil masterpiece. In the top image, you can see that I designed a number of brush tips to work together. Each fill color is a separate brush. In the image above, you can see how these brush tips were used together to create the artwork stamped on the wall. You can see, for instance, that the green creature has a separate custom brush for each color. Stamping these colors into the appropriate areas allows you to simulate the effect of multiple stencils. The same technique was used to create the squid and bubbles.

Chapter 5

Tracing Photographs

Creating striking illustrations in Photoshop is easier than you think when you use photography as your starting point. You don't really need any traditional drawing skills; you simply need to understand which tools are right for the task at hand and how to use them to your advantage. All of the details and divisions of color necessary to create a stunning illustration exist in your photography; you just need to recognize the potential within the image and make use of it.

The technique of illustrating over photography revealed in this chapter does involve tracing, but not exact replication. As you define areas with paths, you can simplify, embellish, or sharpen areas of detail as you see fit. However, simplifying and exercising creative license when rendering detail is only part of what makes this image so striking. This style of illustration also owes a lot of its success to the use of color.

Before you begin, try to change your mental framework a little from the norm. This is not an auto trace effect we're creating here. It is an illustration based on a photo. When tracing, do not trace exactly; try to embellish and introduce a nice sharp style to the image. When adding color, make bold decisions. Think about what you'd like to see rather than what you actually see in the existing photograph. Bearing these factors in mind as you work will ensure that your finished illustrations surpass your source photos each and every time.

The creation of the file and the tools and features used are explained clearly enough for beginners to make their way through this chapter. However, what will present a challenge is the use of tools that require a bit of experience to perfect; mainly the Pen tool and the act of drawing smooth and precise paths.

What you'll learn in this chapter

Creative Techniques and Working Methods

Simplify and stylize

By taking some creative license while creating the outlines of the clouds, I was able to give them a sharp, stylized effect. And it was this effect that dictated the overall style of the finished illustration. In general, the curves are smoother than those in the original photograph, and the detail is minimal in comparison. In this chapter, you'll learn to use only the necessary details provided by the original image, thus simplifying it. As you work in this manner, you'll begin to notice that the result of this is a much more striking image than the original, especially when viewing it from a distance.

Make bold color decisions

In this illustration, the colors are bright and the divisions are bold. Highlights and shadows are intense and far from realistic. And perhaps the most important of all, colors are chosen not by what is indicated in the original image, but by what works best within the finished illustration. As you work your way through, you'll gain an understanding of how powerful the use of color can be, and how to employ this strong use of color in future works.

Photoshop Tools, Features, and Functions

Path area strategies

Drawing with the Pen tool can prove challenging for some. However, taking your time and working methodically can pay off in the long run. In this chapter, I'll show you a strategy for creating black outline art. You'll create the exterior with a solid fill. Then you'll subtract an area from that to create an outline. Then you'll add in fine details. All of this is achieved via the strategic use of path area operations.

Quick Mask and beyond

Often thought of as a tool for simply refining selections, you'll be amazed at what you can do to expedite the creation of selections with Quick Mask. Strategic planning when generating selections, combined with underappreciated paint tools, will have you making complex selections from existing resources with ease.

PART ONE: Create a stylized background

1 Open up the starter.jpg file. This is the image we're going to use as the template for our illustration. Generally, it is easier to see what you're doing when tracing, if the image is less intense. Create a new solid color layer by choosing the Solid Color option from the Create New Fill or Adjustment Layer pop-up menu at the bottom of the Layers palette. When the picker opens, select white as your color and click OK. Reduce the opacity of your new solid color layer to 50% in the Layers palette.

Project files

All of the files needed to follow along with this chapter and create the featured image are available for download on the accompanying Web site in the project files section. Visit www.creativephotoshopthebook.com.

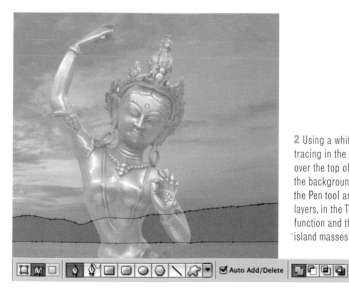

2 Using a white layer as a translucent overlay is very similar to tracing in the real world by placing onionskin or tracing paper over the top of your picture. It is a nice way to work without the background image becoming visually distracting. Select the Pen tool and ensure that it is set to create paths, not shape layers, in the Tool Options bar. Enable the Add to Path Area function and then draw a closed path component around the island masses in the background.

3 Do not trace every bump that is indicated by the image on the background layer. Create a smooth path that is indicative of the landmasses but simpler. With the path visible, create another solid color layer. Choose black from the picker. Here you can see that by having the path active as we create the solid color layer, the path is converted to a vector mask, which is automatically applied to the solid color layer. After this operation, you'll notice that the Pen tool is now set to create shape layers in the Tool Options bar.

ⓘ Creating solid color layers

In addition to using the pop-up menu at the bottom of the Layers palette to create a solid color layer, you can use the main menu if that is what you prefer. Simply choose Layer>New Fill Layer>Solid Color from the menu. This is just one example of the numerous features within Photoshop that can be accessed in more than one place within the workspace.

4 In the Tool Options bar, select the Rectangle tool. Ensure that the Create New Shape Layer option is enabled and unclick the Link button so that the existing shape layer is unaffected by what we do next. Then, click on the Color swatch in the Tool Options bar and choose a rather dark blue color from the picker. If you did not deactivate the Link button, the color of the current layer, which contains the landmasses, would've altered. Click and drag at the bottom of the canvas to create a blue shape layer over the water area.

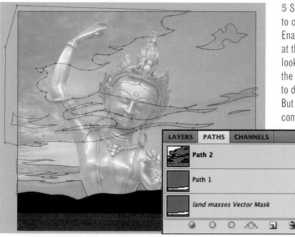

5 Select the Pen tool and, once again, ensure that it is set to create paths and not shape layers in the Tool Options bar. Enable the Add to Path Area function and then take a good look at the sky in the photograph on the background layer. Try to look past all of the rippling cloud details and visually pick out the darkest cloud-covered areas of the sky. Use the Pen tool to draw a series of path components surrounding these areas. But simplify what you see as you create your paths. Make the components look smooth and stylized. Have some fun with it.

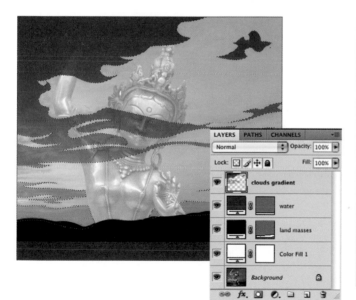

Adding a mask later

You can add a vector mask to any unmasked solid color layer after the fact; you don't necessarily need to create a path before you create your layer. Simply go ahead and create a solid color layer, like we did previously with the white overlay layer. Then create a new path or target an existing path in the Paths palette. With your desired path visible on the canvas and your solid color layer targeted in the Layers palette, choose Layer>Vector Mask>Current Path from the menu.

6 Control(PC)/Command(Mac)-click on the new path thumbnail in the Paths palette to load it as a selection. Return to the Layers palette and click on the Create a New Layer button at the bottom of the palette to create a new, empty layer. Select the Gradient tool. Choose the Foreground to Transparent preset and the linear gradient method in the Tool Options bar. Click on the Foreground Color swatch in the toolbox to select a dark gray foreground color from the picker. Click and drag from the top of the canvas downward to create a gradient within the selection on the new layer.

71

7 Type Control(PC)/Command(Mac)-d to deactivate the current selection. Temporarily disable the visibility of your white solid color layer by clicking on the eye in the column at the left of the Layers palette. Use the Eyedropper to click on an area at the lower left of the sky to choose an orange-brown color as the current foreground color. Press the "x" key to invert the foreground and background colors, sending the new color to the background. Then click on a dark blue-gray region on the canvas to sample it as the current foreground color.

Create a gradient layer

Similar to solid color layers, gradient layers can provide the basis for a simple, graduated sky background.

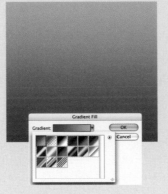

1 Choose the Gradient option from the Fill and Adjustment Layer menu at the bottom of the Layers palette. This will open the Gradient Fill dialog box. Because the last gradient we created used the Foreground to Transparent preset, that is what is selected.

2 Click on the Arrow button to the right of the gradient preview to open the Gradient Preset picker. Choose the option from the upper left within the list of presets. This is the Foreground to Background option and makes use of your previously sampled colors.

3 Now change the angle of the gradient to −90°, flipping it horizontally. You can either enter a numeric value in the angle field or click and drag on the angle control thumbnail to the left of it. Press OK when finished.

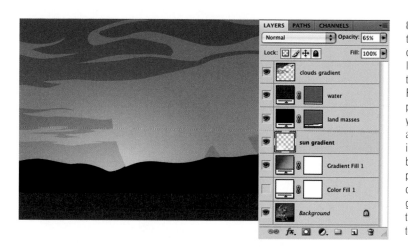

8 Drag the gradient layer down in the Layers palette so that it resides directly above the white overlay layer that we created earlier. Select the Gradient tool and choose the Foreground to Transparent Gradient preset in the Tool Options bar. Set your current foreground color to white and ensure that the gradient method is set to radial in the Tool Options bar. Create a new layer in the Layers palette. With your new layer targeted, click and drag to create a white radial gradient where the sun would be on the horizon. Reduce the layer opacity to 65% to soften the effect.

Alter the gradient layer

Although we've chosen colors from the background photo as our starting point, there is no reason why the sky can't be much more intense than the original.

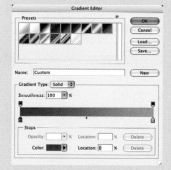

1 Target the gradient layer in the Layers palette. Choose Layer>Layer Content Options from the menu. In the Gradient Fill dialog box, click on the gradient's thumbnail preview to open the Gradient editor. Click on the Color Stop at the left below the horizontal gradient.

2 Click on the Color swatch in the Stops section at the bottom of the Gradient Editor dialog box. This will launch the picker, allowing you to choose a new color for the gradient stop you selected. Choose a more saturated blue and click OK.

3 Now select the Color Stop in the bottom right and follow the same procedure to choose a brighter, more saturated orange. Click OK to close the picker and then drag the midpoint slider under the gradient to the left, until the location reads about 40%.

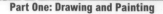

 Beware of banding

When you are making hue/saturation adjustments that affect the underlying gradient fill layers, proceed with caution. Extreme adjustments that vastly alter hue and/or saturation will increase the visible banding in the underlying gradient layer. So try to make gentle adjustments and if you want to drastically alter the colors within the gradient, it is best to edit the fill content of the gradient layer itself rather than using an adjustment layer on top of it.

9 Click OK when you're finished and take a look at the illustration now. The gray clouds now look a little out of place. To remedy this, first target the layer with the clouds on it and then choose Image>Adjustments>Selective Color from the menu. In the Selective Color options, choose Neutrals from the Color menu. Use the sliders to increase the amount of cyan and magenta in the neutral components of this layer (which is more or less the entire layer). The ability to adjust image components separately is a fine example of the benefits of building your file as separate layers.

10 Now, to saturate the colors within the entire background a little more, create a new hue/saturation adjustment layer by clicking the Hue/Saturation button in the Adjustments palette. Simply increase the saturation by 15 and click OK. This little adjustment helps quite a bit without being so drastic that it has adverse effects within the gradient. With your new adjustment layer targeted in the Layers palette, Shift-click on the gradient layer to target all of the layers that make up the background. Choose>Layer>New>Group From Layers from the menu to group them.

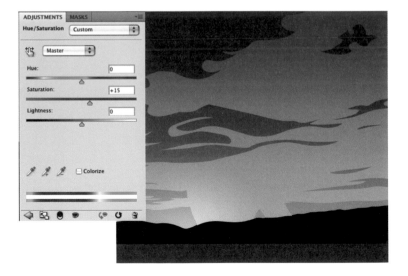

PART TWO: Create the figure outlines

11 Temporarily disable the visibility of your new group and enable the visibility of the white overlay layer once again by clicking in the column to the left of each layer in the Layers palette. We'll enable the visibility of the background group again later on, but for now it will simply get in the way of creating the figure. Select the Pen tool. In the Tool Options bar, set it to create paths instead of shape layers, and enable the Add to Path Area option. Use the Pen tool to carefully create a large, closed path component that surrounds the figure in the underlying photograph.

Editing layer content

A quick way to edit the content of a solid color, gradient, or adjustment layer is to simply double-click on the layer thumbnail in the Layers palette. This will open up the Layer Content options specific to the type of layer you clicked on. For instance, double-clicking on a solid color layer opens the picker and on a gradient layer opens the Gradient Fill options.

12 When you have closed the path component, begin to draw another path component on the inside of the first one. The space between these two components will eventually be filled with black to create a black outline to define the figure; keep this in mind as you carefully create your path components. When you've completed the inside component, ensure that it is still selected and then choose the Subtract from Path Area function in the Tool Options bar. Control(PC)/Command(Mac)-click on an area of the canvas that contains no path to ensure that no single path component is selected.

13 With your path visible (yet no single component selected) on the canvas, create a new, solid color layer from the menu at the bottom of the Layers palette. Choose a black color from the picker and click OK. This creates a new solid color layer that is masked by your path, essentially a shape layer. You'll notice, once again, that the Pen tool is now set to create shape layers in the Tool Options bar; leave it like this. Enable the Add to Shape Area option in the Tool Options bar.

 Changing fill color

The quickest method for changing the fill color of a solid color layer begins by targeting it in the Layers palette. Once the layer is targeted, you can type Alt(PC)/Option(Mac)-Delete on the keyboard to change the fill color of the layer to your current foreground color. To change it to your current background color, type Control(PC)/Command(Mac)-Delete instead.

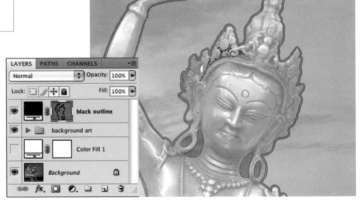

14 Reduce the opacity of the layer to 25% in the Layers palette. The logic for doing this will reveal itself very soon. Use the Pen tool to draw additional closed path components within the solid color layer's vector mask where you want black to appear. These components will reveal the black of the solid color layer. The reason why the opacity of the layer is reduced is because, as you draw within a vector mask on a layer like this, the components effects become visible as you go, even before they're closed, and it can become visually distracting as you work.

15 With the Pen tool set to Add to Shape Area, continue to carefully draw closed path components that trace all of the dark details of the statue. Remember to simplify and stylize details as you see fit. Zoom in and out as necessary while you work. Some areas like her chest, ear holes, and the space between her neck and shoulders will require a two-step process. The first step is to create path components that cover the entire areas. There is a logic to this as well, as we'll be performing a careful subtraction operation next.

Repairing banding

If you find that banding persists in your gradient fill layer, convert the fill layer to pixels by rasterizing it first. Choose Layer>Rasterize>Fill Content from the menu. After you've rasterized the layer, ensure that it is targeted in the Layers palette and then add a bit of noise to it. Choose Filter>Noise>Add Noise from the menu. You'll notice that adding noise breaks up the banding. Try to add as little noise as possible or your gradient will start to appear grainy.

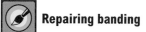

16 The process is much the same as the one you used to create the outline for the figure, except we're working with shape layers right now instead of path components; so the results are immediately visible. Ensure that no path component is currently selected and then choose the Subtract from Shape Area function in the Tool Options bar. With this function enabled, trace the areas inside your black shapes that you want to subtract from the black areas. Remember to create these closed "subtractive" components a fair distance inside the larger "additive" components so that the result is an outline, similar to your original figure outline.

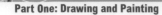
17 Return the opacity of your layer to 100% now that you've finished creating all of the outline art. Ensure that no single path component is selected, but the paths that make up the vector mask on the canvas are all visible. If you can't see the paths, simply target the vector mask and they will become visible. Control(PC)/Command(Mac)-click on the vector mask thumbnail in the Layers palette to load it as a selection. Type Control(PC)/Command(Mac)-Shift-I on the keyboard to invert the selection and press the "q" key on the keyboard to enter Quick Mask mode. In Quick Mask mode, areas that lie outside of your selection are indicated by a red overlay.

 Hiding the vector mask

If you find that the presence of your vector mask is visually distracting, the quickest way to hide it is to use the keyboard shortcut. Type Control(PC)/Command(Mac)-h on the keyboard to hide the vector mask from view. If you want to show it, just type the same keyboard command. When the mask is hidden, this keyboard command reveals it and vice versa.

18 Select the Paint Bucket tool and set your foreground color to black. Click in the background area of the image to fill it with red. This masks the area, thus removing it from your selection. Now, click in the areas between her neck and ears as well as the holes in her ears and crown to fill them with the red overlay, masking them as well. By masking everything except the inside regions of her body, we are ensuring that when we exit Quick Mask mode, we will have a selection that contains only that. Everything else that is masked, indicated by the red overlay, will fall outside of the selection border.

PART THREE: Add regions of color

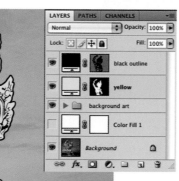

19 Press the "q" key to exit Quick Mask mode. Your mask is now converted to a selection border that surrounds only the inside areas of the figure. Choose Select>Modify>Expand from the menu to expand your currently active selection by only one or two pixels. Do not expand the selection too much or it will stray beyond the outline. Now, with the currently modified selection active, create a new solid color fill layer in the Layers palette. Choose a bright yellow color from the picker and then drag your new, masked, solid color layer beneath the black outline layer in the Layers palette.

Expanding selections

The reason why selections are expanded before using them to create masked solid color layers is to safeguard against thin, hairline spaces between colors. Think of expanding your selections as a form of trapping, by creating an area of slight overlap; there is no risk of the background showing through in-between colors.

20 Select the Magic Wand tool. Ensure that the Contiguous and Use All Layers options are enabled in the Tool Options bar. Click on the yellow area inside her eye outline to select it. Shift-click on the same area in her other eye and the inside of the circle on her forehead too, adding these areas to the active selection. Expand the selection like you did previously and then, with the current selection active, create a new solid color layer. Choose a pale blue color from the picker.

21 Temporarily disable the visibility of your yellow solid color layer. We need to get it out of the way to define different areas of shading which are visible in the underlying statue image. Using the regions on the photograph as a starting point, we're going to create the effect of lights with different colored gels. Select the Pen tool. Ensure that it is set to create paths and that the Add to Path Area function is enabled. Create a series of path components that trace some of the shaded regions on the right of the statue.

 Using both masks

In addition to your vector masks, you can add layer masks to your fill layers as well. Simply target a fill layer that already has a vector mask applied to it and click on the Add Layer Mask button at the bottom of the Layers palette. This will add a layer mask to your layer as well. Using a layer mask will allow you to use paint tools to mask your layer, creating blending effects that can't be achieved via vector masks. In CS4 it is possible to target a vector mask and apply feathering effects to it in the Masks palette. However, if you want to edit your mask intuitively with a brush, you'll need to use a layer mask.

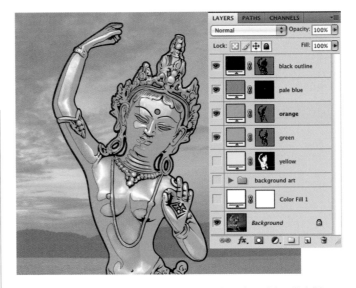

22 Ensure that no single path component is selected, yet the path is still visible on the canvas. Create a new solid color layer and choose a green color from the picker. Drag this layer beneath the blue layer that fills her eyes and forehead circle with color. Switch the pen mode to create paths in the Tool Options bar because it will have automatically switched to shape layers mode. Now draw a series of similar path components, tracing similar areas on the left side. Again, with no single component selected, create a new solid color layer. This time choose an orange color.

23 Disable the visibility of all of your solid color layers except for the black outline layer. Again, set the Pen tool to create paths and enable the Add to Path Area option. This time, use the underlying photo as a guide for creating another series of closed paths that trace the very bright specular highlights on the surface of the statue. Ensure that no single path component is selected and then create a new solid color layer. This time, choose a very light yellow color from the picker. Drag this layer up in the Layers palette so that it resides directly beneath the black outlines layer.

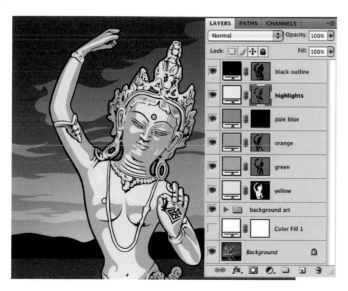

24 Drag your white overlay into the trash in the Layers palette to delete it. It is no longer required. Enable the visibility of any fill color layers that weren't visible and take a good look at your illustration now. It is almost complete, but it needs some interesting shading to finish it off. Again, set the Pen tool to create paths and ensure that the Add to Path Area function is enabled. Take a good look at the green areas of the figure and try to visualize where some darker green shades would help to add a sense of depth.

Rasterizing vector masks

If you wish to edit a layer mask with a paint tool, you'll need to rasterize it. This will convert it to a regular layer mask. Simply target the layer in the Layers palette and then choose Layer>Rasterize>Vector Mask from the menu. Once the mask is converted, you can target it and use any paint tools to edit it, allowing you to achieve effects that simply cannot be performed within a vector mask, like softly blending or blurring the contents of the mask.

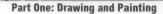
PART FOUR: Shading via gradients

25 Use the Pen tool to create a series of closed path components where you want your shaded areas to go. Load the path as a selection and create a new layer in the Layers palette. Select the Gradient tool. Choose the Foreground to Transparent Gradient preset and select the radial method in the Tool Options bar. Select a darker green foreground color from the picker. With the current selection active and the new layer targeted, create a series of gradients by clicking and dragging. If things are looking too dark, reduce the opacity of the gradient in the Tool Options bar.

Vary the color scheme

When you've completed the illustration, nothing is carved in stone. Have a look at the Layers palette and you'll see that the file is built in a methodically separated, highly editable way. Go ahead and double-click some of the fill layers. Change the solid colors and alter the gradient layer. Layers that are actual pixels will require direct edits via the Image>Adjustments menu. But have some fun and try different color combinations. You may even hit upon something you like better than the original.

26 Use the Pen tool, with the same settings as before, to create a series of closed path components to indicate areas of shadow within the orange areas on the other side of the statue. Load the entire path as a selection and choose a dark orange foreground color from the picker. Use the Gradient tool now, with the same settings as before, to complete your illustration by adding a series of gradients within the selection on the current layer. Use the same logic and procedure as you did while creating your dark green shaded areas. Feel free to edit any vector or layer masks, tweak colors, and add or remove any path components as you see fit, embellishing the illustration further.

Capturing subject matter and combining styles

When you are photographing subjects for the purpose of illustrating over later, it is important to think differently than you would if you were shooting for traditional purposes. You need to light the scene, adjust the aperture, and pose your model in a way that allows you to see differentiation between regions of highlight and shadow as well as keep as much of the subject in sharp focus as possible. The resulting images do not have to be technically perfect with regards to photography as long as the aforementioned criteria are met.

Here you can see how the photograph was used as the basis for the illustration, incorporating the techniques explained in this chapter. As exemplified here, you aren't limited to one particular style only. This piece combines a variety of styles and methods, while using the techniques described in this chapter to illustrate the main visual element within the composition.

Source: Original model photo: Orlando Marques; Hair and makeup stylist: Carla Marques; Model: Josie Lee.

Chapter 6

Illustrating from Sketches

n the previous chapter, you learned how to create stunning illustrations from existing photography. That is an excellent method to create bold and sharp works of art when you have the appropriate materials to trace from. However, what do you do when you lack photographic resources, and all that you possess is an idea of what you wish to create? The answer to this question can be found at the end of any pencil: start with a sketch. Quickly sketching onto paper is a tried and true method for recording visual ideas, and an integral starting point when it comes to illustrating. However, as much as sketching is an integral part of the illustrating process, it is what you create from that sketch within Photoshop that will transform your basic idea into a professional piece of finished art.

When working with a sketch, always remember that it is merely a starting point. Photoshop provides all of the tools necessary to improve upon and embellish the artwork along the way. Using Photoshop to create artwork from sketches allows you to create finished art that is true to your original idea in terms of concept, but vastly superior when it comes to execution. Also, when working from sketches rather than photography, your subject matter is not limited to your available photographs, you're only limited by your imagination.

DIFFICULTY 3.0/5

Much like the previous chapter, we're going to spend a lot of time using the Pen tool here. Obviously a bit of experience and practice will make things easier. However, even if you're new to using the Pen tool, you can make your way through. Apart from Pen tool usage, we'll concentrate on building a layered file, selecting and filling regions, creating shaded gradients, and using vector masks.

What you'll learn in this chapter

Creative Techniques and Working Methods

Refining as you go

As with tracing photography, we'll be using the Pen tool to create the regions and define the outer edges of our artwork. However, when working from a sketch, it is necessary to refine the artwork as you go. You'll need to not only trace the art but also create smooth line work of a uniform thickness, add sharp areas of detail, and define regions of varying color. Whereas, when tracing photography, the idea is to simplify, reduce detail, and use what is already there in a stylized manner. The goal here is to build upon what is being expressed in the sketch. A sketch should be viewed as an idea in progress, as opposed to a photograph, which is often a complete idea captured. Rather than replicate, you're finessing as you proceed when working in this manner.

Constraining graduated areas

The way in which shading is added later in this chapter may seem unorthodox at first. However, as you work your way through, you'll likely develop an appreciation for how intuitive this method is. You'll begin by creating loose gradients in approximate regions. This is an uninhibited and efficient way to get the colors you want in desired areas. The next step is to mask the regions with vectors and create defined areas with sharp edges, containing the chaos and getting just the effect you're after.

Photoshop Tools, Features, and Functions

Magic Wand

Used with a default tolerance setting and with the Sample All Layers option disabled, this tool is your best bet for quickly selecting regions of transparency that are isolated from others by your outline art.

Expand

In order to avoid minor gaps, you'll need to expand all of those quick Magic Wand–based selections before you fill them with color. This simple command found under the Select>Modify menu is your greatest ally here.

Polygonal Lasso

This tool does not often see the light of day. However, in the background of the image, it was the wisest choice for quickly creating a series of random triangular shapes around the edges. It comes in handy from time to time; try not to forget that it exists.

PART ONE: Creating the outline

1 Begin by opening up the sketch.psd file. This is the scanned drawing we're going to use as the basis for creating the illustration on the opposite page. As you can see here, the basic idea exists within the sketch. However, when you look at the finished art on the opposing page, you can see that a lot of refinement and embellishments were made to transform the sketch into a finished piece. The first step in the transformation is to carefully define the outer shape of the figure. Select the Pen tool.

Project files

All of the files needed to follow along with this chapter and create the featured image are available for download on the accompanying Web site in the project files section. Visit www.creativephotoshopthebook.com.

Embellish as you go

Your path doesn't have to follow the sketch exactly, remember the idea here is to improve upon the drawing. Use the sketch as a guide, but create your paths however you think they work best. Don't worry about tracing the sketch exactly; you'll get a much better result if you focus on creating clean line work and smooth curves.

2 In the Tool Options bar, set the Pen tool to create paths, not shape layers, and enable the Add to Path Area function. Zoom in closely on the figure and click once on the outer edge of her to create an anchor point, starting a new path component. Start at the left-most corner of her hair; because this is a sharp corner, it is an ideal place for a corner point. Follow the outer perimeter of her hair upward a little, then click and drag to create a smooth point. Keep the mouse button down as you drag, this will move the direction handles, which defines the curvature of the line on either side of the point.

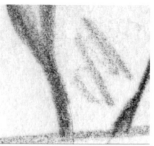

3 Release the mouse button and move upward, further along the outer edge of her hair. Click and drag to create another direction point; when you are happy with the approximate curve of the new line segment, release the mouse button. Use this method to work your way around her hair, creating a curved path component. When you get to a sharp corner, simply click and then move on to the next point, creating a corner point instead of a smooth point. Work your way around the entire perimeter until you get to the place where her chest meets the bottom of the canvas.

4 Hold down the Space bar to temporarily access the Pan tool. Drag upward so that you can see the area below the bottom edge of the canvas. Continue to draw your path so that it dips below the bottom of the canvas and then rises back up to trace the contour of her hand. Do not trace the outer edge of the diamond just yet. When you've traced the contour of her hand and find yourself at the bottom edge of the canvas again, create a point below the canvas and then another point below the canvas at the far left.

(i) Screen modes for panning

In order to work beyond the edge of the canvas, you'll need to be working with a screen mode that allows you to see the area beyond. Select either Full Screen Mode with Menu Bar or Full Screen Mode from the options available in the Screen Mode menu in the Application bar. An even quicker method for toggling through screen modes is to simply hit the "f" key. If you're using Windows, the default view is already a Full Screen option. However, if you're using a Mac, you'll need to choose a different screen mode than the default.

5 Continue to draw your path upward, back onto the canvas, tracing the outer contour until you reach your original point. Click on the first anchor point you created to close the path component. This is the outer perimeter of the woman. If we were to load this path as a selection and fill it with black, like we're going to do shortly, the result would be a solid black shape like a silhouette. What we really want is an outline; this is achieved by drawing additional path components that will subtract when the selection is eventually loaded. Choose the Subtract from Path Area function in the Tool Options bar.

 Editing paths

Use the Direct Selection tool to select individual points of your path components and edit them. You can move anchor by clicking on them and then dragging. When you click on a smooth anchor point, the direction lines will appear. Clicking and dragging on a direction handle at the end of a direction line allows you to reshape the curves on either side of the direction point.

Converting points

You can access the Convert Point tool within the expanded Pen tool button in the toolbar, or by holding down the Alt(PC)/ Option(Mac) key when using the Pen tool. To convert a corner point to a smooth point, simply click and drag on it using the Convert Point tool. Direction lines will appear, curving the line segments on either side of the point as you drag. To convert a smooth point to corner point, click on it once with the Convert Point tool and the direction lines will disappear, removing the direction lines and the curvature from the line segments.

6 With the Subtract from Path Area option enabled, carefully trace the inside areas of the woman, creating numerous, closed path components that will subtract from the outer path when we load it as a selection. Use the sketch as your guide to trace all of the white regions that exist inside the black outline of the sketch and within the outer perimeter defined by your first path component. Trace her skin, the fabric of her shirt, hair highlights, the inside of her glasses, etc. And remember, if you accidentally create a path component using the wrong path area operation, simply select it with the Path Selection tool and change the Path Area function in the Tool Options bar.

7 When you close your last path component, there should be no single component selected within your path. If for some reason, you have a single component selected, use the Path Selection tool or the Direct Selection tool to click on an area of the canvas that contains no path. This will deselect any selected path component(s). Ensure that your new path is targeted in the Paths palette; then click on the Load Path as a Selection button at the bottom of the palette. With the selection active, return to the Layers palette and click on the Create a New Layer button at the bottom of the palette.

ⓘ Auto Add/Delete

When using the Pen tool, by default, the Auto Add/Delete option is enabled. When this option is enabled, points are added to, or removed from, any selected path depending upon where you click. If you click on an existing point, it will be removed. If you click on a line segment, a point will be added.

8 Press the "d" key to set the foreground color to black if it isn't already. Ensure that your new layer is targeted and your current selection is active. Type Alt(PC)/Option(Mac)-Delete to fill the active selection with the current foreground color on the new layer. Type Control(PC)/Command(Mac)-d to deactivate the selection. Select the Magic Wand tool. In the Tool Options bar, ensure that the Contiguous option is enabled, Sample All Layers is disabled, and that the tolerance is left at its default setting of 32. Click on her shirt area contained within the black outlines to load it as a selection.

PART TWO: Filling regions with color

9 Hold down the Shift key and click on her sleeve area as well, adding it to the currently active selection. Click on the Foreground Color swatch in the toolbar to open the picker. Select a bright orange color from the picker and click OK to specify it as the current foreground color. Create a new layer in the Layers palette and drag it beneath the black outline layer. With the selection active, choose Select>Modify>Expand from the menu. Expand the selection by a single pixel or two and then fill the active selection with your new foreground color on the new layer. Deselect.

Fill the remaining areas
Repeat this same method to add a variety of colors to different outlined regions of the artwork.

1 Target your outline layer in the Layers palette and use the Magic Wand to select her face, neck, and hand regions that are surrounded by black outlines. Leave the selection active and then target the underlying layer. Expand the selection by one or two pixels.

2 Select a yellow foreground color and fill the active selection with it. Deselect and target the black layer again. Use the Magic Wand to select her hair highlights. Return to the underlying layer and expand the selection. Select a blue foreground color from the picker.

3 Fill the active selection with your new foreground color. Repeat this method to add some purple into the highlight areas of her glasses frames. Finally, repeat the process again to add some gray into the lenses of her glasses. Keep this selection active.

10 Select the Gradient tool. Choose the Foreground to Transparent preset and enable the radial method in the Tool Options bar. Set the foreground color to white and set the opacity of the Gradient tool to 75%. Click and drag once, starting at the top edge of each lens selection border and dragging outward slightly, to create white highlights at the top of each lens. Next, switch the foreground color to green and add larger gradients into each lens near the bottom. Finally, choose a very light yellow foreground color and create two smaller gradients over top of the green ones you just created.

11 Deactivate the selection and create a new layer. Target the new layer and choose a new, light blue foreground color from the picker. Type Alt(PC)/Option(Mac)-Delete to fill the entire new layer with the foreground color. Drag the layer to the bottom of the stack in the Layers palette. Then drag the sketch layer to the top of the stack. From now on, we'll enable and disable the visibility of the sketch layer as required, making it visible only when it is needed as a guide. Change the blending mode of the sketch layer to multiply and reduce the opacity to 65%.

Create an action

When repeating the same task over and over again, like expanding a selection, create an action to save your time in the long run. To begin, ensure that you have a selection active. Then, in the Actions palette, click on the Create New Action button. Name your action, assign a function key, and click Record. Expand your selection and then click the Stop Recording button in the Actions palette. The next time you want to expand a selection, all you need to do is click on the assigned function key to play the action, which will automatically expand your selection.

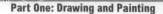

12 Select the Pen tool and ensure that the Add to Path Area option is enabled. Draw a closed path component around the perimeter of her lips, using the same method you used to draw your first path component around the entire woman. Now examine the details of her face that are indicated by the sketch. Create a few thin, closed path components that will add lines of detail to her face. Next, select the Subtract from Path Area option and create two closed path components, surrounding her lips, inside the outer lips path component. Load the entire path as a selection.

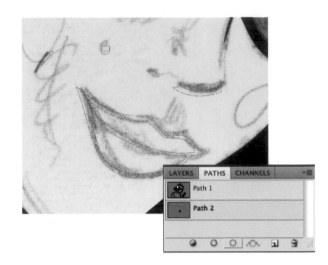

Breaking a curve

When you click and drag on a direction handle with the Direct Selection tool, it moves the direction lines on either side of the direction point, altering the curves of both line segments. However, if you click on a direction handle with the Convert Point tool, it will convert your smooth point to a corner point with independent direction lines. This means that the direction lines do not affect the line segment curve on the other side of the point when moved; only the curve on the same side of the point is affected.

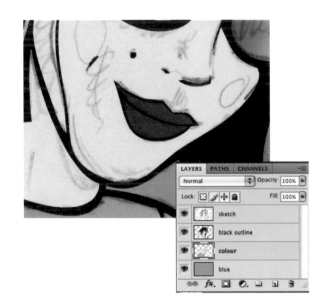

13 Target the layer that contains your black outline art in the Layers palette, and fill the new selection with black on that layer. Deactivate the selection and select the Magic Wand tool. Using the same settings as before, use the Magic Wand to target both empty areas inside the lip outlines. Expand the selection slightly using the Select>Modify>Expand menu option and target the layer that contains your other solid colors in the Layers palette. Fill the active selection with red on this layer and deselect. Select the Pen tool and ensure that the Add to Path Area option is enabled.

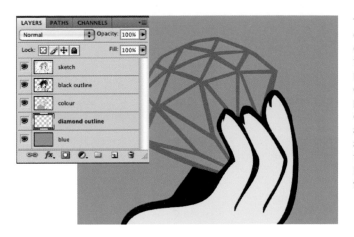

14 Use the Pen tool to draw a closed path component that surrounds the outer perimeter of the diamond shape. Next, enable the Subtract from Path Area function and create a closed path component for each facet on the inside of the diamond shape. Ensure that no single path component is selected and then load the entire path as a selection. Create a new layer and place it above the solid blue layer. Select a purple foreground color from the picker and fill the active selection with it on the new layer. Disable the visibility of the sketch layer to see the illustration clearly.

PART THREE: Shading via gradients and masks

ⓘ Refine edge

Photoshop CS3 and CS4 offer another method for expanding selections. It resides amid a plethora of other features in the new Refine Edge option. When you have a selection active, click on the Refine Edge button in the Tool Options bar. Drag the contract/expand slider to the right to enlarge the selection boundary, expanding the selection. Or, instead of dragging the slider, you can enter a numeric value in the field.

15 Use the Magic Wand tool to select all of the inner facet areas of the diamond. Expand the selection as you've been doing previously and create a new layer. Drag the new layer beneath the diamond outline layer and fill it with a very light purple color. Deactivate the selection and create another new layer. Drag this layer up within the Layers palette, until it resides directly below your black outline layer. Choose an orange foreground color. Use the Gradient tool, with the same settings as before, to create a series of gradients over the areas of her face that require shading.

16 Worry not, all unwanted areas of gradient will be hidden in a moment. Right now, continue to add orange gradients over areas of her neck and hand that will require shading as well. When finished, select the Pen tool and enable the Add to Path Area option. Draw a series of closed path components around only the regions of her skin where you want the orange gradients to be visible. Ensure that no single path component is selected and then choose Layer>Vector Mask>Current Path. This will constrain the visibility of your gradients to the areas within the vector mask's path components.

Create a series of masked gradient layers

Use the same method of creating gradients and applying vector masks to add highlights and shadows to different parts of the illustration across multiple layers.

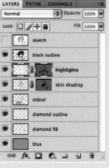

1 Create a new layer beneath the black outline layer. Target it and create some new radial, white to transparent gradients on this layer, in areas where you'd like to add highlights. For a less drastic result, reduce the gradient opacity in places.

2 Select the Pen tool. With the Add to Path Area function enabled, create a series of closed path components to contain your highlight gradients within specific regions on the canvas. Ensure that no single path component is selected and choose Layer>Vector Mask>Current Path from the menu.

3 Use this method to create new, vector-masked layers with different colored gradients on them, indicating the different shades within her shirt and the diamond. Also add some darker shading to her face and neck, using the same procedure.

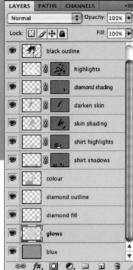

17 Create a new layer and place it directly above the solid blue layer in the Layers palette. Select the Gradient tool. Leave the options set as they were, except increase the gradient opacity to 100%. Choose a very light blue foreground color from the picker, then click and drag to create a large, light blue to transparent gradient in behind the woman's head on the new layer. Repeat this process a couple of times to intensify the gradient. Then choose a light purple foreground color and repeat the same process to add a glow behind the diamond.

PART FOUR: Polygons in the background

Continuing to edit masked layers

Once you've created your gradients and added a vector mask to a layer, it doesn't mean that your layer contents have to remain that way. Remember, in areas where you added shading within a vector mask, you can edit the layer contents whenever you like. Simply target the layer, not the mask, in the Layers palette and edit the layer using any paint tool. You can paint with a brush or add different colored gradients to alter the colors. Paint anywhere on the layer you like, but bear in mind that only areas that aren't clipped by the layer mask will be visible.

18 Create a new layer and select the Polygonal Lasso tool. Enable the visibility of your sketch layer once again. However, ensure that your new layer is presently targeted in the Layers palette. Enable the Add to Selection option in the Tool Options bar and draw a series of polygons on the left side of the canvas, based on what is indicated by the sketch layer. Select the Gradient tool and choose a green foreground color from the picker. Set the gradient opacity to 50%. Click and drag repeatedly, from the edges of the canvas inward, to create a series of gradients within the polygons around the left edges of the canvas.

19 Deactivate the current selection and create
a new layer. Disable the visibility of the sketch
layer. Target the new layer and again draw a
series of polygonal shaped selections. This time,
make them thinner than before, and try to create
them in-between the larger polygons that you
created previously. Use a dark blue foreground
color and the Gradient tool to create numerous
gradients within this selection on the new layer.
Deactivate the selection when you're finished. In
the Layers palette, click on the layer below while
holding down the Shift key to target it too. Choose
Layer>New>Group From Layers from the menu.

 ## Zooming

When creating and editing paths, I
often find myself zooming in close
to edit individual points, and then
zooming out to view the results of
these edits within the entire path.
Rather than always having to switch
back and forth between the Zoom tool
and any path creation or editing tool,
you should familiarize yourself with
the keyboard shortcuts for zooming.
Type Control(PC)/Command(Mac)
"+" to zoom in, or type Control(PC)/
Command(Mac) "−" to zoom out.

 ## Bird's eye view

Holding down the "h" key while you are
zoomed in on an image allows you to
enter bird's eye view. Clicking on the
canvas zooms out and allows you to move
a bounding box around on the image area.
The bounding box dictates the region that
will be visible when you exit bird's eye
view. When the bounding box surrounds
your desired region, release the mouse
button and you will automatically zoom
back in. The area defined by the bounding
box will fill the screen instantly.

20 Click on the group in the Layers palette and hold down the Alt(PC)/Option(Mac)
key. Drag upward until you see a very dark horizontal line appear directly above
the group in the Layers palette and release the mouse button. This creates a copy
of the group directly above the original. Target your newly copied group and then
choose Edit>Transform>Flip Horizontal from the menu. Select the Move tool.
Click and drag to the right, while holding down the Shift key, until the flipped
polygons are moved to the right edge of the canvas.

Other things to consider

Don't feel limited by the content within your sketch. You can add other elements into the composition after the fact. Feel free to incorporate type layers, repeating patterns, or anything else you can think of to add interest and diversity to your illustrated work.

Simple art with extreme color

Your drawing does not have to be overly complicated. You can use a very simple sketch as a starting point, especially if you have a clever color strategy up your sleeve. Here you can see that the illustrated components are very simple, allowing color divisions to create a strong presence within the image. If the illustration and the color usage are both complex, things tend to become overwhelming.

There are no limits

When you choose sketches over photography as your raw resource material, there are no limits when it comes to subject matter. Proven here by the contents of this page, your illustration subjects can be as wild as your imagination.

Chapter 7

Retro Art Effects

There is a certain quality to vintage pop art that usually makes me smile. I am not sure whether it is the perpetually happy and whimsical figures, the coarse halftone patterns and inferior printing, or the gaudy combinations of color. But there is something about that 1950s drive-in style, "everything-is-wonderful" advertising art that is genuinely unique and strangely optimistic.

From a Photoshop artist's perspective, perhaps a major part of the appeal is just how different it is than most contemporary digital art. As far as execution goes, printed retro art was generally done on the cheap. Registration didn't always match up so well, colors overlapped, and halftone screens were overly large. Age is almost certainly another contributing factor to the appeal. Whether the artwork was part of a sign that has spent 40 odd years outdoors or on an old cardboard box that has been sitting in a mothball-ridden attic, the signs of age are always evident. Areas of color become worn, and printed inks will eventually display numerous scrapes and scratches.

Photoshop is a tool that allows us to achieve absolute perfection in almost anything we set out to do. However, in this chapter, I really want to draw your attention to the fact that Photoshop is an extremely useful tool when it comes to methodically reproducing imperfection. Retro art's simplicity of design, rough and imperfect execution, and whimsical nature is a breath of fresh air for those of us who could use a break from the seriousness and perfection of working digitally day to day.

DIFFICULTY 2.5/5

In addition to working with layers, groups, and layer masks, this chapter will venture into the realm of alpha channels and innovative selection methods. Although everything is clearly explained, some users simply find the concept of alpha channels daunting.

What you'll learn in this chapter

Creative Techniques and Working Methods

Recognizing suitable resources

Something as simple as the background you use can be integral in setting the tone for your illustration. Here, a weathered and torn library book succeeds on a number of levels. First, the ragged imperfection of the edges reinforces the feeling of imperfection inherent within retro imagery. Second, the natural and organic color of the paper gives the image a more human feel, grounding it in the natural world as opposed to the digital realm. As you work your way through this chapter it will be hard to ignore the fact that these factors, along with the style of the artwork itself, help to create a convincing effect. You'll develop a sharp eye for recognizing the potential in what will be useful background elements in future retro compositions.

Analysis of common textures

The primary distress effects applied to the artwork are the result of a couple of desktop scans. An unlikely resource was a common slate tile. It was scanned and then converted to grayscale for inclusion within an alpha channel. After you load the channels as selections and use them to mask groups of layers, simulating wear and tear, the potential within everyday textures becomes quite evident. You'll begin to look around you and envision common objects as textures, analyzing the light and dark potential within and visualizing the masked results that can be achieved.

Photoshop Tools, Features, and Functions

Color halftone filter

You can do a lot more with the color halftone filter than simulate the effect of CMYK printing under a microscope. If you carefully arrange the screen angles so that they line up nicely, you can create a beautiful and smooth dot pattern that acts as a valuable resource.

Alpha channel content

When you create a color halftone pattern in an alpha channel, it acts as a convenient and permanent resource to load as a selection border at any point. Learning to create art within channels for the sole purpose of using as selections is something that will benefit you in all manner of projects, not just retro art imagery.

PART ONE: The background and outline art

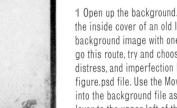

1 Open up the background.jpg file. This is a desktop scan of the inside cover of an old library book. You can substitute this background image with one of your own if you like. If you decide to go this route, try and choose something that conveys a bit of age, distress, and imperfection like this image does. Next, open up the figure.psd file. Use the Move tool to click on your figure and drag it into the background file as a new layer. Drag the contents of the new layer to the upper left of the book cover on the canvas.

Project files

All of the files needed to follow along with this chapter and create the featured image are available for download on the accompanying Web site in the project files section. Visit www.creativephotoshopthcbook.com.

2 Click on the Foreground Color swatch in the toolbar to open the picker. Choose a dark blue color from the picker and click OK. With your newest layer targeted, enable the Lock Transparent Pixels option in the Layers palette. Type Alt(PC)/Option(Mac)-Delete to fill the solid pixels on the current layer with your new foreground color. Change the blending mode of the layer to multiply. Next, open up the tub.psd file. Again, use the Move tool to drag it into your working file as a new layer. Position it beneath the figure on the canvas.

3 Lock the transparency of the tub layer and then fill it with a slightly lighter blue foreground color. Change the blending mode of the layer to multiply and reduce the opacity a little. Open up the shoe.psd file and drag it into your working file as a new layer. Position it to the right of the figure, lock the transparency, and fill the layer with a very light blue foreground color. Repeat this same process one more time to add the sock.psd art to the file as a new layer. Fill the sock with a very light, off-white color.

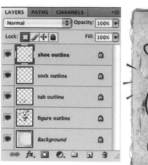

PART TWO: Distress the outlines

Create a texture channel

Use a desktop scan of an ordinary slate tile to create a new alpha channel that will assist in ageing your outline art.

1 Open up the slate.jpg file. Choose Image>Mode>Grayscale from the menu to remove the color information from the file. After converting to grayscale mode, choose Image>Adjustments>Levels and perform a very drastic input levels adjustment, like the one shown here.

2 Choose Select>All and then Edit>Copy from the menu. Return to your working file. In the Channels palette, click on the Create New Channel button. Target the new channel and choose Edit>Paste from the menu. Feel free to use the Move tool to reposition the pasted contents.

3 Click the Load Channel as a Selection button at the bottom of the Channels palette. Target all of your outline art layers and type Control(PC)/Command(Mac)-g to group them. With the current selection active, click on the Add Layer Mask button to mask the group.

4 Type Control(PC)/Command(Mac)-Shift-n on the keyboard to create a new layer. Drag the layer beneath the group in the Layers palette and select the Polygonal Lasso tool. Use the Polygonal Lasso to draw a shape that surrounds the bathtub on your new layer. Select a deep red foreground color from the picker and fill the selection with it. Repeat the same procedure to create a green polygonal shape on this layer that surrounds the shoe. Now use the Polygonal Lasso tool to draw an irregular shaped selection that surrounds the top portion of the background.

Editing masks

You can reintroduce any masked areas by adding white into those areas when your layer mask is targeted in the Layers palette. If too much of your group is masked by your channel-based mask, go ahead and paint white over those areas with a soft paintbrush and a white foreground color to make them visible again. You can also reduce the areas affected by your hue/saturation layer masks by targeting the mask and then filling a selected area with black, hiding the effect in that area.

5 With the current selection active, create a new hue/saturation adjustment layer by clicking on the Hue/Saturation button in the Adjustments palette. Adjust the hue to +111 and reduce the saturation by 76. This creates a hue/saturation adjustment layer with a mask based upon your selection border. Now use the Polygonal Lasso tool to draw a selection border around the sock area. Again, create a new hue/saturation adjustment layer. Set the hue to +21 and reduce the lightness to −29.

6 Expand your group and target the figure outlines layer in the Layers palette. Select the Magic Wand tool. Ensure that the Contiguous option is enabled and that the Sample All Layers option is disabled in the Tool Options bar. Leave the tolerance set to the default value of 32, and click in the figure's empty shirt area that is surrounded by outline art. With your new selection active, create a new layer and drag it beneath the expanded group in the Layers palette. Fill the active selection with a lighter red foreground color and deselect.

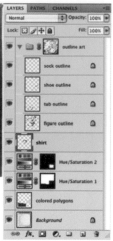

 Nudging

You can use the Move tool to reposition the contents of any layer on the canvas; however, sometimes you may only want to adjust the positioning of something by a few pixels. When you just want to give the contents of your targeted layer a gentle nudge in a certain direction, first select the Move tool. Then try using the arrow keys on the keyboard instead of clicking and dragging the Move tool. The arrow keys make performing very subtle movements an effortless procedure.

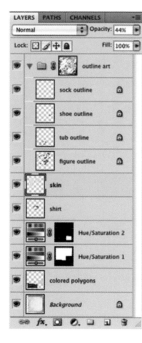

7 Use the Move tool to click and drag a little, offsetting the registration so that the fill color of his shirt doesn't match up with the outline. Again, target the figure outline layer and this time, click in the face area to select it. Then hold down the Shift key and click inside the other areas of skin like his foot, hands, etc. This will add all of these areas to your selection. Create another new layer beneath your group in the Layers palette. Fill the active selection with a flesh-colored foreground color and deselect. Reduce the opacity of the layer to 44%.

8 Duplicate the layer by dragging it onto the Create a New Layer button at the bottom of the Layers palette. Increase the opacity of the duplicate layer to 100% and use the Move tool to offset the position slightly on the canvas so that the color appears to be out of register. Repeat this method of selecting areas with the Magic Wand, filling the selections with different colors on new layers, and offsetting the registration, filling all of the outline art. Fill the remaining areas of the figure outline layer and also fill the outlined areas indicated by the other outline art layers.

PART FOUR: Distress the solid areas

Hide a mask

When you mask a layer or group while a selection is active you'll immediately see the results, as all areas that lie outside of your currently active selection border are masked. Sometimes you may feel that the result is too drastic, and perhaps you want to unmask some currently masked areas to reveal layer contents hidden by the mask. Often, it can be difficult to visualize which areas you want to reveal because they are masked and therefore not visible. However, there are a few ways to remedy this. You can temporarily hide a layer mask by holding down the Shift key and clicking on it in the Layers palette. The mask thumbnail will be covered with a red "x." This will allow you to see your unmasked layer so you can decide which regions need to be revealed. Then, Shift-click on the mask thumbnail to make it visible again and edit the mask's contents.

In CS4, you can hide the mask by clicking on the visibility icon at the bottom of the Masks palette as well. In addition to simply hiding the mask, the density slider in the Masks palette will allow you to reduce the opacity of it, making it partially visible if you like.

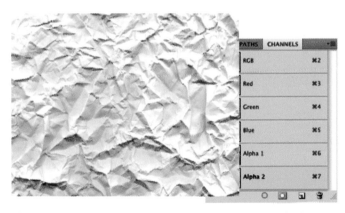

9 Target all of the individual layers that you created, which fill the outlined areas of your artwork, and add them to a new group in the Layers palette. Open up the crumpled.jpg file. Type Control(PC)/Command(Mac)-a to select all and then type Control(PC)/Command(Mac)-c to copy. Once you've copied the crumpled paper image, return to your working file. Create a new alpha channel in the Channels palette. Target the channel and then type Control(PC)/Command(Mac)-v to paste the crumpled paper image into the new channel. Load the new channel as a selection.

10 Target the new group containing your filled area layers in the Layers palette. With the current, channel-based selection active, click on the Add Layer Mask button at the bottom of the Layers palette to mask the group. Masking this group while the crumpled paper–based selection is active will add a nice, subtle distress effect to all of the filled area layers within the group.

PART FIVE: Halftone effects

Create a halftone screen pattern

Clever use of the Color Halftone filter within a new alpha channel allows us to create and store a dot pattern, which can then be loaded as a selection border.

1 Create a new alpha channel in the Channels palette. With this new channel targeted, click on the Foreground Color swatch in the toolbar and select a light gray foreground color from the picker. Then type Alt(PC)/Option(Mac)-Delete to fill the entire channel with it.

2 Choose Filter>Pixelate>Color Halftone from the menu. Enter a maximum radius of 9 pixels and set the screen angles of all four channels to 45°. This will convert the gray contents of your alpha channel to a black-and-white dot pattern.

3 Load the alpha channel as a selection and return to the Layers palette. With your current selection active, create a new layer and place it beneath both of your groups, yet above the adjustment layers, in the Layers palette.

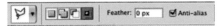

11 With your new layer targeted and the current selection active, select the Polygonal Lasso tool. In the Tool Options bar, click on the Intersect with Selection button. Draw a very rough polygonal selection that overlaps the red background behind the bathtub on the canvas. When you close your polygonal selection, you'll immediately see the results of using the Intersect option. Only areas where your two selection borders overlap remain selected. Fill the resulting selection with a light red color and deactivate the selection. Reduce the opacity of the layer slightly.

Create halftone backgrounds

Use the halftone channel alongside the Polygonal Lasso's Intersect function to create and fill a series of dotted backgrounds for your line art.

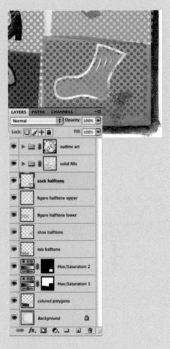

1 Load the channel as a selection again and use the Polygonal Lasso to create a selection border behind the shoe that intersects with the channel-based selection. Fill the area with green on a new layer. Repeat this process to add a light blue pattern behind the lower portion of the figure.

2 Load the halftone channel as a selection again and this time, choose Select>Inverse from the menu. Again, use the Polygonal Lasso to draw a selection border intersecting the area behind the upper portion of the figure. Fill the selection with gold on a new layer.

3 Use this same method to load the channel as a selection, invert it, and draw a polygonal selection that intersects the selected area behind the sock. Fill the resulting selection with green on a new layer. Deactivate the selection.

PART SIX: Embellish and organize

12 Now that the composition is beginning to take shape, let's take a moment and look at things that require a bit of refining to enhance color and contrast overall. Because this file is built as separate layers, performing alterations is easy. First, change the blending mode of the hue/saturation layer that affects the area behind the sock to multiply. Next, change the blending mode of the halftone layer behind the lower portion of the figure to multiply and reduce the opacity. Finally, duplicate the other hue/saturation adjustment layer, change the blending mode to linear burn, and reduce the opacity considerably.

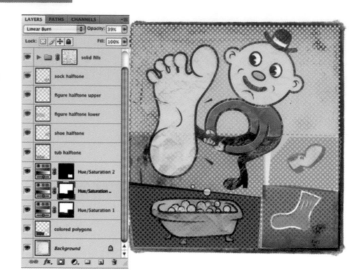

 Halftone density

When creating halftone patterns within channels, screen density depends upon the value of the grayscale shade you're converting. Here, a light gray converted to a halftone produces a dot pattern in which the dots do not touch and are surrounded by white space. If you were converting a very dark gray, there would be light-colored dots, surrounded by areas of black. Try to envision the density of dot pattern you want to create before you fill your channel with a grayscale value; this will help you choose the right shade of gray and ultimately ensure that you get the selection you want from it.

13 Target all of the halftone layers, adjustment layers, and areas that contain solid-colored polygons. Add all of these background-affecting layers to a new group within the Layers palette. After you do this, create a new layer and drag it to the top of the stack within the Layers palette. Select the Brush tool and choose a hard, round Brush preset from the Brush Preset picker in the Tool Options bar. Choose a dark flesh foreground color from the picker and paint some shading onto the figure's skin on your new layer.

14 Keep this layer targeted in the Layers palette and expand the group that contains your outline art. Control(PC)/Command(Mac)-click on the figure outlines layer thumbnail to generate a selection from its contents. Press the Delete key to remove these areas from your currently targeted layer and deselect. Reduce the opacity of the layer to 61%. Use this same method to paint some details into the sock area on a new layer. Then load the sock outline layer as a selection and delete any painted contents of the selected area on your sock detail layer. Deselect and collapse the expanded group.

Viewing layer masks

Although the layer mask thumbnail in the Layers palette provides you with a small preview of the mask's content, it is very small and you can't always see the subtle paint effects that reside within your mask. If you hold down the Alt(PC)/Option(Mac) key while you click on your layer mask thumbnail, it will become visible on the canvas, exactly like you'd see it if you made it visible while hiding the composite channel in the Channels palette. This is a quick method to have a look-back at how you've edited your masks. Alt(PC)/Option(Mac)-clicking on the mask thumbnail again hides the mask and returns the canvas to normal.

15 Return to the Channels palette and load your halftone channel as a selection once again. Invert the selection and create a new layer at the top of the stack in the Layers palette. Choose a darker flesh foreground color than the one you used previously. Paint over shaded areas of his skin within the active selection on the new layer to add darker, halftone shading effects. Next, switch the foreground color to an extremely light flesh color, almost white. Paint within the selection to add highlight areas onto this skin, nose, and hat.

16 Use a variety of colors to paint over various areas of this layer to add shading and highlights within the active selection. Increase and decrease the brush diameter as necessary. Also, try reducing the opacity of your brush and painting over areas of the background to introduce different colors into already existing dot patterns. When you're finished, invert the selection and continue to paint on the current layer until you're satisfied with the results. Deselect.

Inverting keyboard commands

Carefully pay attention to the keyboard commands you use when inverting. You can either invert an image or invert an active selection. Always remember that the keyboard shortcut for inverting an image is Control(PC)/Command(Mac)-I and that for inverting a selection is Control(PC)/Command(Mac)-Shift-I. Remembering when and when not to hold down the Shift key while using these keyboard shortcuts is essential to performing the correct operation each time.

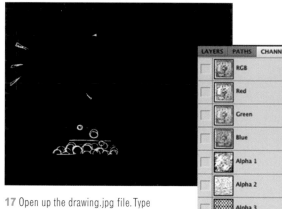

17 Open up the drawing.jpg file. Type Control(PC)/Command(Mac)-I on the keyboard to invert the image, creating a negative of the original. Select all and copy. Return to your working file and create a new alpha channel in the Channels palette. Ensure that your new channel is targeted, and paste the copied, inverted image into your alpha channel. Load the channel as a selection.

18 Create a new layer at the top of the stack in the Layers palette. Set your foreground color to white and fill the active selection with white on the current layer. Deactivate the selection and use the Move tool to position the contents of the layer so that the drawn bubbles nicely overlap the bubbles on the tub outline layer below. Target the top four layers that provide the painted, drawn, and halftone details, and add them to a new group in the Layers palette.

The secrets of successful retro art

Let's take a final look at some of the essential techniques required to produce convincing vintage artwork.

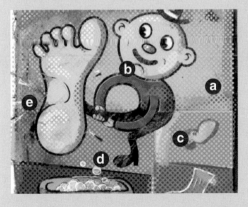

a Starting with an appropriate background image is always helpful. Here an old library book was used, but it can be anything that has a nostalgic feel to it. A background image or texture with an authentic feel will prove much more successful than a flat, solid-colored canvas.

b Using alpha channels as the basis for selections, which are in turn used to mask groups, is an excellent way to create convincing wear and distress. Using appropriate imagery within your channels is very important. Try to choose images containing random patterns and textures, as realistic wear and tear is never orderly.

c Moving layers that contain fill colors offsets the registration between outlines and solid color fills. This poor registration is a telltale sign of quick and dirty printing, resulting in a distinct look that is about as far away from digital technology as you can get.

d The halftone screen effect tends to dominate the overall composition in terms of stylistic methods used. It really adds an authentic feel to the finished art, reminiscent of vintage printing methods.

e Incorporating scanned ballpoint pen art into the composition adds a scratchy, hand-drawn feeling, which contributes to the nondigital overall feel of the illustration.

Incorporating type into your design

Working within the framework described in this chapter allows you to create convincing retro art effects time and time again. However, don't feel limited to illustration only when using this technique; this is an excellent method for working with typographical elements as well. A little distress and halftone pattern here and there within your letterforms will make them feel right at home in your retro compositions.

Other type-integration methods

Feel free to get a little creative when adding typographic components to your retro imagery; you aren't strictly limited to the Type tool. In the top image I used a ballpoint pen to draw the Z's, giving the image a tactile and whimsical charm. In the bottom image, I actually cut out a series of letters from an old newspaper and placed them in the image after scanning. The yellow paper and naturally distressed ink of the scanned letters add to the convincing retro effect.

Chapter 8

Coloring Comic Art

Not only does Photoshop provide the tools necessary to create stunning images from beginning to end, but it also provides the necessary tools for individuals performing a specific task as part of a larger creative process. In this chapter, we'll be donning the hat of the comic book colorist. A colorist contributes more to the process of comic art creation than merely filling in spaces between the lines. In addition to obviously adding color, the colorist is responsible for refining the light and shadow within the existing ink drawings as well as creating the mood within each panel via color.

As you shall soon find out, the task facing the colorist is not as effortless as it may appear. Ideally, each region of different color would be surrounded by black outlines in the ink drawing. That way, automatically generated selections could be filled on underlying layers. However, there is no sense in sacrificing the quality of the ink drawing by placing such a rigid restriction on the black-and-white artist. By taking a creative approach, a capable colorist can work colorful magic within any piece of supplied art. An innovative combination of tools, methods, and patience is the key to bringing any black-and-white drawing to life via color in Photoshop.

DIFFICULTY 3.0/5 The tools and features used in this chapter are not exactly what I would describe as advanced. However, you will need to spend a fair amount of time carefully isolating regions and filling them with solid and graduated colors. Proficiency in painting and creating paths are both valuable assets here.

What you'll learn in this chapter

Creative Techniques and Working Methods

Setting the mood

When you look at a black-and-white drawing, it can sometimes be difficult to visualize the end result. Initially, the art may feel static and lack feeling. However, as you begin to add color methodically while working your way through this chapter, you'll see how integral color is to providing the essential atmosphere required to generate a mood within the image. From the earliest stages, where you create a graduated background, the importance of color becomes evident. Immediately the scene has a dark, wet, and murky feeling; and this is simply the combination of two colors that allows you to achieve this.

As you begin to add color to the image, layer after layer, you'll develop an understanding of how powerful it can be. Choosing the right colors and implementing them with intent will allow you to control the atmosphere and overall feeling in every image you colorize. Also, you'll learn to separate different components on different layers, allowing you more control later on should you decide to perform any edits after the fact.

Envision light sources

When you begin to add gradient highlights to regions of the image, study the black artwork carefully, as it will often give you an indication of the direction of light. For instance, the leprechaun has a dark shadow on his back, behind his legs, and on the back of his hat. This shadow is very dark and lets us know that the area in front of him, where the explosion emanates from his hands, is extremely bright. Taking this as our cue, we're going to create a very bright burst of yellow in this crucial area and complement the effect by adding yellow gradient highlights to the front of the figure and the rocks he resides upon. By paying attention to the visual cues that already exist within the black-and-white artwork, you'll learn to make color and shading decisions that are grounded in a semblance of realism, resulting in a more compelling image at the end of it all.

Photoshop Tools, Features, and Functions

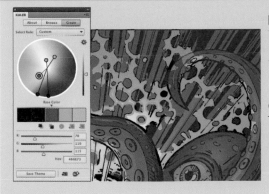

Kuler

This application, now available in the Extensions palette within Photoshop CS4, can provide massive assistance when it comes to developing color themes. Create your own, borrow from others, or share the results with everyone else.

Quick Mask

This tool is your best friend when you want to manually create a selection using elements of your imagery as a visual guide. Painting in Quick Mask mode will allow you create intricate selections that isolate regions of the image that are not completely contained within black borders.

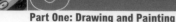

PART ONE: Preparing the outline art

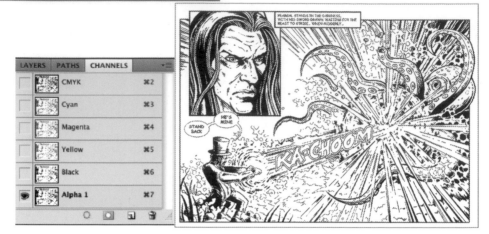

1 Open up the ink.jpg file. Choose Select>All and then Edit>Copy from the menu. Close the file and then choose File>New from the menu. In the New options, the height, width, and resolution will match that of your copied art. Choose CMYK mode, a white background, and click OK to create a new working file. In the Channels palette, click on the Create New Channel button at the bottom of the palette. With the new channel targeted, choose Edit>Paste from the menu to paste your copied art into the new channel. Click on the Load Channel as a Selection button at the bottom of the Channels palette.

Project files

All of the files needed to follow along with this chapter and create the featured image are available for download on the accompanying Web site in the project files section. Visit www.creativephotoshopthebook.com.

2 Click on the CMYK composite channel instead of the alpha channel in the Channels palette and return to the Layers palette. Choose Select>Inverse from the menu to invert the selection and then click on the Create a New Layer button at the bottom of the Layers palette. Press the "d" key on the keyboard to set the current foreground color to black. Target your new layer in the Layers palette and then type Alt(PC)/Option(Mac)-Delete to fill the currently active selection with black on the new layer. Choose Select>Deselect from the menu to deactivate the selection and target the background layer in the Layers palette.

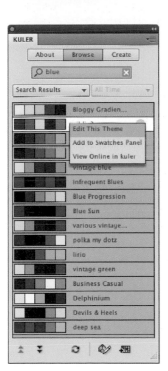

PART TWO: Exploring Kuler

3 Color can make or break any illustration. And when it comes to choosing colors for your comic art, you may find a little assistance in developing your color scheme helpful. Kuler is Adobe's Web application that allows you to create, research, and even share your color schemes online. Schemes can be shared with the rest of the world and downloaded as Adobe Swatch Exchange files. It is worth checking out, even just to see what other artists have come up with. Visit http://kuler.adobe.com/.

⚠ Check your channel options

When working with alpha channels, by default, selected areas are white and color indicates masked areas. The instructions here assume that you are working with the default Channel Options settings. However, the default settings can be changed at any point. If you find that your selections are inverted compared to those discussed within this chapter, you need to change your Channel Options. Simply double-click on your alpha channel thumbnail in the Channels palette to access the Channel Options. In the Channel Options, ensure that color indicates masked areas and not selected areas.

4 In Photoshop CS4, you don't have to worry about accessing Kuler via a Web browser; you can access it within Photoshop by choosing Window>Extensions>Kuler from the menu. You can browse existing themes by clicking on the Browse button. There are a couple of pull-down menus that will aid you in finding what you're after or you can simply type a keyword into the search field. Here you can see the results that appeared when I simply typed the word "blue" into the search field. You can edit a theme, view it online in Kuler, or export it to the Swatches palette by clicking on the little triangle to the right of your selected theme's name and choosing the desired option.

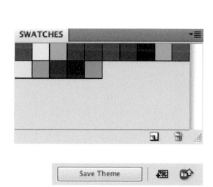

5 You can click on the Create button at the top of the palette to create a color theme of your own. Or, if you choose the Edit Theme option from the pop-up menu mentioned in the last step, you'll end up in the Create section of the palette as well. When creating a new theme, a good starting point is to choose an option from the Rule menu and then go from there. Dragging a color around on the color wheel will move all colors around properly to adhere to the rule that you have chosen. You can edit the brightness of the targeted color via the vertical slider to the right of the color wheel, or edit the RGB components directly below.

6 When you hit upon a theme that you like the look of, you'll want to export it to the Swatches palette, or at the very least you'll want to save it. Both of these options are available at the bottom of the Create section of the Extensions palette. If you're feeling generous, there's also a button there to upload your theme to Kuler online. Clicking that button will launch your designated Web browser. You can sign in there and save your theme. Kuler is an excellent tool for working with and developing harmonious color themes. However, it is merely an option. If you find it more intuitive to choose colors on the fly from the picker, so be it. However, if you decide to use Kuler, I suggest you export your themes to the Swatches palette and access the colors from there. It is a nice storage area for colors. However, to keep things organized you may want to clear the Swatches palette before adding your custom color themes to it. This process is outlined in depth in Chapter 1.

PART THREE: Adding color

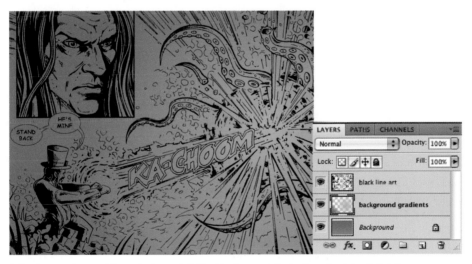

7 Use the Rectangular Marquee tool to draw a rectangular selection border that surrounds the background of the main panel, but does not stray beyond the black border. Click on the Foreground Color swatch in the toolbar and choose a teal color from the picker. Next, click on the Background Color swatch and choose a green background color from the picker. Select the Gradient tool. In the Tool Options bar, choose the Foreground to Background preset and enable the linear method. Drag from the top of the selection to the bottom while holding down the Shift key.

8 Create a new layer and then select a much lighter blue foreground color from the picker. Switch the gradient method to radial and choose the Foreground to Transparent Gradient preset in the Tool Options bar. Click and drag from the center of the explosion on the ink drawing outward, creating a new radial gradient within the selection on the new layer. Choose a muted green foreground color from the picker and change the gradient method to linear. Click and drag from the bottom left corner of the selection inward a little to change the color of that area. Deselect.

9 Select the Magic Wand and target the black line work layer in the Layers palette. Enable the Contiguous option and disable the Sample All Layers option in the Tool Options bar. Leave the tolerance set at 32. Click inside a "KA-CHOOM" letter to select that area. Then hold down the Shift key and click inside each remaining letter, adding those areas to the selection. Create a new layer and drag it beneath the current layer. Select a bright yellow foreground color and fill the selection with it on the new layer. Repeat the procedure again to select and fill the area surrounding the letters with orange.

PART FOUR: Defining regions and graduated fills

Manually filling areas with color

To create more areas of solid color, we'll need to use the Brush tool and the Eraser together, as there are no more closed black boundaries.

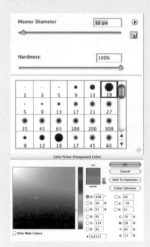

1 Deselect and choose the Brush tool. Choose one of the hard, round Brush presets from the Brushes Preset picker in the Tool Options bar. Specify a diameter of around 10 pixels and choose a bright green foreground color.

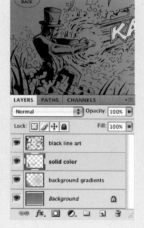

2 Set the opacity and flow to 100% in the Tool Options bar. Use the brush to paint color into areas of the leprechaun's clothing on the current layer. Increase or decrease the diameter as required. Feel free to stray outside of the lines.

3 Use this method to paint different colors into remaining areas of the leprechaun as well as the rocks. Select the Eraser tool. Set up the tip and options like your brush, and erase any painted areas that extend beyond the outlines. Increase or decrease the diameter as required.

10 Use this method to paint color into areas of the monster as well. Increase or decrease the brush diameter as required to carefully paint his skin, eye, the underside of his tentacles, suction cups, and his spots. Don't be too fussy when painting around the edges because, as you already know, you can erase any unwanted paint. Take extra care when painting in areas where two colors meet. Use very small brushes, and paint one color over the other wherever required. To achieve the soft blending effect around the center of the explosion, erase the sharp painted edges using a very large, soft brush tip and a low opacity setting.

Create shaded areas

Use the Gradient tool within path-based selections to add highlights and shadows to the artwork.

1 Enable the Lock Transparency function for this layer in the Layers palette. Select the Pen tool. Set it to create paths and enable the Add to Path Area function in the Tool Options bar. Draw a series of path components to indicate highlight regions on the leprechaun's clothing. It is fine if the path components extend beyond the edge of the leprechaun's color fill.

2 Click the Load Path as a Selection button in the Paths palette and select the Gradient tool. Select the Foreground to Transparent preset and the Radial option. Choose a light green foreground color, then click and drag within the selected areas to add graduated highlights to the leprechaun's clothing.

3 Because the Lock Transparency option is enabled, only painted pixels are affected ensuring that the new highlights don't stray beyond the figure's edge. Use this method to add highlight and shadow areas all over the leprechaun. Vary the gradient colors and also create smaller, bright yellow highlights within existing highlights.

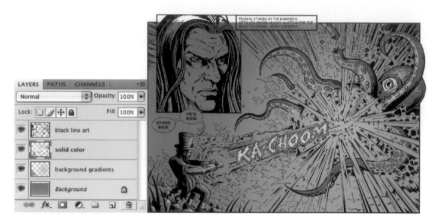

11 Repeat this method over and over again to add highlights and shadows onto the monster and the rocks underneath the leprechaun on the current layer. Remember that your paths can stray beyond the edges, because the Lock Transparency option will ensure that you do not affect transparent pixels. Select the Magic Wand tool. Ensure that the Contiguous, and Sample All Layers options are disabled in the Tool Options bar. Click on a yellow region inside the lettering to select all regions of this color on the current layer. Choose Select>Modify>Contract from the menu and contract the selection by a few pixels.

Envision light sources

Take a good look at the ink drawing before you begin adding any shadows or highlights on separate layers. In this drawing, the explosion areas will provide the brightest light. Therefore, for example, the leprechaun should have all his highlight areas based upon which side of him is facing the light source. That means his front is brightly lit and as a result of this, the shadow areas need to be created on his backside. It is very important that you examine the art and make a mental note of the lighting situation before you proceed with shading, otherwise the results will be unsatisfactory.

12 Select the Gradient tool and enable the linear method. Choose a red foreground color and drag from the bottom of the selection upward to create a red to transparent gradient inside the letters. Next, use the Magic Wand to select the orange outline color and then add a similar gradient into that area. Finally, use the Pen tool to draw a series of path components indicating small sharp highlights within the letters. Load the path as a selection and fill it with white. Deselect and then use the Pen tool to create a series of path components within the water, defining regions of shadow.

13 Load the path as a selection and select the Gradient tool. Choose the radial method and use the Gradient tool to add large, teal and green, foreground to transparent gradients into the selection on the current layer. Reduce the gradient opacity if you find that the results appear too strong. Now, use the Pen tool to define regions of highlight within the water. Load the path as a selection and then use the Gradient tool to introduce some gradients into the active selection using very light foreground colors and varying gradient opacity.

Create a hand-painted selection

In Quick Mask mode you can create a complicated selection border by painting with the Brush tool. This creates a temporary channel which loads as a selection when you exit.

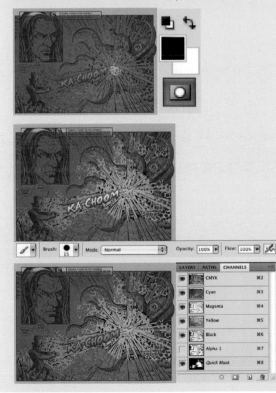

1 Create a small selection in the explosion area using the Lasso tool. Click on the Quick Mask Mode button in the toolbar. Immediately, you'll see that the surrounding areas are covered with a red overlay. This indicates masked areas. Removing the red overlay from certain areas creates selected areas when you exit Quick Mask.

2 Select the Brush tool and choose a hard, round Brush preset. Set the opacity and flow to 100 and hit the "x" key to switch the background color, which is white, to the foreground color. Carefully paint with white to create selected areas of the explosion and crackle effect. Increase and decrease the size of the brush as required.

3 You'll likely end up removing the overlay in certain areas accidentally. To remedy this, simply paint over those areas using black to mask them once again. You'll find yourself unmasking and masking, back and forth, until your temporary Quick Mask is complete, looking something like this.

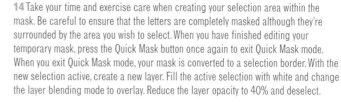

14 Take your time and exercise care when creating your selection area within the mask. Be careful to ensure that the letters are completely masked although they're surrounded by the area you wish to select. When you have finished editing your temporary mask, press the Quick Mask button once again to exit Quick Mask mode. When you exit Quick Mask mode, your mask is converted to a selection border. With the new selection active, create a new layer. Fill the active selection with white and change the layer blending mode to overlay. Reduce the layer opacity to 40% and deselect.

Do not be alarmed

I know at this point we're including the letters in our selection that you meticulously masked previously to ensure that they would not be included. But do not fret. All of that work was not a waste of time. We'll be using the fruits of your Quick Mask labors shortly to mask a group of layers, revealing the words once again and staying true to the spirit of what you created within your mask.

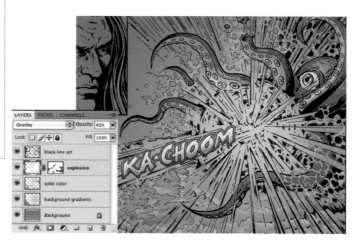

15 Click the Add Layer Mask button in the Layers palette to mask the new layer. Select the Gradient tool and a black foreground color. Within the mask, create a series of radial, black to transparent gradients to soften any hard edges you wish to blend into the background. Control(PC)/Command(Mac)-click on the layer's thumbnail (not the mask), to load a selection from the layer's contents. Use the Lasso tool to circle the word area while holding down the Shift key so that the new selection includes the words too. Choose Select>Modify>Contract from the menu and shrink your selection just like you did earlier with the lettering.

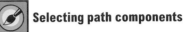

16 Create a new layer and ensure that it is targeted in the Layers palette. Select the Gradient tool and use it to create numerous radial, foreground to transparent gradients within the active selection on the new layer. Use a variety of yellow and very light yellow foreground colors. Change the blending mode of the layer to overlay, deselect, and create a new layer. Select the Brush tool. Choose a large, round, soft Brush preset. Paint light yellow into the area at the center of the explosion and into the area surrounding the leprechaun's hands on your new layer.

Selecting path components

Generally, when loading selections from paths, I recommend that no single path component be selected so that the resulting selection is based upon all of the path components. However, when adding gradients into selections, especially when working with more than a single gradient, you may wish to generate a selection from only select components within a path and not all of them. Use the Path Selection tool to select the components you'd like to load as a selection. With your components selected, load the path as a selection. The resulting selection will be based upon the selected components only.

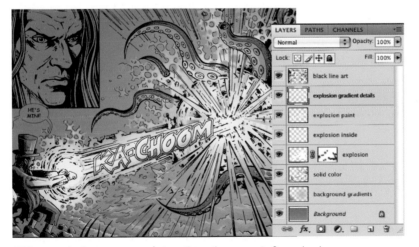

17 By now you've become very good at creating path components. So go ahead and draw some path components inside the explosion area that add detail, and also create horizontal streaks going across the lettering. Load the path components as selection borders and fill them with radial, foreground to transparent gradients on another new layer. Use an orange foreground color for some areas, and use gold and yellow for others. Also don't be afraid to add smaller, different colored gradients on top of existing ones. Deactivate the selection when finished.

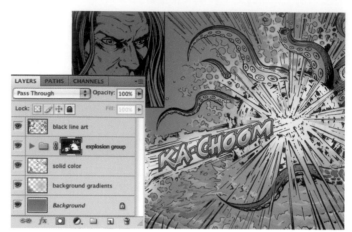

18 With your current layer targeted in the Layers palette, hold down the Shift key and click on the lowest explosion layer. This targets both layers as well as all layers in between, effectively targeting all of your explosion layers. Type Control(PC)/Command(Mac)-g to group them. Expand the group and Control(PC)/Command(Mac)-click the bottom layer to load a selection from the layer's contents. Target the group and then click on the Add Layer Mask button at the bottom of the Layers palette. Once again, your words that were originally masked, as well as the leprechaun's arms, become clearly visible. Collapse the group.

Embellish the explosion

Continue to work on your explosion outside of the masked group, adding bursts of light and hot centers.

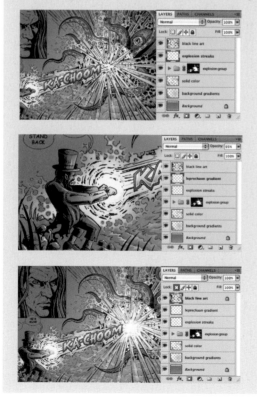

1 Use the Pen tool to draw a series of path components to represent streaks of light emanating from the large explosion's center. Load the path as a selection and add radial, light yellow to transparent gradients into the selection on a new layer.

2 Deactivate the selection and create another new layer. Use the Gradient tool, with the current options and foreground color, to create a small radial gradient over top of the leprechaun's hands on the new layer. Reduce the opacity of the layer slightly.

3 Target the black outline layer and enable the Lock Transparency option. Select the Brush tool. Use a soft, round Brush preset to paint over areas on this layer that are at the center of both explosions. Use red and orange foreground colors as you paint.

19 Next we're going to add a bit of color into some of the streaks indicated by the black line art. The top half of the background is looking a bit too monochromatic. To remedy this, examine the image and try to visualize what outer streaks you'd like to alter the color within. Use the Pen tool to draw a series of path components in these regions. Load the path as a selection and choose a blue foreground color that is quite different from the background.

Add streaks of color

Use the Gradient tool to add different colored streaks into the background; then mask your layer to avoid covering any main elements and to soften the effect.

1 Create a new layer and drag it below the black line art layer. Set the blending mode of this layer to color and then use the Gradient tool to add large, radial, foreground to transparent gradients into the active selection on this layer. Deselect.

2 Keep the current layer targeted, and Control(PC)/Command(Mac)-click on the solid color layer thumbnail to load a selection from the contents. From the menu choose Layer>Layer Mask>Hide Selection so that the streaks do not overlap the monster.

3 Target the new layer mask in the Layers palette. Select the Gradient tool and set the foreground color to black. Create black to transparent, radial gradients within the mask to gently blend the layer contents into the background in the image center.

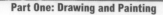

20 Drag the lock on the background layer into the trash within the Layers palette, converting it to a normal layer. Target all of the layers, except the black line art layer, and add them to a new group. Now, use the methods employed so far to create a number of new layers containing the artwork for the inset, text box, and speech bubbles. Fill selections with color and gradients. Paint and erase to fill specific areas with solid colors. Fill path-based selections with gradients to add highlights and shadows. When you're finished, add all of these layers to a second group.

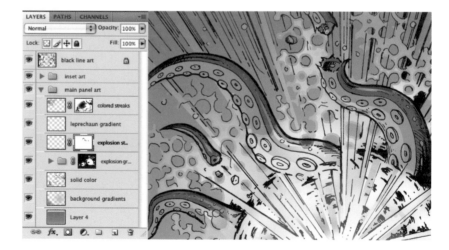

21 Now that your comic book art is complete, it does not mean that you cannot make further adjustments. Simply expand either group to access individual layers and masks. I added a mask to the layer that contained the explosion streaks, and used it to soften the effect in areas where they overlapped the tentacles. However, this is just one example of what can be done. Take a good look at the illustration and feel free to edit and embellish the way you like.

Where to go from here

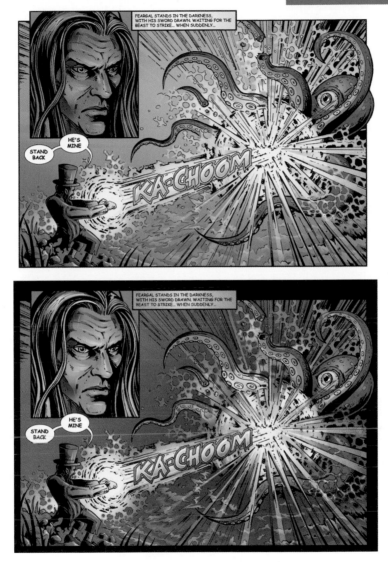

This file is built in a way that lends itself to further editing. By separating the color methodically on layers, it is easy to insert adjustment layers in-between these things within the Layers palette. As you can see here, a few carefully inserted and masked adjustment layers can begin to change the overall feeling. I am relying mostly upon hue/saturation adjustments here. However, the bottom image uses an invert layer as well. It is interesting to note that a yellow/green background makes the explosion seem like it is even brighter, really illuminating the scene. Also noteworthy is the effect that the invert layer has on the white border. By surrounding the image with black, the content suddenly seems more ominous.

PART TWO
Unconventional Methods

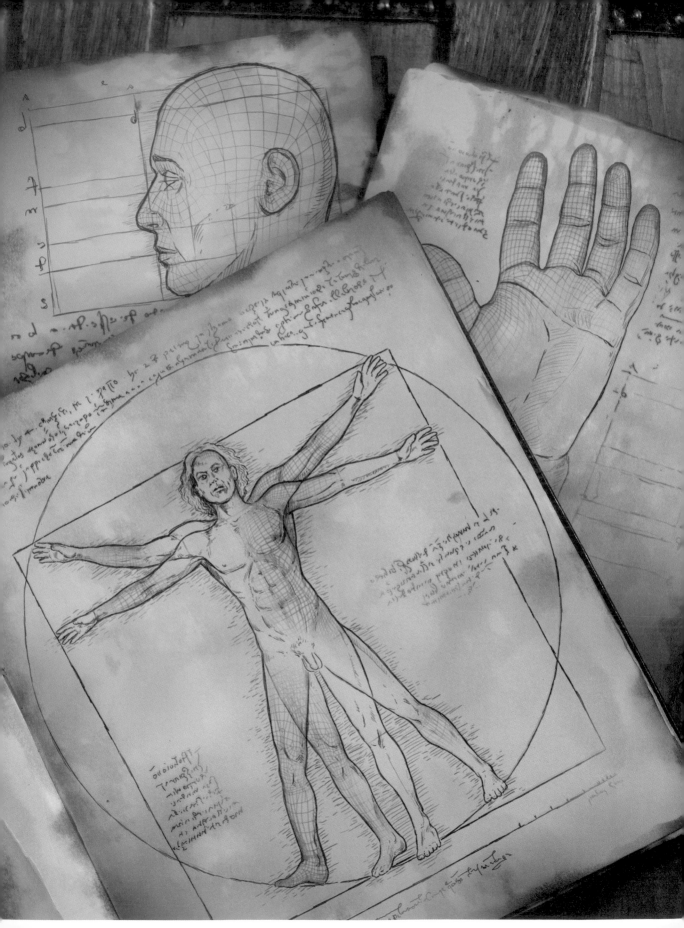

Chapter 9

Antique Effects

When you look at this image, the last thing you're likely to think of is a hairdryer. I imagine that proves true with a thermal fax machine as well. However, as weird as it may sound, those two very things are essential ingredients in creating the antique sketch effect you see here. Alongside Photoshop, unlikely and technologically inferior tools can prove quite useful when you're trying to create an authentic antique effect.

When you think about very old works of art like the sketches of Leonardo da Vinci, it isn't just the beauty of the drawings and the subject matter that captures your attention. Equally beautiful is the process of age itself. Paper turns color over the years. It becomes stained by moisture. It is affected by environmental factors, and edges become darkened from centuries of handling. There is a certain beauty in the randomness of these tactile signs of age, and it is randomness that is often overlooked in the all-too-perfect world of digital art.

I honestly can't tell you what made me do it. But one day I just tried using a hairdryer on some blank thermal fax paper. The heat forced it to darken around the edges and bleed inward on the page. The first thing that came to mind was the darkened edges of very old documents and drawings. I looked at it longer and began to ponder the usefulness of the black-and-white burn effect before me. I immediately began thinking of alpha channels and how they translate grayscale data into selection borders. And just like that the idea was born.

DIFFICULTY 3.0/5 A familiarity with all things layers will be beneficial in terms of ease while working your way through this one. Alpha channel experience is helpful, but not required. Also, if you've got some experience drawing paths with the Pen tool, it'll make things easier for you.

What you'll learn in this chapter

Creative Techniques and Working Methods

Bringing the real world into alpha channels

In this chapter, I'll reveal everything you need to know to get your thermal fax machine and hairdryer working for you as creative tools. You'll learn to use these tools to produce the random and tactile raw materials essential to the antique effects you see here. By the end of it, you'll master the art of using real-world black-and-white art as the content of alpha channels. You'll make selections from those channels, and you'll make fantastic multilayered Photoshop masterpieces from those selections.

A modular approach

If you look at the main illustration at the beginning of this chapter, you'll notice that it contains three different illustrations on three separate pages. The overall feel from page to page is the same, yet the content of each drawing is different. As you work your way through this chapter, you'll develop an understanding of the modular approach I take when creating an illustration like this. It begins by creating the art on a single page. A number of layers and resources are used. Then all elements are grouped and masked. Taking this process as your cue, you'll run through the paces repeatedly, adding art to different areas, using exactly the same methods over and over. Not only will you see the inherent logic within this technique, you'll also pick up speed as you move along.

Photoshop Tools, Features, and Functions

Alpha channels

These are essential tools for bringing the sketches and thermal fax pages into the artwork. Not only are they crucial for this integration, but also an understanding of what alpha channels are capable of is partially responsible for the inspiration for this chapter.

Layer blending modes

The antique effect is created across a series of layers that work together. Some are originals and some are duplicates. Opacity and blending modes vary. But what is truly exceptional here is the overall effect that can be achieved when a diverse set of blending modes work together while stacking up layers.

Vector masks

While building up effects on layers, you can spend your energy concentrating on the textural feeling itself rather than accuracy. Take comfort in the fact that after you've created just the right layer effect, you can neatly trim the group with a layer mask so that it doesn't stray beyond the edge of the page.

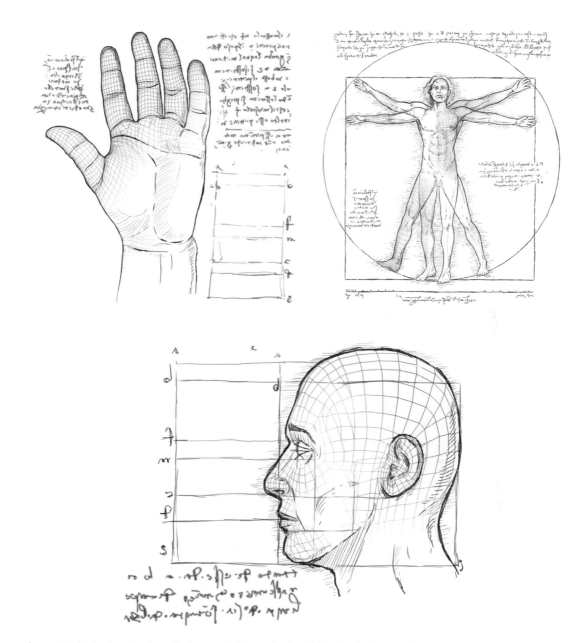

A good illustration is a direct result of the materials you begin with. That is why hours and hours were spent creating these initial sketches. Although the thermal fax/hairdryer effects will dictate the overall feel, these sketches provide the subject matter. They were based upon original sketches by Leonardo da Vinci; however, polygons and wire mesh have been included to convey the subtle fact that we're working digitally as well.

PART ONE: Real thermal fax effects

1 The first step is to print out all of the original sketches. Then, take the printed sketches to a thermal fax machine. One at a time, insert each sketch into the thermal fax machine and press the Copy button. This will make an exact copy of your original sketch on thermal paper. In addition to copying your sketches, make a few copies of a blank piece of paper, simply to get a couple of blank thermal pages as well.

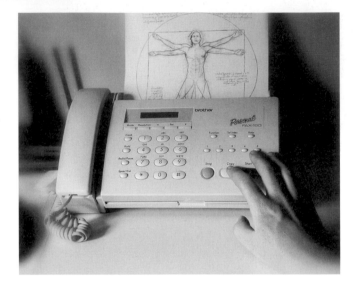

 Project files

All of the files needed to follow along with this chapter and create the featured image are available for download on the accompanying Web site in the project files section. Visit www.creativephotoshopthebook.com. The initial sketch files can be found there. And for those of you who don't have access to a thermal fax machine, hairdryer, or simply want to focus on the Photoshop work in this chapter only, all the scanned thermal pages are included in this folder.

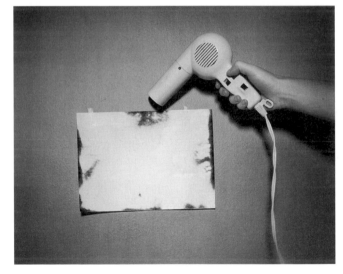

2 Tape one of your blank pages to a wall or another flat surface. Plug in your hairdryer and ensure that it is set to the hottest setting. Activate the hairdryer and move it close to the paper. Immediately you'll begin to see the paper darken when the hot air hits it. Use this technique to darken the blank sheets of thermal paper around the edges only. These will be used later to create a dark edge effect on the pages within the illustration.

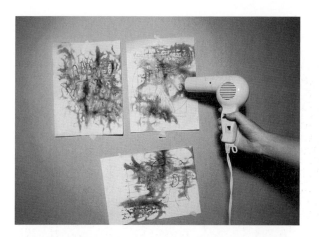

3 Now tape your thermal copies of the sketches to the wall or another flat surface. When using the hairdryer on these, concentrate on burning the centers of each page. Try moving the hairdryer back and forth quickly. It is fine if the image becomes obscured by the burn effect. You'll notice the paper will ripple slightly and the high points of the ripples will be darkest.

4 Open up the background.jpg file. This shot was carefully set up on an antique wooden trunk to lend a sense of authenticity to the final result. The pages you see here are already looking a bit aged. The corners are rounded slightly and the pages are a bit darker around the edges. Notice how the empty pages are set up to overlap each other. Each page will provide the background for one of the sketches and have an antique effect applied to it.

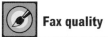 **Fax quality**

Most fax machines, even old thermal ones, will have a number of quality settings to choose from. The best quality is not necessarily required for what we are doing here. When you are copying your sketches to thermal paper, experiment with a variety of settings. What you're after is something that, although it may omit lighter details from the sketches, copies the majority of the artwork so that it is dark and legible. The scans included on this CD were copied on an old fax machine using the medium-quality setting, which provided the clearest result.

5 If you've done your own thermal effects using the hairdryer and copies of the illustrations, the next step is to scan each piece of paper. Envision the destination of each sketch within the background and actually rotate your pages on the scanner to approximate the angle before you scan them. You can rotate them in Photoshop later if necessary, so don't worry about being too accurate. Also, scan your blank pages with the thermal effects applied to them.

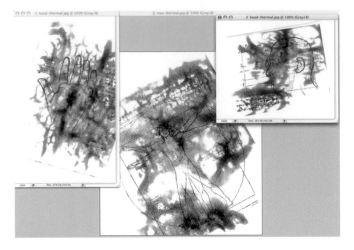

PART TWO: Incorporating the first drawing

Scanning and tonal adjustments

If you're scanning your own burned thermal fax pages, ensure that they are scanned and saved in grayscale mode. This isn't absolutely necessary, but it is helpful as the scans are destined for alpha channels. Also, it would be ideal if you could adjust your scanner driver preferences so that an automatic tonal adjustment is performed ensuring that the white backgrounds within your files contain 0% black. If you don't have this option, simply perform a very quick tonal adjustment via the Brightness/Contrast option in the Image>Adjustments menu.

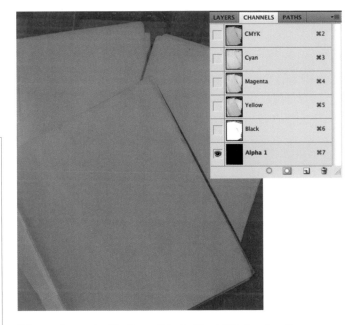

6 Open up the man.jpg file. Choose Select>All and Edit>Copy from the menu. Return to the background.jpg file, your working file. In the Channels palette, click on the Create New Channels button to create a new alpha channel. With the new alpha channel targeted in the Channels palette, click in the column to the left of the CMYK composite channel to enable the visibility of all channels. Your alpha channel will be visible as a red overlay, similar to traditional rubylith.

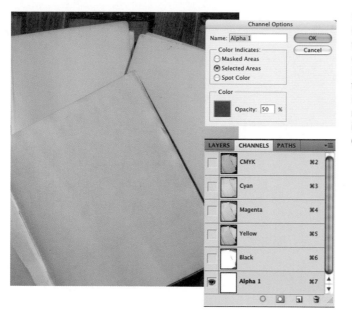

7 With your new channel targeted in the Channels palette, choose Channel options from the Channels Palette menu. In the Channel options, you'll notice that the default setting is for color to indicate masked areas. Change this so that color indicates selected areas instead. When you click OK, you'll immediately notice that the red overlay disappears from the image window as the background of your alpha channel becomes white instead of black.

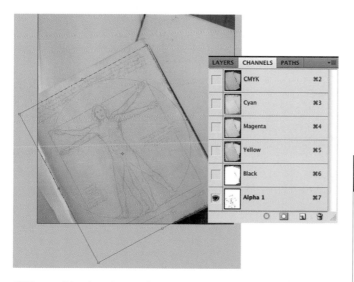

8 With your alpha channel targeted, choose Edit>Paste from the menu. You'll notice the colored areas within the pasted sketch appear as a red overlay in the image window. Choose Edit>Free-Transform from the menu. Hold down the Shift key while you drag a corner point inward to reduce the size of the pasted art proportionately. Move the mouse pointer to the outside of the bounding box until it changes to indicate rotation. Click and drag to rotate the contents to the same angle as the large page. Click in the center of the box and drag it onto the main page to position it.

Select, copy, and paste

As you add sketches and scanned thermal effects into each channel, you'll be doing a lot of copying and pasting. Therefore, it is beneficial to familiarize yourself with some keyboard shortcuts:

- Control(PC)/Command(Mac)-a is "select all"
- Control(PC)/Command(Mac)-c is "copy"
- Control(PC)/Command(Mac)-v is "paste"

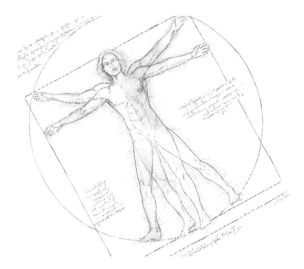

Sampling color

When you click on a color with the Eyedropper tool, the foreground color is automatically replaced with the new color. However, if you hold down the Alt(PC)/Option(Mac) key and click on a color within the image, the background color will be replaced instead of the foreground color.

9 When you're satisfied, press the Enter key to apply the transformation. Although viewing the new channel against the rest of the image is handy for positioning, disable the visibility of the CMYK composite channel by clicking on the eye in the left column. This will allow you to view the channel by itself. Click the Load Channel as a Selection button at the bottom of the Channels palette. You'll notice that because you changed color to indicate selected areas, the black regions of the channel are selected rather than the white regions.

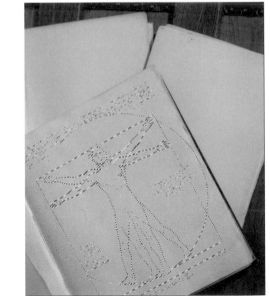

10 Return to the Layers palette and click on the Create a New Layer button at the bottom of the Layers palette. As soon as you create a new layer, the CMYK composite channel will become visible once again, and your alpha channel's visibility will be automatically disabled. This is a handy way to return to the regular workspace. With the current selection active, target your new layer. Select the Eyedropper tool and click on a brown area of the background to sample it. The foreground color will automatically change to your newly sampled color.

11 Ensure that your new layer is targeted and choose Edit>Fill from the menu. In the Fill dialog box, use your current foreground color, a blending mode of normal, and 100% opacity. Pay attention to these settings as you'll use them over and over again while filling selections throughout this chapter. Type Control(PC)/Command(Mac)-d to deactivate the current selection and change the blending mode of the layer to multiply. Click the Add Layer Mask button at the bottom of the Layers palette to add a mask to the layer.

(i) About filling

When you choose Edit>Fill from the menu, you have a number of choices as to how to go about filling. You can choose a color, a blending mode, and an opacity setting. However, throughout this chapter, we'll be using the default settings, which are the current foreground color, a normal blending mode, and an opacity setting of 100%. If you use the keyboard command Alt(PC)/Option(Mac)-Delete, your current layer or active selection is automatically filled using these settings.

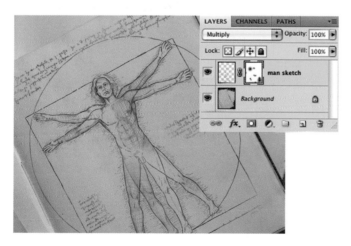

12 Target the layer mask in the Layers palette and select the Gradient tool. In the Tool Options bar, choose the radial method and the Foreground to Transparent Gradient preset. When you target the mask, your foreground color automatically switches to black because you have changed what color indicates in the Channel options earlier. This is perfect for masking. Click and drag with the Gradient tool to draw small, black to transparent, radial gradients within the mask in areas that you wish to gently fade from view. For a more subtle masking effect, try using the Gradient tool with a lower opacity setting.

PART THREE: Thermal effects via channels and layers

13 Open up the man-thermal.jpg file or a scan of your own version of this thermal-affected sketch. Select all and copy. Return to the working file and create a new alpha channel in the Channels palette. Paste your copied image into the new channel and then enable the visibility of the composite channel within the Channels palette. Choose Edit>Free-Transform from the menu. Use the visible CMYK image as your guide to resize, rotate, and reposition the image you pasted into the channel. Do your best to get it to match up nicely with the sketch on the main page within the image.

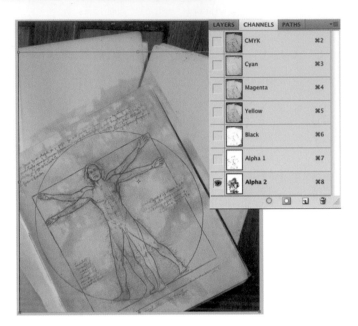

Color opacity

In the Channel Options dialog box, you'll notice that at the bottom, there is an area where you can change the opacity of the red overlay. When you are displaying the CMYK composite channel at the same time as your alpha channel, there may be instances where you find that the red is too faint to really see what you're doing. Increasing the opacity in the Channel Options will help with channel visibility. The downside, however, is that the more you increase the opacity, the less transparent the overlay becomes. Ideally, you'll address this on an as-needed basis depending upon your existing channel preview circumstances.

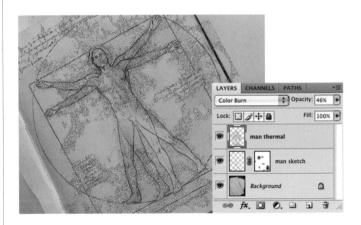

14 Load your new channel as a selection. In the Layers palette, create a new layer. Ensure that your selection is active and that the new layer is targeted. Use the Eyedropper to sample a beige color from the image and then fill the active selection with the new foreground color on the new layer. Change the layer blending mode to color burn and reduce the opacity of the layer to 46%.

15 With the current selection still active, create a new hue/saturation adjustment layer by clicking on the Hue/Saturation button in the Adjustments palette. Increase the saturation by 61 and reduce the lightness by 9. When you create an adjustment layer, your active selection is used to create a mask and then becomes deactivated. Right-click(PC)/Control-click(Mac) on the adjustment layer's mask thumbnail and then choose the Add Layer Mask To Selection option from the pop-up menu that appears. This will reload your selection. With the new selection active, create a new layer and ensure that it is targeted in the Layers palette.

16 Change the blending mode of the new layer to color burn and reduce the opacity to 30%. Use the Eyedropper to sample a slightly darker brown color from within the image and then select the Gradient tool. Ensure that the Foreground to Transparent Gradient preset is selected and that the radial method is enabled in the Tool Options bar. Click and drag to create a few gradients within the selection on the current layer. This will add a darkening effect in these areas. Add as many as you think are needed and then type Control(PC)/Command(Mac)-d to deactivate the selection.

Individual channel options

Earlier on, we changed what color indicates in your channels by accessing the Channel options via the Channels Palette menu. When you do it this way, every subsequent channel you create uses the same options. However, you can edit the options for individual channels after the fact. To do this, simply double-click on any alpha channel in the Channels palette. The Channel Options dialog box opens up, allowing you to alter the options for that specific channel only.

Part Two: Unconventional Methods

17 Drag the current layer onto the Create a New Layer button in the Layers palette to duplicate it. Change the blending mode to multiply to darken the effect further and then choose Filter>Blur>Gaussian Blur from the menu. Enter a radius value sufficient enough to considerably soften the contents of the duplicated layer. Now that the overall page is looking good, it is time to begin darkening the edges. Open up the edge1.jpg file or a desktop scan of your own. Select all and copy.

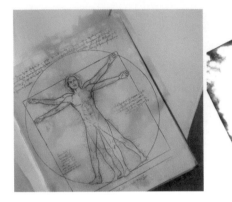

Begin darkening the edges of the page

Now the blank thermal page scans that were burned around the edges only, will be put to good use.

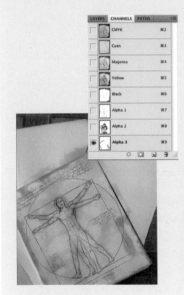

1 Create a new channel in your working file and paste the copied image into it. Enable the visibility of the composite channel and position it over the appropriate area. This included scan was already rotated on the scanner; however, you may need to rotate your own.

2 Load the channel as a selection and create a new layer. Target the layer and fill the active selection with a newly sampled, dark brown foreground color. Change the layer blending mode to color burn and reduce the opacity to 15%. Deselect.

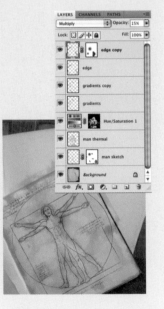

3 Duplicate this layer and change the blending mode to multiply to darken the effect. Add a layer mask and then use the Gradient tool to add radial, black to transparent gradients into the mask to soften any areas on this layer that appear too dark.

146

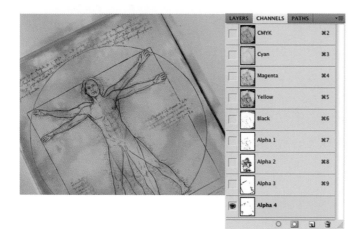

18 Open up the edge2.jpg file or use another of your own scans. Again, select all and copy. Return to your working file and paste it into a new alpha channel. Enable the visibility of the CMYK composite to aid you in positioning the contents of the channel on the page. The included file was rotated on the scanner; however, especially if you're using your own file, you may need to use Free-Transform to resize and rotate the channel contents. Load the channel as a selection and then create a new layer in the Layers palette.

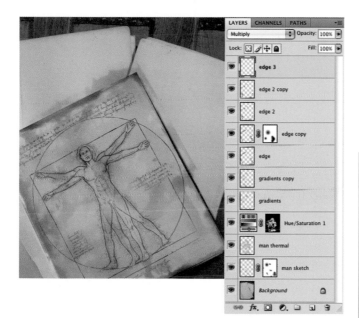

19 Use the Eyedropper to sample a different dark brown color and fill the active selection with that color on the new layer. Deselect and reduce the opacity of the layer to 16%. Duplicate the layer, change the blending mode to color burn, and increase the opacity to 24%. Open up the edge4.jpg. Again, copy the image and paste it into a new channel within your working file. Position it using the CMYK composite channel as your guide. Load it as a selection and fill the selection with dark brown on a new layer. Change the blending mode to multiply and deselect.

Channel color

Sometimes, when previewing an alpha channel against the CMYK composite channel, red simply isn't going to be as visible as another color would be. You can alter the color overlay of your channel by clicking on the Color swatch in the Channel options. This launches the picker, allowing you to change the display color of your channel to another color that will be more visible against the CMYK composite channel. Your display color can vary from channel to channel; they don't all have to be the same.

Part Two: Unconventional Methods

20 Create a new layer and select the Gradient
tool. Ensure that the gradient is still set to radial
and that the Foreground to Transparent preset
is selected in the Tool Options bar. Set the
blending mode of the layer to darken and ensure
that you have a dark brown foreground color
specified. Click and drag on this layer, creating
gradients in various sizes, using varying opacity
settings, to darken areas of the page on the
underlying layers with smooth blends of color.

 Cleaning up channels

When you are working with a file
like this, it doesn't take long for the
Channels palette to fill up and for file
size to swell. Go ahead and delete
any alpha channels you wish from
the palette after they've been used.
You don't need to hang onto them as
storage areas for your selections once
you've filled a selection with color on
a layer. You can load a selection from
the layer at any point by Control(PC)/
Command-clicking on its thumbnail in
the Layers palette.

21 Target your top layer, hold down the Shift
key and click on the initial sketch layer, which
sits directly above the background layer in
the Layers palette. This will target both the
layers and all the layers in-between. Choose
Layer>New>Group From Layers from the menu
to add them to a group. Select the Pen tool,
ensure that it is set to create paths, and that the
Add to Path Area option is enabled in the Tool
Options bar. Carefully trace the outer edge of
the page with the Pen tool, drawing a closed
path. Choose Layer>Vector Mask>Current Path
from the menu to clip the group.

22 Now repeat what you've done with different resource materials. Follow the same process that you used to create the antique man illustration, using different resource files and a different position on the canvas. Use the hand.jpg and hand-thermal.jpg files for your first two channels and subsequent layers. Then follow the process employed previously to build up layers with varying colors, masks, and blending modes to create the antique effect. To build up the edge effect on a series of layers, use the edge4.jpg file as your resource. When finished, add the layers to a group and clip it with a vector mask.

Examining the hand group

Although the contents of your group will likely differ, this is exactly how I achieved the effect.

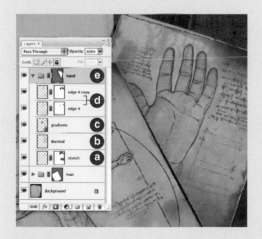

a The channel-based hand sketch selection is filled with brown on this layer. The blending mode is set to multiply and a mask is used to soften areas that are too strong.

b The channel-based thermal hand selection is filled with a lighter brown on this layer. The blending mode is set to color burn and the layer opacity is reduced to 77%.

c Brown to transparent, radial gradients reside on this layer. The layer blending mode is set to multiply, thus darkening the underlying layers.

d The channel-based edge selection is filled with brown on this layer. The layer blending mode is set to color burn and the opacity setting is 28%. The layer is duplicated and the blending mode of the duplicate layer is set to multiply. The opacity is increased to 51% and both the layers are masked. Gradients are used within each mask to hide areas that are too prominent.

e All of these layers are added to a group and a path is drawn around the edge of the page. The path is used as the basis for a vector mask that clips the group and ensures that no artwork extends beyond the edge of the page.

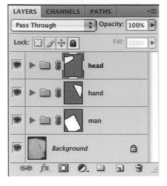

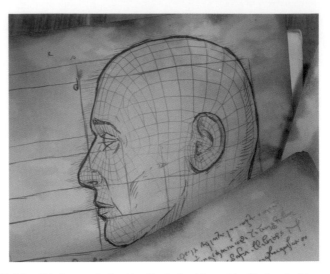

23 Now it is time to repeat the entire procedure for a third time. This time, use the head.jpg file, the head-thermal.jpg file, the edge5.jpg file, and the edge6.jpg file to create the same effect on the remaining page. Use the now familiar method of creating channel-based selections and building up the antique effect on a stack of layers. Experiment with different colored fills, various blending modes, layer masks, and opacity settings. When you're finished, add all of these layers to a group as well. Then clip the group with a vector mask so that the drawing and the age effect do not stray beyond the edge of the page.

Where to go from here
The methods used to create this effect lend themselves nicely to repetition and experimentation.

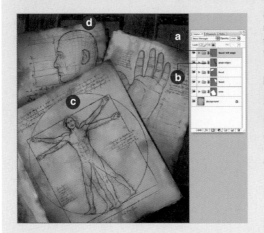

a Use sections of some of your resource files to generate selections and a new stack of layers, adding an antique effect to the page that is partially visible at the lower left of the image. When finished, clip it with a vector mask.

b Use the same method to add the antique effect to all of the little bits of pages that are sticking out beneath the main pages. This will ensure that all pages, wholly or partially visible, will have the same antique effect applied to them. Carefully clip the desired areas with a vector mask.

c Because this file is built as a series of layer groups, you can edit any layer at any time. If you feel that an effect needs to be made stronger or weaker, alter the blending modes and opacity settings of the necessary layers to make it so. Have some fun experimenting here.

d If you're not entirely satisfied with the accuracy of your vector masks, never be afraid to zoom in closely and edit the vector mask's individual points and line segments with the Direct Selection tool.

Focus on the edges

To create this image, the same thermal fax technique was used, but instead of copying sketches and then burning them with the hairdryer, only blank sheets of thermal paper were used. This provides the ability to focus only on the edges when creating multilayered burn effects, leaving the actual sketch unaffected.

Staining paper ahead of time

Another method for ageing paper is to stain it before you scan it. The two scanned pages shown here are simple, unbleached paper samples purchased at a Japanese paper shop. The edges were torn off and then a pot of tea was brewed.

The wet tea bags were removed from the teapot and then rubbed along the edges of the paper, allowing it to bleed into the paper from the edges inward. Then a brush was used to paint the tea over the entire paper area. Once the pages had dried, they were scanned. As you can see here, the tea stain method produces a convincing antique paper background effect, without the aid of alpha channels or layer stacks.

Putting the stained paper to good use

These two images are excellent examples of the tea-stained papers in use. Although the effect is quite different than the thermal fax paper effect, the antique and aged feeling is certainly there.

Chapter 10

Photocopier Meets Photoshop

Photoshop, to many, represents perfection. But while we strive to achieve perfection, let us not overlook the beauty of imperfection. If you're an urban dweller, pay attention to what is surrounding you as you wander the streets. You'll notice photocopied flyers and posters plastered all over the place. You'd be hard pressed to find a better example of imperfect, yet beautiful, artwork. This is the art of the underground scene. Local bands and underground artists do what they can with what they have. There is an evident do-it-yourself aesthetic inherent in the majority of urban poster art.

This low-fidelity appearance is more a result of available tools and failing monetary resources rather than a conscious attempt at style. Regardless of intent, a certain style prevails. Poor registration, inferior image quality, and cut-and-paste typography all contribute to the urban underground look. However, the most prominent element is the look achieved by using a poor-quality photocopier to put it all together. Generally these collages are photocopied on machines in desperate need of servicing or even dangerously low on toner. Not the sort of thing found at a professional copy shop, but rather like something you'll find in a local convenience store.

Remember, just because Photoshop has an arsenal of tools that lend themselves to achieving perfection, it doesn't mean that you cannot turn the tables and create convincing imperfection. The limit to what you can achieve with Photoshop's tools and functions is dictated by your own willingness to explore less-than-obvious methods. To create tactile and distressed underground poster art effects, all you need is access to a good old-fashioned photocopier, an enthusiasm for Photoshop, and a willingness to experiment.

DIFFICULTY 2.5/5

Although this chapter is a simple montage, you'll need to know how to create text layers and change fonts. You'll also need to know how to use simple selection tools and some very basic experience with the Free-Transform command will be helpful. A bit of experience drawing simple paths is beneficial toward the end as well.

What you'll learn in this chapter

Creative Techniques and Working Methods

Virtual scissors and glue

In order to get that authentic cut-and-paste look, you have to take a very simplistic approach to isolating elements and compositing in Photoshop. When isolating different bits and pieces, you'll learn that rough selections are more believable than precise ones. A bit of white space around a dark rectangle or an accidentally angled cut will help the finished composition look convincing. When you piece things together, you'll quickly see the merit in this sort of hasty montage technique. This is no place for precise selection tools or grids to assist in perfect alignment. This is intended to look like a real photocopied do-it-yourself gig poster. If you're used to creating slick, photographic compositions in Photoshop, this chapter will definitely open your eyes to new possibilities.

Deterioration tactics

When you run artwork through a photocopier, there is always some deterioration in quality. In general, this is the type of thing we are conditioned to avoid. However, this chapter will get you thinking about the beauty within the result of that deterioration and have you searching for ways to emulate and enhance the effect. After you create copies for a number of generations, it is almost impossible to ignore the unique quality of the deterioration and you can't help but notice the potential in the random distress that occurs.

Photoshop Tools, Features, and Functions

Brightness/Contrast

With infinitely better tonal adjustment tools like curves and levels available, it isn't very often we reach for something as simple as the brightness/contrast adjustment. However, this time, it is a simplistic result that we're after. Here, the goal of the image is an inferior, not superior, appearance. Enabling this feature's legacy format deteriorates the quality even further.

Smart objects

Placing the finished poster file into the large background image allows you to create a flexible final composition quite easily. Keeping the poster as a smart object allows you to tweak the poster design at any point, even long after you think you're finished.

Blending and opacity

Authentic results are not always the result of complicated procedures. Creating the effect of the poster being glued to a surface can be as simple as overlaying the image with a texture layer. The secret to success is combining just the right layer blending mode with the perfect opacity setting.

PART ONE: Prepare, print, and photocopy

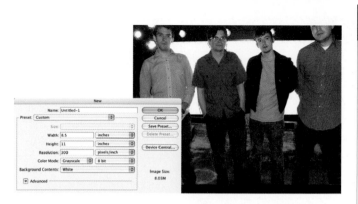

1 Open up the neinphoto.jpg file. This is a press photo used by an American band known as The Nein. The Nein will act as the subject for the urban poster art you'll be creating here. To simulate the appearance of cutting with scissors, use the Polygonal Lasso tool to draw a very rough polygonal selection around the outside of a single band member in the image. Now, create a new file. Specify a white background and grayscale color mode. Set the canvas size to something that is similar in size to the paper you'll be printing everything out on.

2 Return to the neinphoto.jpg file. Hold down the Control(PC)/Command(Mac) key. Click inside the selection border and drag the contents of the selection into your new grayscale file as a new layer. Continue to hold down the Control(PC)/Command(Mac) key and position the layer on the canvas to allow space for the band members. Use this method to add each band member to the grayscale file. To fit them on the canvas, you'll likely have to rotate one band member. To do so, target the appropriate layer in the Layers palette and then choose a 90° rotation option from the Edit>Transform menu.

Project files

All of the files needed to follow along with this chapter and create the featured image are available for download on the accompanying Web site in the project files section. Visit www.creativephotoshopthebook.com.

You can follow along from the beginning, creating and printing out your own grayscale files. Or, if you don't want to seek out a photocopier on your own, you can access the already photocopied and scanned files in the same archive. These supplied files will be referred to by name throughout the tutorial. Feel free to use them or substitute files of your own as you work.

Editing text

When you have a type layer targeted in the Layers palette and the Type tool selected, you can edit any of the type options in the Tool Options bar. This will affect the entire contents of the type layer. However, if you click on an area of type on the canvas, which activates the type layer, it becomes necessary to select type in order to edit it. Either click and drag to select a portion of the text or double-click to select it. Once your text is selected, it can then be edited.

Source: Nein press photo courtesy of Casey Burns/The Nein.

3 Next, choose Layer>Flatten Image from the menu to flatten the layers. Choose Image>Adjustments>Brightness/Contrast from the menu. Enable the Use Legacy option offered in the Brightness/Contrast dialog box so that you are removing shadow and highlight detail when adjusting. Adjust the brightness and contrast sliders to increase the contrast and decrease the range of grays within the image. This is the first step in image deterioration that is necessary to produce a convincing effect. When you've completed the adjustment, print the image in black and white on an ink jet or laser printer.

Creating text

Very simple typography set against black, white, or gray backgrounds will help to lend a sense of authenticity to your design.

1 Create a new grayscale file identical to your previous file. Select the Horizontal Type tool. Click on the canvas to add a type insertion point. Enter some text and press the Enter key to create a new, editable type layer.

2 While the Type tool is selected, you can alter the font, size, color, and other attributes of your type layer in the Tool Options bar. Choose an appropriate font like American typewriter. Now, create another type insertion point and add some different text using a different font.

3 Target your background layer and use the Rectangular Marquee to create a selection beneath a line of type. Use Edit>Fill from the menu to fill the selection. Then target the overlaying type layer, ensure that you've selected the Type tool and change the color of the type to white.

4 Use the aforementioned techniques to add all of the necessary text to your page on a series of layers. Try different shades of gray, as well as black, behind white text. Try duplicating type layers by dragging them onto the Create a New Layer button at the bottom of the Layers palette. Move the duplicated type around the canvas with the Move tool. In addition to experimenting with different grays in the background, try changing some of your black type to gray as well. Fill your page with options until you're satisfied, and then flatten the image. Print this page in black and white as well.

Create some basic shapes
Again, simplicity is the key to a design like this, especially when creating backgrounds and borders.

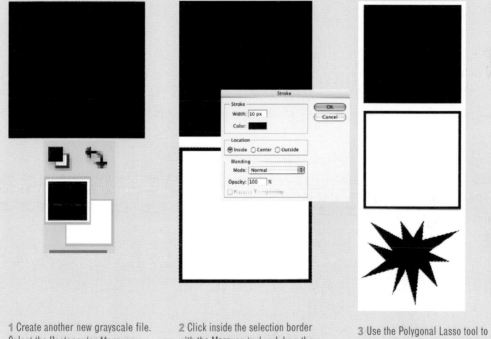

1 Create another new grayscale file. Select the Rectangular Marquee tool. Hold down the Shift key while clicking and dragging to draw a square selection. Press "d" to set the foreground color to black, and type Alt(PC)/Option(Mac)-Delete to fill the selection with it.

2 Click inside the selection border with the Marquee tool and drag the active selection border down on the canvas beneath the square. Choose Edit>Stroke from the menu. Select "inside" as the location and "black" as the color. Enter a width value and click OK.

3 Use the Polygonal Lasso tool to create a primitive starburst shaped selection on an empty area of the canvas. Use the same methods you used previously with the first square to fill your starburst with black. Print this file in black and white as well.

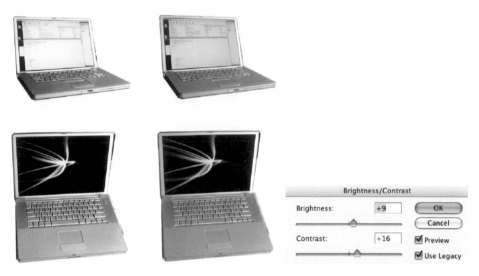

5 Open up the computers.jpg file from the CD. This grayscale file has already had the computer images placed in it and has been flattened. All that you need to do here is snap up the contrast a little. Choose Image>Adjustments>Brightness/Contrast from the menu. Again, enable the Legacy option to deteriorate the image and adjust the sliders to increase the contrast overall. Print this final file in black and white and then gather up all of your printouts.

Making copies
The best way to get that rough, photocopied look is to gather up your printouts and find a neglected copier.

1 Convenience stores are the best places to find copiers that are rarely maintained. The lack of maintenance often results in a grittier result, which is exactly what we're after. Get out your printouts and make at least one photocopy of each.

2 Try copying the copies a few times. With each generation, the quality deteriorates and the signature look of the copier becomes more apparent. Crumple some copies, flatten them, and then copy them again. Incorporating this crumple technique will distress your copies even more.

3 When you're finished, gather up the copies and head home. There is a good chance that you'll have a lot to choose from. Lay everything out on the floor to have a good look. Choose the best of the bunch and scan them.

PART TWO: Prepare the background

6 Again, all of the photocopied and scanned files that were used to create this poster are included on the CD. They will be referred to by name for the rest of this chapter. However, feel free to substitute photocopies of your own if you like. To begin creating the poster, open up the paper.jpg file from the CD. This desktop scan of a folded piece of paper will act as the background in the multilayered file you'll create. Something as simple as starting with an authentic background can be very powerful in helping to achieve a convincing result. Every little bit helps.

Choosing fonts

For your poster art to look authentic, it should definitely look like a computer was not involved in its creation whatsoever. This especially rings true when it comes to choosing fonts. American Typewriter and Stencil are both fonts that are available when typesetting with traditional tools. As a result of this, it is entirely believable that the typesetting on the poster could've been accomplished by traditional means. Adding the photocopied look to a slick modern font will display the technique we're describing, but at the same time it will ruin the authenticity of the final poster design by displaying something that is clearly impossible.

7 Choose Layer>New Fill Layer>Solid Color from the menu. When the New Layer dialog box opens, set the blending mode to multiply and click OK. When the picker opens, choose a dark pink color and click OK to create your new solid pink layer. Next, click on the Create a New Layer button at the bottom of the Layers palette. With the new layer targeted, use the Rectangular Marquee tool to draw a square selection. Press the "d" key to set the current background color to white. Type Control(PC)/Command(Mac)-Delete on the keyboard to fill the new selection with white.

8 Type Control(PC)/Command(Mac)-d on the keyboard to deactivate the current selection. Open up the shape.jpg file and use the Rectangular Marquee tool to draw a selection around the square that has the stroke around it. Hold down the Control(PC)/Command(Mac) key, click inside the selection border and, while holding the mouse button down, drag the contents of the selection into your working file as a new layer. Change the layer blending mode to multiply and then choose Edit>Free-Transform from the menu. Hold down the Shift key while dragging a corner handle outward to increase the size proportionately.

 Lighten then darken

Almost every photocopier has a setting that allows you to lighten or darken the copied image. When you're copying the original, try using a very light setting so that a lot of the detail and tonal range disappear. Then, try copying this initial copy with a darker setting, enhancing the contrast while copying the image of reduced detail and tonal range.

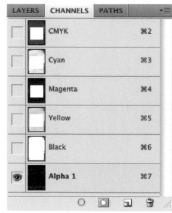

9 Click and drag within the bounding box to position the layer contents. When it frames the white box on the layer below, press the Enter key to apply the transformation. Return to the shapes.jpg file and deactivate the selection. Choose Image>Adjustments>Invert from the menu to invert the color of the shapes image. Now, use the Rectangular Marquee tool to draw a selection around the inverted square shape. Choose Edit>Copy from the menu. Return to your working file. In the Channels palette, click on the Create New Channel button at the bottom of the palette to create a new alpha channel.

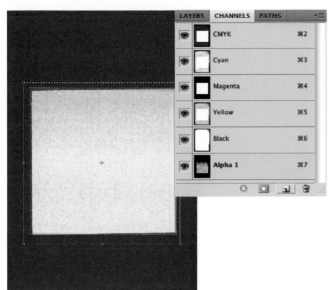

10 Click in the column to the left of the CMYK composite channel in the Channels palette to make it visible at the same time as your alpha channel. Your alpha channel will preview against the background as a red overlay. Ensure that the alpha channel is targeted in the Channels palette and then choose Edit>Paste from the menu to paste the copied rectangle into the channel. Use Free-Transform to increase the size and position the square so that it overlaps the large white square, exactly like you did with the outlined square earlier. Press Enter to apply the transformation.

The Nein

I often listen to music when I spend countless hours in my studio and every once in a while I come across a band like The Nein that sparks an idea. I thought this band was the ideal subject to display such an anti-technology technique. They hail from the USA and their album Wrath of Circuits has an inherent fear of technology about it. This disc was released by Sonic Unyon Records in Canada. If you'd like to hear their music you can find out more from http://www.sonicunyon.com.

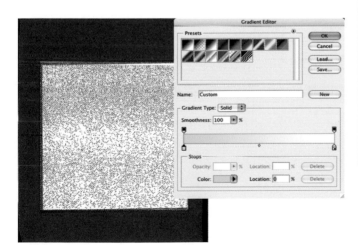

11 Control(PC)/Command(Mac)-click on the alpha channel thumbnail to generate a selection from its contents. In the Layers palette, with the current selection active, click the Create a New Layer button. Target your new layer at the top of the Layers palette and select the Gradient tool. In the Tool Options bar, choose the linear gradient method and then click on the Gradient preset thumbnail to edit the gradient. Choose any two-color Gradient preset as a starting point, then click on the Color Stop at the left, below the gradient. Click on the Color swatch to launch the picker and select a light blue color.

12 Use this same method to change the color stop beneath the gradient at the right to a different, darker blue. Drag the gradient midpoint to the right slightly and click OK. Your new gradient will be selected as the preset when you exit the Gradient Editor. Click and drag, from the bottom up, within the current selection on your new layer. This will add your new gradient into the selection. Deactivate the selection and change the blending mode of the layer to multiply.

PART THREE: Add the main components

Adding a figure

Follow this process to create a figure, complete with a giant laptop on his head.

1 Open up the band.jpg file and use the Polygonal Lasso tool to draw a polygonal selection around one of the band members. Control(PC)/Command(Mac)-click inside the selection and drag the contents into your working file as a new layer.

2 With the new layer targeted, choose Edit>Free-Transform from the menu. To rotate, move the mouse pointer outside the bounding box, then click and drag. Shift-drag the corner of the box to increase the size proportionately. Press the Enter key to apply the transformation.

3 Open up the computers.jpg file. Select a laptop with the Polygonal Lasso and drag it into your working file as a new layer. Use the Free-Transform function to rotate, resize, and position the laptop so that it overlaps the figure's head.

13 Use the Polygonal Lasso tool to draw a selection that surrounds only the screen of the laptop in your working file. Open up the eyes.jpg file. In the eyes.jpg file, draw a polygonal selection around one of the eyes in the image. Copy the selected area and return to your working file. With your current selection active, choose Edit>Paste Into from the menu to paste the eye into the image as a masked layer. Target the new layer thumbnail in the Layers palette (not the mask) and use Free-Transform to resize and position the eye.

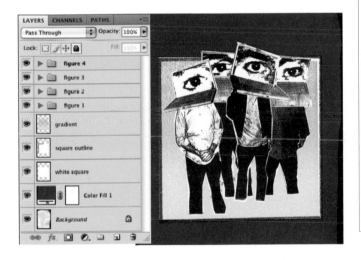

Linking the unlinked

When you have a selection active and you choose the Paste Into option from the Edit menu, your copied artwork is pasted into the file as a new layer. This layer is automatically masked and the active selection determines which areas of the new layer will remain visible. When you create a masked layer this way, the mask and the layer are not linked in the Layers palette. If you want to move both the layer and the mask together, it is necessary to link them by clicking in the space between the two thumbnails in the Layers palette. You'll see a link icon appear in this area. Masks are linked to layers here because if the groups containing the layers are moved, we want the masks to move with them.

14 Click in the area between your new layer thumbnail and the mask thumbnail in the Layers palette to link them. Now, target the current layer and then Control(PC)/Command(Mac)-click on the laptop layer and the figure layer in the Layers palette so that all three layers are targeted. Choose Layer>New>Group From Layers from the menu to add these layers to a group. Now, repeat this procedure three times to add the three remaining figures, add laptops on their heads, put eyes on the laptop screens, link any unlinked masks, resize and rotate as required, and then add each set of layers to a group until you have a separate group for each figure.

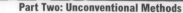

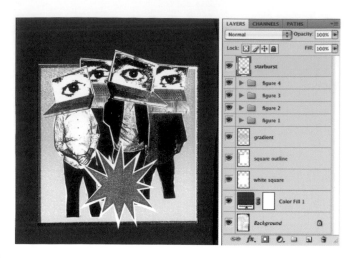

Another duplication method

When you are using the Polygonal Lasso tool, try right-clicking(PC)/ Control-clicking(Mac) on the contents of your layer on the canvas. You will see a pop-up menu appear offering you several functions to choose from. Included on the list is the option to duplicate the layer. Try using this method, you may find it even quicker than dragging layers onto the Create a New Layer button at the bottom of the Layers palette. This method works with any selection tool.

15 Return to your shapes.jpg file. If you have left the file open, there is a chance that it is still inverted. Choose File>Revert from the menu to revert it back to the original positive state. If it isn't currently open, reopen the shapes.jpg file. Use the Polygonal Lasso tool to draw a selection border around the starburst shape. Hold down the Control(PC)/Command(Mac) key, and then click inside the selection border and drag it into your working file as a new layer. Use Free-Transform to increase the size and position the layer on the canvas as shown here.

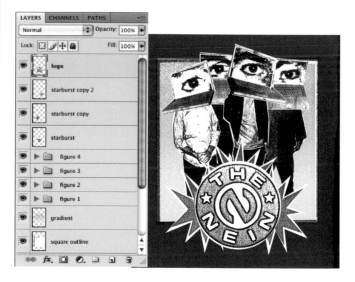

16 Drag your starburst layer onto the Create a New Layer button at the bottom of the Layers palette to duplicate it. Use the Move tool to drag it over to the left and then down slightly on the canvas. Duplicate this layer too, and then move it to the right. Open up the logos.jpg file. Click and drag with the Elliptical Marquee tool to select the logo at the upper right. Hold down the Shift key to create a circular selection as you drag. Control(PC)/Command(Mac)-drag the selected logo into the working file as a new layer. Use Free-Transform to adjust the size and position.

17 Return to your logo.jpg file. This time use the Elliptical Marquee tool to draw a selection around the black logo at the lower right of the canvas. Copy it and return to your working file. Click on the Create New Channel button at the bottom of the Channels palette to create an alpha channel. Double-click the new channel thumbnail and when the Channel Options appear choose Selected Areas in the Color Indicates options and click OK. Paste the copied art into your new channel and then enable the visibility of the CMYK composite channel by clicking in the column to the left of it in the Channels palette.

PART FOUR: Typographic elements

(i) Constrained rotations

When you are rotating the contents of a layer or selection with Free-Transform, try holding down the Shift key while you click and drag outside of the bounding box. When you do this, your rotations will be constrained to 45° increments.

18 Use Free-Transform to increase the size of your pasted selection and position it within the channel so that it overlaps the logo in the composite channel. Press Enter to apply the transformation and then open up the type. jpg file. Use the Polygonal Lasso tool to draw a selection around the "sonic unyon presents" that is set against a dark background. Copy it and return to your working file. Paste it into your targeted alpha channel and then use Free-Transform to adjust the size and position it at the upper left within the channel. Load the channel as a selection.

19 With the new channel-based selection active, return to the Layers palette and create a new layer. Click on the Foreground Color swatch to choose a light green foreground color from the picker. Type Alt/Option-Delete to fill the active selection with the foreground color on the new layer and then deselect. Set the blending mode of the layer to multiply in the Layers palette and select the Polygonal Lasso tool. Use the Polygonal Lasso to draw selections that cover each large eye. Then fill these selections with the same color on the current layer and deselect.

 Lighten via blending

If you double-click a layer thumbnail in the Layers palette, you will access the layer style box which, in addition to a plethora of other options, allows you to control the blending of the layer. In this case, simply direct your attention to the top slider in the "blend if" section. Drag the left slider underneath the "this layer" bar to the right. This will lighten all of the shadow areas on the layer. This is a handy way to lighten all of the black components of your photocopied art on a layer. The advantage of doing this versus a color adjustment is that you can always go back to this dialog box and edit or reset your adjustment.

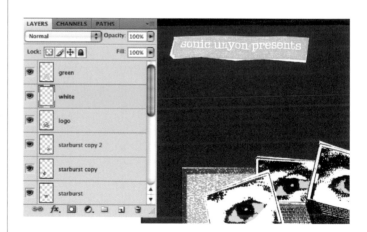

20 Create a new layer and drag it below the top layer in the Layers palette. Use the Polygonal Lasso to draw a shape that roughly surrounds the "sonic unyon presents" box on the top layer. Ensure that the new layer is targeted and then press "d" on the keyboard to set the background color to white. Type Control(PC)/Command(Mac)-Delete to fill the selection with the background color and then deselect. Return to the type.jpg file, reopen it if necessary.

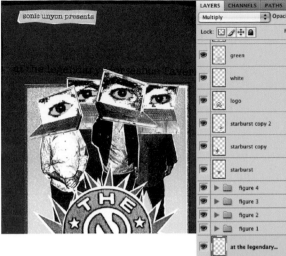

21 Use the Rectangular Marquee to draw a selection around the black against white "sonic unyon presents" type. Copy it, return to your working file, and paste it in as a new layer. Drag the layer to the top of the Layers palette and change the blending mode to multiply. Use Free-Transform to adjust the size and angle of the layer contents as well as position it over the other "sonic unyon presents" artwork on the canvas. Repeat this method to add the "live at the horseshoe" text on a new layer. Drag the new layer beneath the figure groups in the Layers palette.

Distorting

Each piece of photocopied text that is brought into this image as a new layer is resized and rotated by using the Free-Transform function. However, if you look at the word "live" you'll notice that it has been distorted. To distort, rather than scale, while using Free-Transform, hold down the Control(PC)/Command(Mac) key while you drag a corner handle of the bounding box.

22 Now, return to the type.jpg file. Use the Polygonal Lasso to select a section of type, copy it, and then paste it into the working file as a new layer. Use Free-Transform to size, rotate, and position it. Repeat this method over and over again until you've added all of the necessary text elements to the poster. Leave the blending modes for all of these new layers set to normal as you add them. Move the layers up and down within the palette as you see fit.

23 The poster design is complete, but it doesn't look weathered or distressed enough on the surface. To remedy this, we'll incorporate a photo of the real thing. Open up the texture.jpg file. This is a photo of extremely weather-beaten poster art. Select all and copy. Paste it into your working file as a new layer and drag the new layer to the top of the stack in the Layers palette. Change the blending mode of the layer to hard light and reduce the opacity to 26%. Save and close your poster file with all of the channels and layers intact.

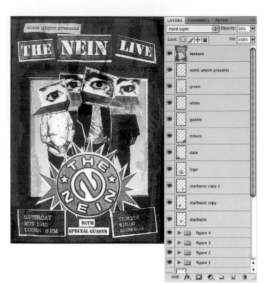

PART FIVE: Application methods

Put your poster up on the wall

Add your poster to a background image as an editable smart object, carefully tracing it with the Pen tool.

1 Open up the wall.jpg file. Then, choose File>Place from the menu. Navigate to your layered poster file on your hard drive and open it. This will place your poster file into the wall image file as a smart object.

2 The smart object is placed into your file surrounded by a Free-Transform bounding box. Resize and rotate the smart object while placing it to the left of the canvas. Press Enter key to commit the transformation.

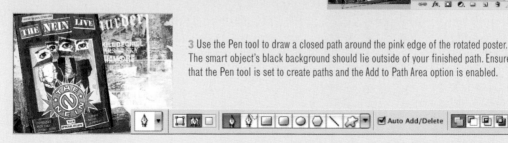

3 Use the Pen tool to draw a closed path around the pink edge of the rotated poster. The smart object's black background should lie outside of your finished path. Ensure that the Pen tool is set to create paths and the Add to Path Area option is enabled.

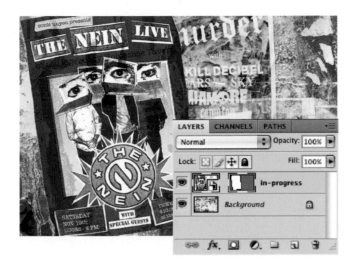

24 With your new path selected and your smart object targeted in the Layers palette, choose Layer>Vector Mask>Current Path from the menu to clip your smart object with the path. You will see a vector mask added to your smart object in the Layers palette. If you wish to edit your poster at any point, all that you need to do is double-click on the smart object in the Layers palette. This will open a new document containing a layered version of the poster. You can make any changes you like to the poster file. Once you save the changes, the smart object will automatically update within this file, reflecting the changes you made.

Examining the poster you've created
A successful urban poster art effect is the culmination of a number of essential ingredients.

a Converting your images to grayscale and then enhancing the contrast is an excellent way to get started. It allows you to create simple, high-contrast images that lend themselves nicely to real-world photocopier degradation without losing any essential detail.

b Scanning the photocopied results and then using the Polygonal Lasso tool allows you to create an imperfect and choppy composition. Because most real-world underground posters are put together by manually cutting and pasting, a choppy Photoshop selection technique is necessary to ensure an authentic look.

c Creating areas of color that overlap the imagery on a layer with a multiply blending mode simulates authentic silkscreen-printing effects. Usually, urban posters that are silkscreened are hastily created with poor registration and as a result, colors overlap and tend to look sloppy.

d Now, even though we started with a folded piece of paper in the background, the results were still a little too crisp looking. Adding a photo of actual torn-up posters on the top layer helps to provide a gritty, textured effect.

Try varying your color scheme

Because this style of urban artwork is comprised of flat, solid colors, it lends itself nicely to hue/saturation adjustments. As is evident in these poster designs for The Weekend, a hue adjustment, after all is said and done, can open the door to a plethora of new color combinations. Sometimes you'll be taken by surprise to see how well a color combination that you'd never think to try will work out.

Source: Original Weekend press photo courtesy of Teenage USA Recordings.

Other inferior devices

Although we explored the thermal qualities of old fax machines in the previous chapter, they can also be used to deteriorate, just like an old photocopier is used in this chapter. The central figure in this composition is the result of copying and re-copying black-and-white printouts with a fax machine instead of a photocopier. With fax machines, you're likely to see line patterns form rather than the random noise patterns caused by photocopying. In any case, it still helps to create a wonderfully distressed result.

Source: Model photo courtesy of Paul O'Connor: www.paulandpaul.co.uk.

Chapter 11

Urban Lowbrow Art

There is evidence of a reckless approach inherent in the majority of urban art. This, along with pop-culture subject matter, is what some argue sets it apart from the world of mainstream art, giving it the derogatory sounding tag of being "lowbrow." However, with a lack of mainstream acceptance comes a sense of freedom. Not only is no subject too taboo, but the techniques of execution are less limited than within mainstream art. Paint is thrown around with abandon, new elements are added on top of old, and the visual result has an incredibly loose feel to it. This is something that is rarely achieved or even addressed in the world of digital art. Things are often very contrived and the feeling of abandon is rarely even attempted. The recklessness and abandon that the paint slingers take for granted is something that we Photoshop artists must carefully plan and calculate. In order to achieve similar results, it is up to the digital artist to devise a process that mimics the techniques of the real-world approach. This process is outlined step-by-step within this chapter. So lower your chair, lean back, and let's create an urban lowbrow masterpiece.

The techniques used in this chapter are not overly complicated, but there is a lot going on here. A vast array of tools and features are used. You'll explore everything from bitmap conversions to layer stacks, alpha channels, type layers, masks, groups, the Pen tool, native filters, and more. If anything within this chapter is remotely daunting, it is the quantity of techniques explored.

What you'll learn in this chapter

Creative Techniques and Working Methods

The importance of materials
As you work your way through the following pages, you'll notice the inclusion of many real-world resources. When a dripping paint effect is required, we'll opt for an actual photo of just the thing. Rather than a digital simulation, an appropriate paper scan is used to create an authentic unbleached parchment background. All of the primary elements are converted drawings or photos. The results are helped by the fact that no single element is entirely computer generated. By the time you finish this chapter, it will become obvious that if you want the finished result to feel real, it is best to begin with real-world resources.

Visualize puncture effects
Converted and adjusted black-and-white art is an infinitely useful tool when compositing. The usefulness of this as a resource extends beyond the obvious use as an image component on the canvas. By creating selections from the art and hiding regions of groups via masks based on the selections, you'll learn to puncture holes in artwork that is composed of multiple layers, revealing the background layer beneath.

Intentionally compose within groups
The central primary elements within this image, the car, the figure, etc., are all contained within a single group. By treating the group as a self-contained collage within the greater scheme of the image, you can work on the content as an independent component. Then, after the fact, you'll learn that the entire group can be integrated into the composition by simply altering the blending mode.

Photoshop Tools, Features, and Functions

Threshold method
Using bitmap mode's threshold method is very effective. When you choose the threshold method, there are no halftone screens or patterns generated from the shades of gray within the image. The result is a simple, high contrast, black-and-white image.

Native filters
Another method for achieving high contrast is to use a couple of native filters that reside within Photoshop. The stamp and photocopy sketch filters can prove very useful when it comes to converting color and grayscale images and will help preserve a little detail where the bitmap conversion method will not.

Alpha channels
When it comes to incorporating converted components into the composition, we'd be nowhere if it weren't for alpha channels. They provide unparalleled control and flexibility when it comes to creating custom selections from black-and-white data.

PART ONE: Building the background

1 To get started, open up the bkd.jpg file from the CD. This will act as the background layer in our new working file. Next, open up the black-and-white heart.jpg file. Type Control(PC)/Command(Mac)-a to select all of the image contents and then type Control(PC)/Command(Mac)-c to copy the contents of the selection. In the bkd.jpg file, click on the Create New Channel button at the bottom of the Channels palette. With your new alpha channel targeted, type Control(PC)/Command(Mac)-v to paste the copied black-and-white image into your alpha channel. Click on the Load Channel as a Selection button at the bottom of the palette.

Project files

All of the files needed to follow along with this chapter and create the featured image are available for download on the accompanying Web site in the project files section. Visit www.creativephotoshopthebook.com. However, do not feel restricted to using these files only. Feel free to follow along and incorporate background imagery and textures of your own as you work through the chapter. Also, rather than using the supplied outline art files, you can create your own outline art using the methods described earlier in either Chapter 5 or Chapter 6.

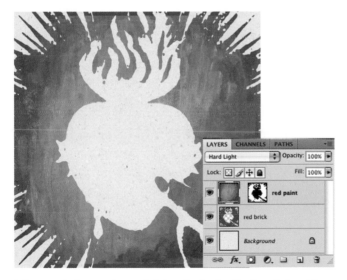

2 Return to the Layers palette and click on the Create a New Layer button at the bottom of the palette. Target your new layer and click on the Foreground Color swatch in the toolbar to access the picker. Choose a color similar to red brick and click OK. Type Alt(PC)/Option(Mac)-Delete to fill the active selection with the new foreground color. Leave the selection active and open up the redpaint.jpg file. Select the contents of the redpaint.jpg file and copy. Return to the working file with the active selection and choose Edit>Paste Into from the menu.

3 Use the Move tool to drag the contents of the layer up to the top of the canvas area. Ensure that the layer is targeted in the Layers palette and not the mask. Because the mask isn't linked, it will remain in position as you move the layer contents. Change the layer blending mode to hard light and then duplicate the layer by dragging it onto the Create a New Layer button. Change the blending mode of your duplicate layer to soft light. With your current layer targeted, Shift-click on the layer directly above the background layer, targeting the top three layers. Type Control(PC)/Command(Mac)-g to add the targeted layers to a new group.

Mask your group

Punch a hole in your paint effects by using the contents of a new channel as the basis for a mask.

1 Open up the ace.jpg file. Select the contents of the file and copy them. Return to your working file and create a new alpha channel in the Channels palette. With your new channel targeted, paste the copied contents from the other file.

2 Click in the column to the left of the CMYK composite channel to enable its visibility. You will now see your alpha channel appear as a red overlay on top of the image. This will aid you in repositioning your pasted art.

3 Position the pasted art within the paint area to the right. Load the channel as a selection and then target your group in the Layers palette. Choose Layer>Layer Mask>Hide Selection from the menu to mask this area of the entire group.

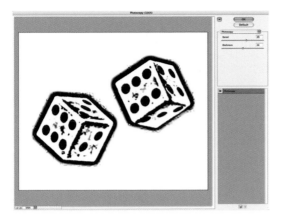

4 Open up the dice.jpg file. We're going to use the photocopy filter here as it will produce a high-contrast result with a halo around the perimeter of the dice. The photocopy filter uses the current foreground and background colors to produce its results; so in order to create a black-and-white effect, we need to set the foreground and background colors to their default black-and-white state. Press the "d" key on the keyboard to set the foreground and background colors to their default state. Choose Filter>Sketch>Photocopy from the menu. Adjust the detail and darkness settings until your dice look something like this. Apply the filter.

Incorporate the dice

Place your converted dice into another channel and use the resulting selection to punch another hole in the paint.

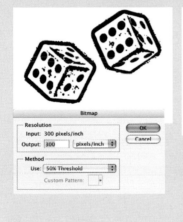

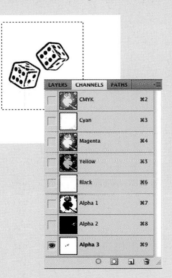

1 Choose Image>Mode>Grayscale from the menu. Then, choose Image>Mode>Bitmap to access the bitmap conversion options. Choose 50% threshold as the method and leave the output set at the current resolution. This will vary depending upon the resolution you're working at.

2 Click OK to convert your image. Then select the contents of the image and copy them. Return to your working file, create a new alpha channel, and invert it by typing Control(PC)/Command(Mac)-i. Paste your copied dice into the new, inverted channel.

3 Enable the visibility of the composite channel. Position your selection contents to the left and then load the channel as a selection. Invert the selection by typing Control(PC)/Command(Mac)-Shift-i. Target the group's mask in the Layers palette and fill the selection with black.

PART TWO: Introducing painted textures

5 Deactivate the dice selection. Open up the bluepaint.jpg file and use the Magic Wand to select a range of blue color from within the image. Hold down the Control(PC)/Command(Mac) key and drag the selected paint into the working file as a new layer. Choose Edit>Free-Transform from the menu. Click and drag within the center of the bounding box to reposition the contents; then Shift-click and drag a corner point to resize the contents of the bounding box proportionately. Press the Enter key to apply the transformation. Reduce the opacity of the layer and change the blending mode to luminosity.

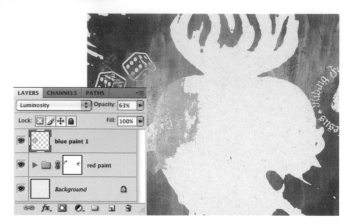

Finish the blue paint effect

Repeat the process of dragging selected regions of blue into the image and then add a solid blue background on an underlying layer.

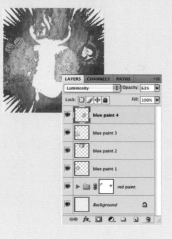

1 Return to the bluepaint.jpg file and use the Magic Wand to select another, different range of color. Again, hold down the Control(PC)/Command(Mac) key and drag it into the working file. Use Free-Transform to resize and position it; change the mode to luminosity and reduce the opacity.

2 Use this method to add a couple more layers from the same bluepaint.jpg file. Control(PC)/Command(Mac)-click on the thumbnail of one of these layers to generate a selection from the contents. Then Control(PC)/Command(Mac)-Shift-click on the remaining blue paint layer thumbnails to add them to the selection.

3 Create a new layer and drag it below all of these new layers in the Layers palette. Choose a light blue foreground color from the picker and use it to fill the active selection on your new layer. Deactivate the selection.

PART THREE: Adding the main components

6 Target all of the blue paint layers and group them in the Layers palette. Open up the figure. jpg file. This file, like the original heart.jpg file, has been prepared ahead of time. Both images were converted to grayscale and then converted to bitmap mode, as you did previously to convert the dice after the photocopy filter was applied. Use the Move tool to click anywhere on the image and drag it into the working file as a new layer. Reposition the layer contents toward the upper left of the canvas. Drag the new layer to the top of the stack in the Layers palette.

7 Now open up the edges.jpg file. This is another prepared image that was created by converting poor-quality scans of photocopied pages to bitmap mode. If you like this sort of look, be sure to read Chapter 10 where photocopy effects are explained in greater detail. Use the Move tool to drag the edges.jpg image into the working file as a new layer. Position the layer so that it touches the top of the canvas and change the blending mode to multiply. Open up the car.psd file and drag it into the working file as a new layer. Position the car layer at the bottom of the canvas.

(i) The conversion process

In order to convert an image to bitmap mode, it must be converted to grayscale first. After you convert your image to grayscale, it is a good idea to examine the overall contrast within the image. Perform any tonal adjustments you think will be necessary for a successful conversion while you're working in grayscale. Once you've got things looking the way you want them, then go ahead and convert the image to bitmap mode. Once the image is in bitmap mode you cannot perform any tonal adjustments, so remember to make any adjustments while you are in grayscale mode.

8 Open up the righthand.jpg file. Duplicate the background layer and ensure that the foreground and background colors are set to black and white. Target the bottom layer and then choose Filter>Sketch>Stamp from the menu. Adjust the sliders so that there is a good balance between contrast and detail. Click OK to apply the filter and then target the top layer that is hiding the effect. Now choose Filter>Sketch>Photocopy. Apply a fairly dark photocopy effect and then change the blending mode of this layer to multiply. Choose Layer>Flatten from the menu to flatten the image.

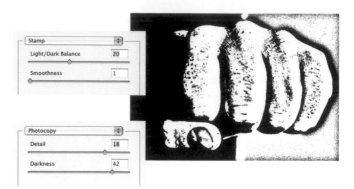

Incorporate hands into the design

Add the selected hand to your working file; then repeat the entire process to alter and then add the other hand as well.

1 Select the Pen tool, ensure that it is set to create paths, and that the Add to Path Area option is enabled in the Tool Options bar. Draw a closed path component that surrounds the hand and includes a bit of the perimeter.

2 In the Paths palette, click on the Load Path as a Selection button. Copy the selected contents and return to your working file. Paste the copied art into the file as a new layer and use Free-Transform to adjust size, rotation, and position.

3 Open up the lefthand.jpg file and repeat the process. Apply filters to the original background and duplicate layers. Flatten the file and encircle the hand with a path. Load the path as a selection and copy. Paste the art into the working file and transform the layer contents.

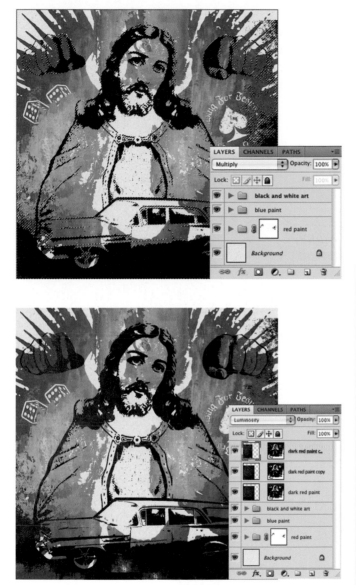

9 Target all of these black-and-white layers and add them to a new group within the Layers palette. Ensure that the new group is targeted in the Layers palette, and set the blending mode of the group itself to multiply. Now that you can see the entire composition clearly, select the Magic Wand tool. Disable the Contiguous option, and then enable the Sample All Layers option in the Tool Options bar. Leave the tolerance set at the default value of 32 and click on a black area of the canvas. This will select all visible areas of the same black color.

Gathering resource materials

When collecting resource materials to use within your urban art illustrations, primarily main image components, bear in mind the conversion process. The image of Jesus is a photograph I took of a mural painted onto the side of a religious supply store. I knew it was an ideal candidate for conversion because, although the original was in color, there was enough contrast between the outline and fill colors to indicate that conversion to black and white would be successful. And although the low-rider car is a photo of an actual car, I examined the image and found that the same qualities were present. It is important to look for areas of preexisting contrast in your photographs or scans to ensure that the image contains detail and is properly represented when you convert to bitmap mode.

10 Open up the darkred.jpg image. Select and copy it. Return to your working file and, with the current Magic Wand selection active, choose Edit>Paste Into from the menu. Use the Move tool to reposition the contents of the layer toward the left of the canvas. Change the blending mode of the layer to hard light. Duplicate the layer. Target your newly duplicated layer and now duplicate it too. Target the second duplicate layer and use the Move tool to move the layer contents upward and to the left a little more. Change the blending mode of the layer to luminosity.

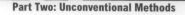

11 Target all of the dark red paint layers in the Layers palette and group them. Use the Pen tool to create path components outlining areas like the car windows and the front of his gown. Generate a selection from the path and fill the active selection with brown on a new layer. Drag the layer down beneath the group that contains the black-and-white artwork in the Layers palette. Reduce the layer opacity slightly, revealing some of the painterly texture beneath. Use this same method again to add color into his skin and hair on other layers beneath the group containing the black-and-white art.

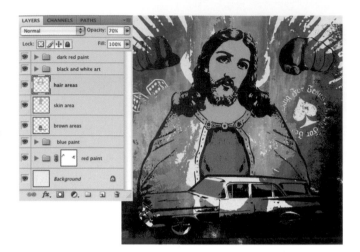

PART FOUR: Bitmaps and type layers

Add the heart

A scanned drawing, converted to bitmap mode, provides the basis for the heart-shaped selection within a new alpha channel.

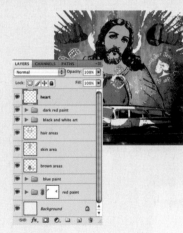

1 Open up the sacredheart.jpg file. Choose Image>Mode>Bitmap from the menu. Use the 50% threshold method and then invert the image. Copy the inverted bitmap and create a new alpha channel in your working file. Paste the copied art into the channel.

2 Load a selection from the channel and then create a new layer in the Layers palette. Drag your new layer to the top of the stack in the Layers palette. Fill the active selection with a light beige foreground color on the new layer.

3 Deactivate the selection and then use the Move tool to reposition the contents of the layer so that the heart is sitting directly on top of his chest area. Keep the foreground color set to the same beige and select the Horizontal Type tool.

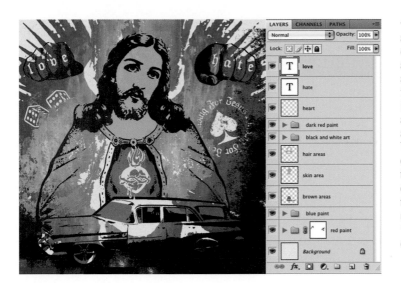

12 Click on the hand at the right to add a text insertion point in that area of the canvas. Type the word "hate" and press the Enter key. Try to select an appropriate font from the available fonts in your system that are listed in the Tool Options bar. Also enter a sufficient size to cover the hand as shown here. Choose Edit>Free-Transform from the menu. Click and drag outside of the bounding box to rotate it and then place the type directly over the knuckles. Press Enter to apply the transformation and then use the same method to add the word "love" across the knuckles of his other hand on another type layer.

PART FIVE: Additional paint effects

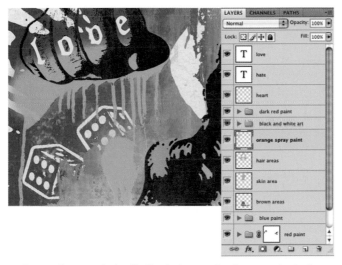

13 Open up the spraypaint.jpg file. Use the Lasso tool to draw a rough selection containing some of the dripping paint and copy it. Create a new alpha channel in the working file and paste the copied paint into it. Generate a selection from the channel and create a new layer in the Layers palette. Fill the active selection with a new, bright orange foreground color. Deactivate the selection and use Free-Transform to resize the contents of the new paint layer. Position it over the hand at the left and drag the layer beneath the group that contains the black-and-white art.

No fonts, no problem

You may find that you're lacking an appropriate font on your system for the love and hate knuckle tattoos in your illustration. If this is the case, worry not, there are plenty of appropriate fonts out there on the Web. Simply do a search for gothic free fonts like I did here, and you'll find numerous hits offering a vast number of appropriate fonts available for free personal use.

14 Use this method to add dripping paint clusters on a variety of layers in different colors. Explore different positions on the canvas as well as within the Layers palette hierarchy. Repeat the entire procedure using the brushy.jpg file and the overspray.jpg file as the resources for new alpha channel–based selections. Load the channels as selections and fill the selected regions with color to produce similar effects in different colors on a variety of layers. Vary the position of your layers but ensure that they remain below the black artwork group in the Layers palette.

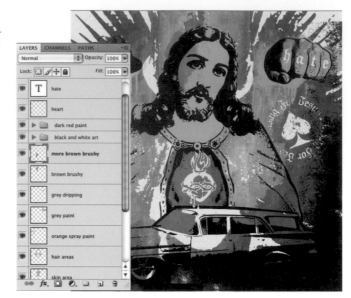

 Don't stop there

Take a good look at your file. It contains numerous layers and alpha channels. You do not have to limit yourself to stopping because the illustration is complete. There are endless opportunities when you consider the resources available within the file. For instance, I duplicated one of the blue paint layers, changed the blending mode to overlay, and increased the opacity to 100%. After that, I dragged it out of the group and closer to the top of the stack within the Layers palette. Finally, I moved it down to the bottom of the canvas. This is just one very simple example of what can be done. Have some fun and experiment with what else you can do within the file.

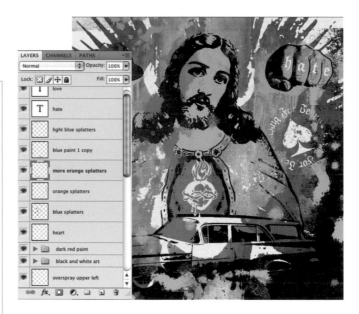

15 Now, use the splatters.jpg as the resource for an alpha channel–based selection. Again, fill the selection with a variety of colors on different layers. Move them up or down within the palette, transform and reposition the layer contents as necessary. Feel free to duplicate and perform transform operations on your new layers as well as existing paint layers.

Don't limit yourself in terms of subject matter

This technique lends itself to any subject, so don't feel limited to traditional lowbrow subject matter and iconography. Here you can see that the effect is equally as compelling when applied to a more esoteric theme like ancient stone monuments. Feel free to take the methodology explained here and apply it to any subject of your own choice.

PART THREE

Real World Photoshop

Chapter 12

Sketch and Dry Brush Effects

At this point, I'm going to assume that you've all seen the effects of third party prefab sketch filters. Granted, these products have improved over the years, but personally, I can spot filters like these a mile away. The reality is that to the experienced eye, these filters really don't look anything at all like authentic sketch effects. In this chapter, I have taken it upon myself to tell you that there is a much better way to do things. The old saying "if you want something done right, do it yourself" comes to mind when one ponders creating authentic sketch and brush effects in Photoshop. That is why, rather than rely on a prefab filter effect, I go back to the drawing table and get those trusty old pencils out.

There are those who will argue that some digital tools, combined with a pressure-sensitive tablet can indeed result in an authentic sketch look. This is somewhat true, but before you go this route, hold up a piece of onionskin paper and look at the fine random and fibrous texture within it. Draw a few lines on it and look at how different each stroke is from the next. The same rings true when it comes to creating dry brush or splattered paint effects. Start with the real thing and in the long run you'll be much happier.

When it comes to Photoshop, a vast array of tools and features are ideally suited to the creation of convincingly tactile art. However, the secret to success lies in understanding what the most effective and efficient procedure is, even before you launch Photoshop. By preparing certain image components ahead of time, in just the right manner, you're setting up your Photoshop workflow ahead of time. Then, when you launch Photoshop and get to work, the process is a pleasure, not a struggle, and the results are impressive indeed.

DIFFICULTY 3.0/5

You'll need a basic understanding of how the Layers palette works; however, things like alpha channel uses are explained in enough detail that even first-timers should be able to work their way through this chapter. A very basic understanding of shape layers, path creation, and the Lasso tool is required.

What you'll learn in this chapter

Creative Techniques and Working Methods

Preparation of image components

As you read through this chapter and begin the process of creating the featured illustration on the previous page, you'll not only create something impressive but also gain an understanding of this fundamental process. The tactile art components that are prepared ahead of time act as building blocks within the Photoshop environment.

In this case, the building blocks are pencil sketches, dry marker drawings, dry brush strokes, and paint drips. Although the materials and processes used to create these initial components add considerably to the feeling of this particular illustration, the actual content could be anything you like. It is the way in which these materials are prepared, and the fact that they are prepared separately is important. So when you complete this chapter, you'll take away with you the knowledge required to execute this process utilizing any tactile art material.

You'll think about how black will translate into a selection when placed in an alpha channel. You'll ponder how sketches will overlap when using the multiply layer blending mode. You'll imagine how shape layers will work alongside your drawings. And, perhaps most importantly, you'll have a clear vision of the results in mind before you enter the Photoshop workspace.

Photoshop Tools, Features, and Functions

Channel options

Control the behavior of your alpha channels before you generate selections from them. Knowing how to set up Channel options to suit your resources will expedite your workflow in the long run.

Shape areas

Understanding which shape area functions to use and when to use it will help you master working with shape layers. Create new layers when you begin to draw with the Pen tool, or edit existing layers with clear intent. This feature allows you to add to, or subtract from, shape layers with ease.

Free-Transform opacity

The capabilities within the Free-Transform operation are vast and certainly no secret. However, few people realize that you can alter layer opacity while performing transformations at the same time.

PART ONE: Preparing the actual drawings

1 It all starts with a sketch. Having a plan is very important. If you go into this with no plan, you'll find yourself throwing things together and the final composition will suffer. The initial sketch can be very rough, but it should give you a basic idea of where the image components will fall within the canvas area, and how they will look.

Project files

All of the files needed to follow along with this chapter and create the featured image are available for download on the accompanying Web site in the project files section. Visit www.creativephotoshopthebook.com.

2 Because I wanted to maximize detail in the sketched components, and really draw attention to the roughness and random textures inherent within pencil drawings, I worked at a larger size than the final output. First, sections of the sketch were enlarged and printed out on separate sheets of paper.

Skipping ahead

The first two parts of this chapter describe the process of preparing and creating art before entering Photoshop. If you aren't interested in this aspect and just want to get busy creating the featured image, go ahead and skip forward to Part Three of this chapter. However, those of you interested in using these methods to generate original works of your own, follow along from the beginning, substituting your own content prepared in the same manner.

3 The next stage involves placing a sheet of tracing paper over each sketch and sourcing an appropriate drawing tool. I prefer to use a relatively soft graphite pencil like a 2H to trace each sketch. The advantage of this is that the lead is deposited generously and the paper tends to get a little dirty as your hand brushes up against your pencil strokes. All of these real-world imperfections will contribute nicely to the authentic feel of the final result.

 Tape preparation

If your tape selection is limited, you can use a fairly adhesive tape, provided you prepare it properly first. Simply take a piece of tape and stick it on your clothing somewhere. Jeans or cotton T-shirts work well for this. Peel the tape off your clothing and due to the amount of fibers and lint that remain on the tape, it is noticeably less adhesive. Now it is safe to use for affixing your tracing paper to your printout.

4 In order to prevent the tracing paper from moving, I have found that it is a good idea to tape the tracing paper to your printout. Using some low-adhesion tape will ensure that you don't tear the paper. I began to trace one of the printouts.

5 After tracing the basic outlines and details, I began to embellish the drawing a little. Thickening up the outlines around prominent areas made them stand out. In this case, the outlines of the skull, the eye sockets, the nose, teeth, and the wrestler underneath. I began to add shading as well.

 **Tracing advice**

Sometimes, when tracing, you'll find that the underlying printout is simply too strong for you to clearly see what you're drawing on your sheet of onionskin or tracing paper. When this happens, simply tear off an additional sheet or two of tracing paper and place it between the printout and the sheet you're drawing on. The added sheets will decrease the strength of the printout as seen through the tracing paper, but it will still remain visible enough to draw over.

6 Removing the tracing from the printout allows you to have a clear look at it and see what needs to be done from here. This is the ideal time to enhance any shaded areas, now that you can see the drawing clearly. This is also the time to erase anything you think looks overdone or cluttered.

7 Don't be afraid to make more than one attempt at drawing something. Sometimes you'll need to trace something a few times to get it right. Trace the image and then trace the tracing. Repeat this process, improving upon it each time until it is perfect. If you are creating art of your own, scan all of your finished drawings. If not, you will be prompted to open the downloadable project files by name soon enough.

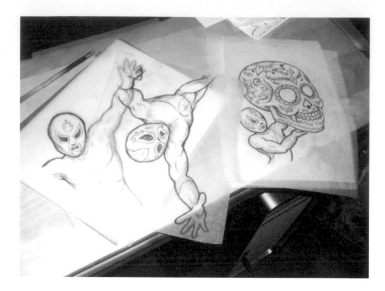

PART TWO: Working with markers and ink

8 Now we'll move from pencils to dried up magic markers. Some people discard markers when they lose moisture, but these are valuable tools. Save your drying markers to create nice dry brush style line work with them. Convincing dry brush effects are very difficult to create digitally. So start with the real thing instead. Here I've drawn a section of detail that can be repeated over and over again to form a pattern in the image background.

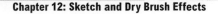

9 To create convincing dry brush effects, you'll have to use a drying brush. Whether you use watercolor paints or India ink doesn't matter. Black is ideal, but color will also work as the scanned art will ultimately be converted to grayscale along the way as it enters an alpha channel later on. You'll need a rough brush, ink or paint, and some paper.

10 To create a convincing dry brush stroke, dip your brush and then begin painting. When you start to run out of paint or ink, keep on painting, these strokes will give you the best effect. Paint strokes until your brush is completely dry before you dip it again and repeat the process. Have some fun creating interesting brush stroke–based shapes.

While you're at it

When I'm creating messy tactile components to incorporate into digital art, I tend to create a lot more resources than are required for the current project. Basically, if I'm going to make a mess with ink, I'll create an abundance of these things while I'm at it; the more diverse the better. Then I archive all of the results and save them as possible resources for future projects. This saves you the trouble of dealing with messy materials again in the future and can help to expedite your next project.

11 To create a dripping or splattered paint effect, dip your brush until it is dripping wet. Then shake it over the top of your page to add some paint drops to it. There will be areas that are as thick as puddles. Gently tilt the paper to make the paint run and blow on it to accelerate the effect. Be warned, this can get very messy.

12 Now, take a rag or cloth and crumple it up into your hand. Dip the cloth or rag into a puddle of ink or paint. Then, using a circular motion, rub ink or paint onto a separate sheet of paper. This is an excellent way to create wispy cloud shapes. Scan everything when it dries.

PART THREE: Building the background

13 Now, if you have created your own image components, now is the time to scan them all and save them as separate files. You will need to substitute them as required as we work through the rest of the chapter. If you're using the project files, now is the time to download them if you haven't already. Open up the sketch.jpg file. This will act as our template on the bottom while assembling the image components on a series of layers.

14 Choose the Solid Color option from the Create New Fill or Adjustment Layer menu at the bottom of the Layers palette. When the picker appears, choose a pink color and click OK. This will create a solid pink layer that covers the sketch. This pink layer will act as the illustration's background, but remember the sketch is always underneath. Whenever you need a template to assist with placing an element into the composition, you can temporarily disable the visibility of the pink layer, allowing you to see the sketch below.

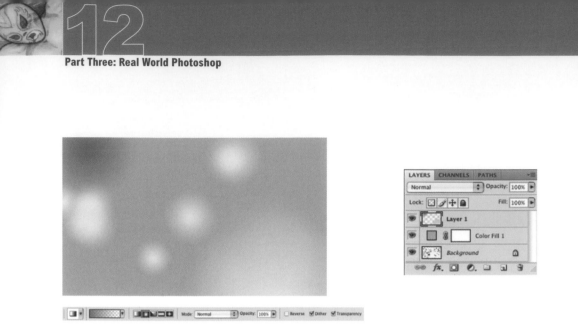

15 Click the Create a New Layer button at the bottom of the Layers palette to create a new layer. Ensure that this new layer is targeted in the Layers palette and select the Gradient tool. In the toolbar, select the Foreground to Transparent Gradient preset, and the Radial Gradient option. Click on the Foreground Color swatch and select a purple color from the picker. Create a gradient on the new layer in the upper left of the canvas. Then repeat this process to select very light pink foreground colors and create a series of gradients on the new layer, similar to those shown here.

PART FOUR: Creating a pattern

Controlling channel-based selections

How selections are generated can be changed beforehand or afterward, whichever you prefer.

1 When you generate a selection from an image pasted into a channel, by default, white areas are selected and black areas are not. The degree to which they are selected depends upon just how white or black they are. If this image were loaded as a channel-based selection, the background would be selected instead of the drawing.

2 If you want the art to be selected instead of the background, you can simply invert the selection after the selection has been generated by choosing Select>Inverse from the menu. Alternatively, you can invert the image within the channel before a selection is generated from it by choosing Image>Adjustments>Invert.

3 By double-clicking on a channel thumbnail in the Channels palette, you can open the options for that channel. Color Indicates is set to Masked Areas by default; this means that selections are generated from white areas. However, if you want to generate selections from the dark regions instead, simply switch the Color Indicates to Selected Areas.

16 Click on the Create New Channel button at the bottom of the Channels palette. Your new channel will automatically become targeted in the palette and visible in the image window. Open up the scan4.jpg file. Now, we are going to paste this image into the new channel, but because it is a black sketch on a white background, the pasted art will appear as it is, white background and all, sitting against a larger, black background. To remedy this, choose Image>Adjustments>Invert from the menu. Now that the drawing is white against a black background, select all by typing Control(PC)/Command(Mac)-A and copy by typing Control(PC)/Command(Mac)-C.

17 Return to your working file and type Control(PC)/Command(Mac)-V to paste the copied art into your new alpha channel. Control(PC)/Command(Mac)-click on the channel thumbnail in the Channels palette to load it as a selection. Return to the Layers palette and create a new layer. Select a very light pink foreground color from the picker. Ensure that the new layer is targeted and then type Alt(PC)/Option(Mac)-Delete to fill the selection with the new foreground color on the new layer. Type Control(PC)/Command(Mac)-D to deselect.

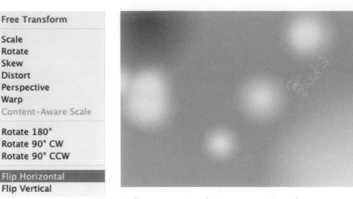

Free Transform

Scale
Rotate
Skew
Distort
Perspective
Warp
Content-Aware Scale

Rotate 180°
Rotate 90° CW
Rotate 90° CCW

Flip Horizontal
Flip Vertical

18 Now, zoom out so that you can see the entire canvas area. This will give you a good understanding of the size relationship between your newly created pattern component and the rest of the image. You want it to be quite small when compared to the size of the canvas so type Control(PC)/Command(Mac)-T to access Free-Transform. Shift-drag a corner handle inward to reduce the size. When you're satisfied right-click(PC)/Control-click(Mac) inside the bounding box. When the pop-up menu appears, choose the Flip Horizontal option and then press the Enter key on the keyboard to apply the transformation.

19 Press the "v" key to quickly access the Move tool. Hold down Alt(PC)/Option(Mac), and then click on the pattern component. While holding down the mouse and keyboard button, drag to duplicate the layer. Position it beside the original, taking into account the angle. Repeat this process a number of times until you've created a row out of duplicate layers. Control(PC)/Command(Mac)-on all of the other layers that make up this row in the Layers palette so that they are all selected and then type Control(PC)/Command(Mac)-E to merge them into one.

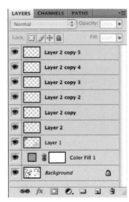

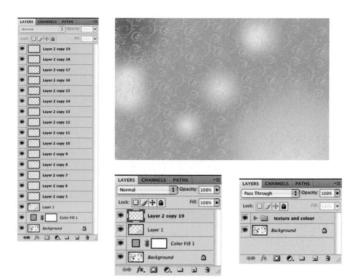

20 Now perform the same operation to make a number of duplicates of your newly merged layer. Position them so that they are slightly offset from each other, yet they fill the entire canvas area. Select the original merged layer and all of the duplicates in the Layers palette and merge them into a single layer like you did on the previous page. With this layer targeted, also target the layer with the gradients as well as the solid pink layer in the Layers palette. When all three are targeted, type Control(PC)/Command(Mac)-G to group them. Double-click the name of the group to highlight the name. While the text is highlighted, enter a new name. Feel free to name the group something appropriate.

PART FIVE: Incorporating scanned sketches

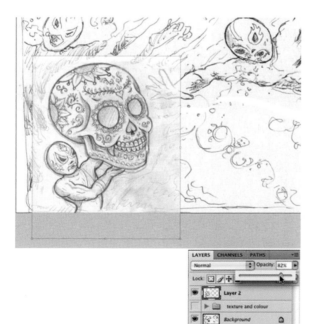

21 Temporarily disable the visibility of your new group by clicking on the visibility icon to the left of it in the Layers palette. Next, open up the scan1.jpg file. Select all and copy. Return to the working file and paste the copied art in as a new layer. Enable the Free-Transform command to resize and position the pasted art based on the underlying sketch. Note that you can reduce the opacity of your layer while the Free-Transform command is active. This will help you see the sketch underneath even as you're resizing. When you're satisfied, return the opacity to 100% and then apply the transformation. If you do not return the opacity to 100% before you apply the transformation, you can do it afterward. It is up to you, the order does not matter.

22 Open up the scan2.jpg file. Copy the art and paste it into the working file as a new layer. Use Free-Transform to resize and position it according to the template beneath. To rotate, simply click and drag outside the bounding box. Remember that you can alter layer opacity at any point to assist you. Apply the transformation and change the layer blending mode to multiply.

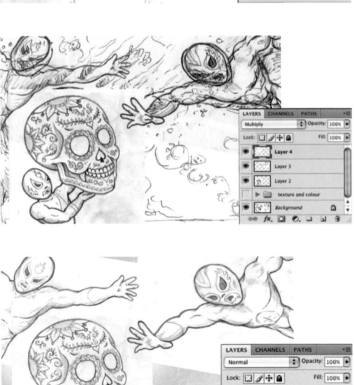

23 Open up the scan3.jpg file. Repeat the process to paste the art from this file into the working file as a new layer. Use Free-Transform to resize and position the art at the top left of the canvas. Change the layer blending mode to multiply. You'll notice that changing the blending modes of these two layers makes the underlying sketch far too prominent. Fear not, we'll address that.

24 Target the three sketch layers in the Layers palette and merge them. The multiply effect, where the three layers overlap each other, is preserved within the new layer. However, the blending mode of the new layer is defaulted back to normal, so the multiply effect applied to underlying layers is lost. Enable the visibility of the underlying background group once again, hiding the unsightly sketch.

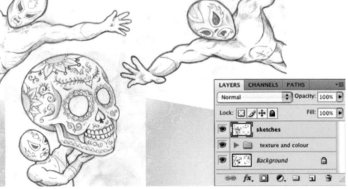

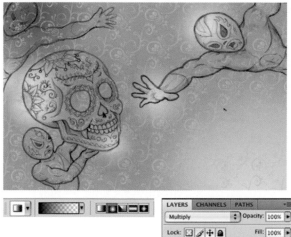

25 Change the blending mode of the layer to multiply. Click on the Add Layer Mask button at the bottom of the Layers palette to mask the layer. Target the layer's mask in the Layers palette and select the Gradient tool. Enable the radial method and choose the Foreground to Transparent Gradient preset in the Tool Options bar. Set the foreground color to black. Begin to create small, radial gradients within the mask to hide edge areas of the overlapping pages that appear too dark against the background.

PART SIX: Adding authentic dry brush strokes

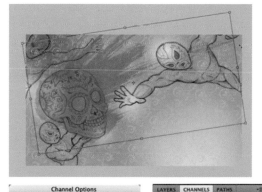

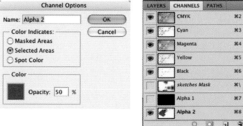

26 Open up the scan5.jpg file. Use the Lasso to draw a closed selection around a large dry brush shape. Copy the selected area. Return to your working file and create a new alpha channel. Double-click the channel's thumbnail in the Channels palette to access the Channel options. Change the Color Indicates option to Selected Areas and click OK. When you exit the Channel options you'll notice that your channel, which used to appear black, is now white. Paste the copied art into the new channel. While the selection is active, enable the visibility of the CMYK composite channel by clicking in the column to the left of it in the Channels palette. Now that you can see the image, use it as your guide as you resize, rotate, and position the pasted art in the channel via Free-Transform.

27 After you apply the transformation, load the channel as a selection. Disable the visibility of the composite channel and then return to the Layers palette. While the selection is active, create a new solid color layer with a light yellow fill. Reduce the opacity of the layer slightly and then duplicate the layer by dragging it onto the Create a New Layer button at the bottom of the Layers palette. Reduce the opacity of the duplicate layer even more and then use Free-Transform to flip it horizontally, rotate, resize, and reposition it on the canvas.

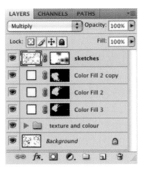

28 Create a new alpha channel. Paste your copied dry brush stroke into the new channel. Because you haven't copied anything since copying the last brush stroke, this will be pasted each time you paste until you copy something else. Again, use Free-Transform to resize the pasted art in the channel. Load it as a selection and then create a white solid color layer while the selection is active. Drag it beneath the yellow layers in the Layers palette and drag the sketch layer to the top of the stack.

29 Create another new, empty channel and then return to scan5.jpg. Select different dry brush strokes with the Lasso, one by one. Copy them. Paste them into the new channel in the working file. Resize, reposition, and rotate them via Free-Transform. Do this until your channel contains four brush strokes and looks a little like this. Load the channel as a selection and then, while the selection is active, create a new dark pink solid color layer. Drag it beneath the rest and change the blending mode of this layer to multiply.

30 Repeat this process again. Select dry brush strokes from the scan5.jpg file, copy them, and paste them into a new channel. Use Free-Transform to alter them. This time arrange them so that the channel looks a bit like this. Load the channel as a selection and then, while the selection is active, create a new solid color layer. This time, specify a light orange fill color and change the layer blending mode to multiply.

31 Return to the scan5.jpg file. Draw a lasso-based selection around the small dry brush stroke in the upper left-hand corner. Copy it and return to the working file. Paste this into a new alpha channel. Load a selection from the channel and, while the selection is active, create a new solid color layer. This time, specify a purple fill. Drag this layer up above all of the other fill color layers in the Layers palette so that it resides directly beneath the sketch layer. Use Free-Transform to adjust the size, rotation, and positioning of the stroke so that it is similar to that which is shown here.

Stacking and blending layers

By duplicating layers and varying blending modes, you can enhance and brighten specific image components.

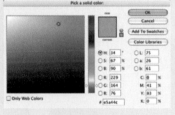

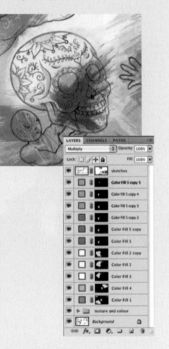

1 Change the blending mode of the current layer to linear burn. Don't be alarmed just yet. We'll improve upon this right now. Duplicate the layer and then change the blending mode of the duplicate to hard light. There, that's better. Now, duplicate the layer again and select the Move tool.

2 Use the Move tool to move the contents of the newly duplicated layer up and toward the right of the canvas, creating an offset effect. Now, duplicate this layer and then double-click on the newly duplicated layer's thumbnail to access the picker. Change the layer's fill color to orange.

3 Change the blending mode of the layer to multiply and move it down and to the right with the Move tool. Duplicate this layer and then move it up and to the left a little. And finally, duplicate this layer and use Free-Transform to scale it down and move it over near the eye at the right of the canvas.

PART SEVEN: Adding painted, wispy clouds

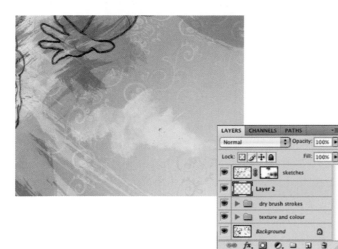

32 For the sake of order, select all of the dry brush solid color layers in the Layers palette and group them. Name the group something appropriate. Next, open up the scan6.jpg file. The initial procedure here is exactly like what you did previously with the dry brush strokes. Draw a lasso-based selection around a section of painted cloud. Copy it and return to the working file. Paste it into a new channel. Load the channel as a selection, but don't create a solid color layer this time. In the Layers palette, create a new layer. Click on the Foreground Color swatch in the toolbar to open the picker. Select a very light yellow color from the picker. Type Alt(PC)/Option(Mac)-Delete to fill the active selection on the new layer with the new foreground color. Do not deselect.

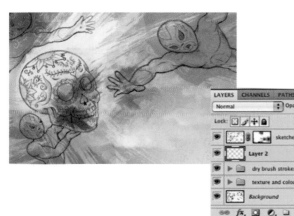

Move carefully

When you are trying to duplicate the contents of an active selection within the same layer, it is very important that you Alt(PC)/Option(Mac)-drag while clicking inside a selection border. If you accidentally Alt(PC)/Option(Mac)-drag outside of a selected area with the Move tool, it will duplicate the entire layer. You may not notice this in the image window right away, but have a look in the Layers palette and you'll see that your layer has been copied.

33 Select the Move tool. Your selection border will likely be visible only in small clusters due to the nature of this channel-based selection. Position the Move tool over a selected area. When you are confident that the tool lies completely inside a selection border, hold down the Alt(PC)/Option(Mac) key and drag to another area of the canvas. This will duplicate the contents of the selection within the same layer. Make a number of duplicates using this method, and feel free to alter size, shape, and rotation via Free-Transform. Repeat this entire process to create different cloud shapes on this layer, generated from different portions of the scan6.jpg file. Try filling some of the new channel-based selections with white instead of yellow. The results are subtle, but add to the overall tactile, painterly feel. Deactivate any active selection.

34 Select the Pen tool. In the Tool Options bar, ensure that the Pen tool is set to create shape layers as you draw. The Shape Area option will automatically be set to create a new shape layer. At the right, in the Tool Options bar, click on the Color swatch. This will open the picker. Select a lime green color from the picker. After you've specified the color of the new shape layer, zoom in on the figure at the lower left. Carefully draw a closed shape that fills the inside of his head with color. It doesn't have to be perfect as imperfection is part of the overall feel of this image. However, try not to stray outside of the black outline on the sketch layer above.

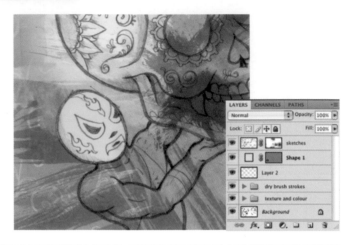

 Editing shapes

When you're using the Pen tool to create shapes, you can edit the line segments, points, or Bezier handles quickly with the Direct Selection tool. To temporarily access the Direct Selection tool while the Pen tool is selected, simply hold down the Control(PC)/Command(Mac) key. When you are finished editing your shape components directly, release the Control(PC)/Command(Mac) key and the Pen tool will return.

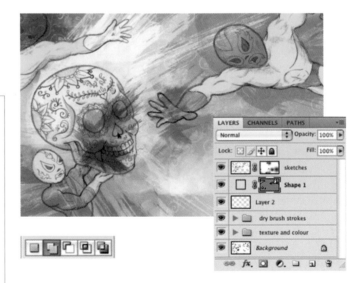

35 In the Tool Options bar, enable the Add to Shape Area option. This will allow you to create further shapes on the same layer in addition to the existing shapes. Use the Pen tool to create a solid shape that fills this figure's glove with the same green color. Repeat the process with the other two figures, adding green fill areas to torsos, arms, and legs.

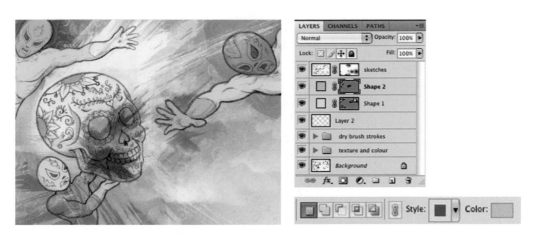

36 Return to the Tool Options bar. Click on the Create New Shape Area option and set the color of the new shape layer to a light orange. Use the Pen tool to draw a closed shape around the head of the figure at the upper left of the canvas, filling it with orange. Then, enable the Add to Shape Area operation and draw some more closed shapes within the same layer. Create shape areas that fill the right figure's gloves and the center of the flowers on the skull with color.

37 Repeat this process to create another new shape layer. This time, specify a purple fill color. Initially create a shape that fills the figure's hand at the upper left with color. Then, enable the Add to Shape Area operation and draw a closed shape that fills the figure's shirt at the lower left with purple. This figure's pants have a strap that comes up over one shoulder. Rather than meticulously draw around that area, just let it be filled with purple for now. We'll fix that up with another shape layer next.

38 Again, enable the Create New Shape Layer operation in the Tool Options bar, and specify a light blue fill color. Carefully draw a closed shape around the skull. Ensure that you do not include the large flowers within the shape area as you draw. Carefully draw around them. When you have closed this shape, enable the Add to Shape Area operation in the Tool Options bar. Now, draw additional closed shapes within the same shape layer that fill remaining areas of the figures with light blue. Pay special attention to filling the pants and shoulder strap of the figure at the bottom left. Although this area is filled with purple on the underlying layer, this obscures it perfectly.

39 Next, enable the Subtract from Shape Area operation in the Tool Options bar. With this function enabled, draw a closed shape around the perimeter of one of the eye holes in the skull. As you begin to draw, you'll immediately notice the results of the Subtract operation as it literally cuts a hole in the shape surrounding it. With this operation enabled, draw closed shapes around the other regions of the skull that should not be filled with blue.

PART NINE: Add shading and painted details

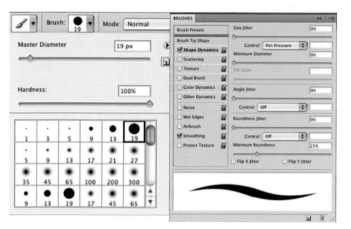

40 Let's continue to impose order on the chaos inside the Layers palette. Group all of the shape layers and name the group. This is also a good time to name the clouds layer if you haven't already. Now, the shape layers we just created are an excellent way to fill areas with color. However, when I look at the illustration in its current state, it seems a little too flat, lacking fine detail. To remedy this, we're going to paint some shaded regions, highlights, and colored details onto the figures. Begin by selecting the Brush tool. Select a hard, round Brush preset from the list of options in the Brush Preset picker in the Tool Options bar. Open up the Brushes palette and have a look at the properties of the Brush preset you'll be using. I use a pressure-sensitive tablet and here you can see that the stylus pressure controls the size of the brush I'm using. If this is not your cup of tea, feel free to disable shape dynamics.

41 Also, it is important to point out that we're not doing any form of advanced painting here; so if you don't use a tablet, it doesn't matter. Create a new layer and zoom in on a region of the image that requires flat, colored detail. Set your brush tip diameter accordingly and select an appropriate foreground color from the picker. Set the opacity of the brush to around 70% or 80% in the Tool Options bar. This will still allow for a subtle layered effect to be built up within the layer as you paint strokes that overlap each other. Carefully paint some solid color into the desired region on the new layer. When you're finished, apply some paint into other regions that require the same color. After that, choose a different foreground color for another region. Repeat this process until all of the solid detail regions are painted.

42 Create a new layer. This time, either select a very soft, round Brush Tip preset from the Brush Preset picker, or simply reduce the hardness of your current brush to zero. Also reduce the opacity of the brush to around 40% in the Tool Options bar. We are going to gently build up paint in shaded regions on this new layer. The process is the same as before. Simply select a color and start to paint it into the appropriate region on this layer. Take your time and paint the appropriate dark colors into areas that require shading, changing your brush size and opacity as required. Choose lighter colors to paint highlights onto raised or protruding areas within the image. To create a very dark or very light region, build up numerous strokes in the same area.

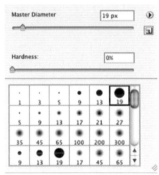

PART TEN: Throw some paint around

43 Open up the scan7.jpg file. This file contains all the drips and paint splatters. We're going to use these to further the overall feeling of tactile imperfection within the image. Use the Lasso to draw a rough selection border around a single paint drip, cluster of drops, or section of splatter. Copy it and return to the working file. Create a new alpha channel and paste the copied art into it. Feel free to alter the size of the pasted art in the channel via Free-Transform. Load the channel as a selection and then return to the Layers palette. Create a new layer and fill the selection on the new layer with the color of your choice. Feel free to alter the blending mode to give the splatter a translucent appearance. This selection was filled with blue before I deactivated it. Then the blending mode was changed to multiply.

44 Repeat this procedure over and over again until you have a multicolored splatter effect across the entire canvas. Feel free to move your splatter layers above or below each other. When you're finished, select all of the splatter layers in the Layers palette and group them. Name the group and then drag it above the sketch layer so that it sits at the top of the stack in the Layers palette.

PART ELEVEN: Final adjustments

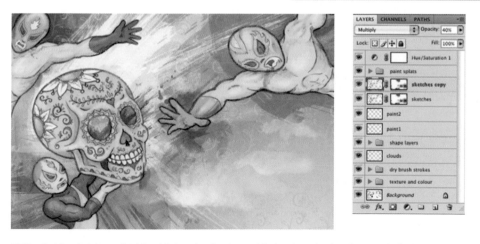

45 Now that the sketches, paint drips, dried marker drawing, and dry brush strokes have been used effectively; take a break and have a good look at the final result. In my opinion, the color is lacking overall. It looks a little faded or washed out. In the Adjustments palette, click on the Hue/Saturation button to create a new hue/saturation adjustment layer. When the sliders appear in the Adjustments palette, increase the saturation greatly by around 40. You will immediately notice the color within the image spring to life. Now the only thing lacking is the density of the blacks within the image. To remedy this, duplicate the sketches layer. Reduce the opacity of the duplicate layer to around 40% so that the results are not overpowering.

A practical application

Bits and pieces of this technique can come in handy when you are creating something a little more conventional. In this editorial illustration, the method of using the sketch on a layer with a multiply blending mode works well. Although this chapter's illustrated patterns and brush stroke effects are entirely absent in this composition, the way that the sketch blends with the photographed page looks authentic and conveys a tactile feeling.

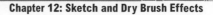

Same techniques, different media

Although the media has changed in this instance from dry brush India ink and pencil sketches to felt-tipped pen and watercolor, the core of the process remains more or less the same. The solid regions of the alien bodies were filled using shape layers, then detail and shading was painted onto a series of layers above. This process of building an image from scanned tactile components can incorporate almost any form of traditional media.

Chapter 13

Simulated Screen-Printing

Many years ago, I used to work as a one-man art department at a silkscreen-printing house. This was so long ago that for the first year or so there was no computer at all in the art department. I used to do all of the original artwork and color separations manually. When it came to adding shading to the designs, I used to have all of these great peel-and-stick halftone sheets made by Letraset at my disposal. There were different densities to mimic different percentages of color where required. There were different patterns to choose from, mainly dominated by dots and lines. But for some reason, I always tended to gravitate toward the line patterns. There was just something about them that captivated me.

Perhaps even more important than the act of working with those primitive materials were the wonderfully primitive results at the end of it all. Thick inks were squeezed onto garments through the fine line work of the screen patterns. It was hard to keep colors in register throughout the duration of the print run, and the artwork often had gaps between colors or unwanted overlaps. At the time it used to frustrate me, and when we eventually began using digital tools, quality was much easier to maintain. However, with many years of using Photoshop under my belt, I find myself coming full circle. Those halftone line patterns still interest me.

Screen-printing is a process that is fraught with limitations. However, it is those very limitations that provide the beauty. Compelled by imperfect beauty, I developed a process to effectively emulate this aesthetic in Photoshop. I guess the romance of cutting out those pieces of halftone screen with an x-acto knife just stuck with me somehow.

Even though features like alpha channels are used, first-timers will likely be able to figure things out by following along carefully. You need a basic understanding of selection tools, image modes, layers, and the Color picker to make your way through this chapter with ease. The thing that you'll need the most is patience as core techniques are used over and over again for different elements.

What you'll learn in this chapter

Creative Techniques and Working Methods

Positive thinking

When a design is color separated for screen-printing, a film positive is created for each color. Areas of 100% black are going to reproduce as 100% of that particular color, and coarse halftone screens are used to create percentages of those colors. Each positive is used to create a separate screen in which ink will be forced through with a squeegee onto the desired surface. Usually all screens are crudely registered on a carousel-like device, and ink is applied to the surface, one color at a time.

Now, when it comes to working in Photoshop, we're going to prepare our separations ahead of time. As a result of this, it is very important to visualize your design and then create the necessary components ahead of time. Each color or shade is prepared as a separate piece of black-and-white art. And each scanned piece utilizes layers, channels, bitmap conversion methods, and other tools to make it part of an authentic-feeling silk-screened design. By the time you finish this chapter, not only will the preparation stage make sense, but also you'll walk away with the knowledge necessary to realize ideas of your own using these techniques.

Photoshop Tools, Features, and Functions

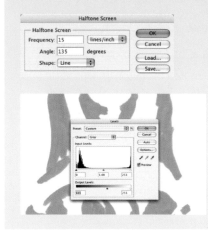

Halftone Screen

This is the lovely feature responsible for all of those great line patterns in the opening image. When you convert to a bitmap, this is one of the features available. It really is a powerhouse of control although it may seem primitive. We'll make extensive use of the Line option in this chapter, but I encourage you to check out the other options, especially the dot pattern method.

Controlling density

Back in the old days, you were limited to different screens ready made for different values of color. In Photoshop we can alter the density of color ahead of time. This effectively removes any limitations. In this chapter, you will develop an understanding of how the darkness of the gray will translate into a halftone pattern, and what to do to the color ahead of time to control this.

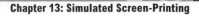

Manually separated drawings

The first step is to draw all of the different elements within the illustration. I began by drawing the outline art for each element with a black felt-tipped pen. Then, I placed a sheet of tracing paper over each drawing. On the tracing paper, with black marker, I covered areas that would require halftone shading in the final composition. Precision isn't really important at this stage as the end result will appear rough and off-register anyway. Doing this creates the equivalent of a separate mechanical "positive" for the shading color.

Project files

All of the files needed to follow along with this chapter and create the featured image are available for download on the accompanying Web site in the project files section. Visit www.creativephotoshopthebook.com.

I used this method to create a "positive" for each different shade or highlight color. This resulted in a number of different "positives" to accompany each drawing. Afterward, I scanned all of them separately and saved them as individual files.

Essential wave and creature components

The large waves are comprised of three different drawings. Here is the black outline. Although this does not actually appear in the image as seen here, it is integral to providing a framework for the shading as well as defining the solid regions of color.

These dark areas will be used to shade the solid regions beneath the crest of the wave.

The dark areas in this image will be used to create the shading beneath the curly bits at the top of the wave.

Here's a quick composite of all three files, simply for reference. Some areas have been lightened in this image to express the differentiation between the individual files. When the files are overlaid on each other, it gives you an idea of how they'll be positioned together in the final illustration.

Just like the wave on the previous page, the creatures are initially comprised of a series of drawings.

Again, here's an example of how all of the different pieces will fit together. The finished art will look different when the halftone effect is generated and different colors are used, but these separate drawings are the building blocks.

PART ONE: Build the first wave

1 To get started, the first thing you're going to need is a working file. Create a new file that is 11 inches wide and 11 inches high, at a resolution 150 ppi, in CMYK mode. This resolution is specified assuming you'll be using the project files to follow along. However, if you're going to use scanned drawings of your own, feel free to work at a much higher resolution. Go ahead and leave the background contents set to white or transparent or background color, it doesn't matter. Click on the Foreground Color swatch in the toolbar. When the picker opens, select a bluish purple color and click OK. Type Alt(PC)/Option(Mac)-Delete to fill the entire background layer with your new foreground color.

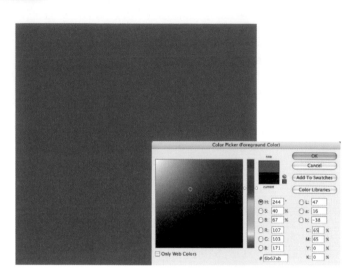

Magic Wand or Quick Selection tool

Pressing "W" on the keyboard is your shortcut to either the Quick Selection tool or the Magic Wand tool. Both tools inhabit the same area within the toolbar. The first time you launch Photoshop, the Quick Selection tool is visible. However, depending upon which tool was used last, the visible tool could be one or the other. Pressing "W" on the keyboard will immediately select whichever tool is visible. However, if it is the hidden tool that you wish to access instead, simply hold down the Shift key while you press the "W" key.

2 Open up the wave1.jpg file. Select all by typing Control(PC)/Command(Mac)-A on the keyboard. Then copy the selection contents by typing Control(PC)/Command(Mac)-C. Return to your new, purple working file, and paste the copied art into it as a new layer by typing Control(PC)/Command(Mac)-V. Quickly select the Move tool by pressing the "V" key on the keyboard. Use the Move tool to drag the wave layer to the left side of the canvas until it touches the left edge. Drag it upward as well so that it nearly touches the top of the canvas. Select the Magic Wand tool.

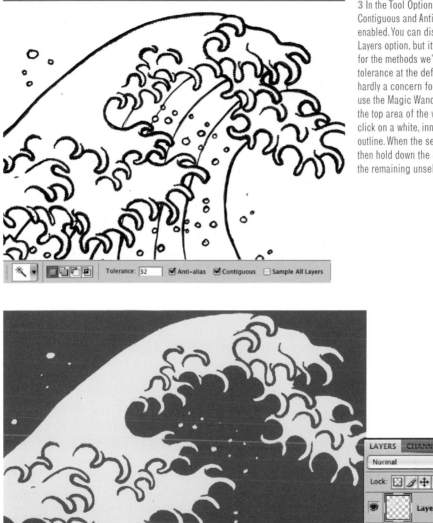

3 In the Tool Options bar, ensure that the Contiguous and Anti-alias options are enabled. You can disable the Sample All Layers option, but it's hardly a concern for the methods we'll use here. Leave the tolerance at the default value of 32. Again, hardly a concern for the way we're going to use the Magic Wand tool. Click once inside the top area of the wave. Ensure that you click on a white, inner area, and not a black outline. When the selection is generated, then hold down the Shift key and click inside the remaining unselected top areas.

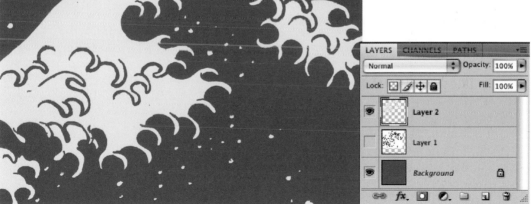

4 Now, while you're holding down the Shift key, click inside the round bubble shapes as well to add them to the selection. When you've selected the top of the wave and all of the bubbles, disable the visibility of the wave layer and then create a new layer above it by typing Control(PC)/Command(Mac)-Shift-N. Click on the Foreground Color swatch in the toolbar and select a light blue foreground color from the picker. With the new layer targeted and the current selection active, type Alt(PC)/Option(Mac)-Delete to fill the selection with the current foreground color. Deactivate the selection by typing Control(PC)/Command(Mac)-D.

Reset warnings

After disabling a warning, you may find that at some point you'll want to enable it again. Choose Photoshop>Preferences>General from the menu. Simply click on the Reset All Warning Dialogs button at the bottom. This will bring back any disabled warnings.

5 Target the wave layer and enable its visibility. Now, use the Magic Wand tool and the same methods to carefully select all of the lower, vertical curved regions within the wave. Disable the visibility of the wave layer and create another new layer. With your new layer targeted and your current selection active, select a dark plum foreground color from the picker. Fill the active selection on the new layer and then deactivate the selection when you're finished.

If you miss a spot

When you're generating selections from the wave layer and then filling them on other layers, you might miss a section or two. If this is the case, you'll surely notice it when you disable the visibility of the wave layer. Worry not, you can use the same procedure to select missing areas, then just fill them with the correct colors on the appropriate layers. And remember, if the color you're after is no longer the current foreground color, you can quickly sample it from the image with the Eyedropper tool.

6 Open up the wave2.jpg file. Choose Image>Mode>Grayscale from the menu to convert the image and discard any color information. Photoshop will likely prompt you to use the black-and-white conversion method instead. Granted, black and white offers you much more control when converting but we're after a quick and dirty method here. In the dialog box, check the "don't show again" box because we're going to do this a lot in this chapter. Then click the Discard button to complete the conversion. After this, all subsequent conversions will be performed without interruption.

7 Now, to create the halftone effect, we're going to convert the current grayscale image to a bitmap. But before you do that, you need to understand how halftone conversion works. Essentially, the density of the black, meaning how dark the color is, defines how dense the resulting halftone pattern will be, meaning how close together the lines within the pattern will be. The idea is that from a distance, the halftone, even though it is made up of sections of solid color, looks like a shade or percentage of that color. Why does this matter? you may ask. Well, the reason is that we need to lighten the scanned images before converting them, because we want to see the lines. As you can see here, the grayscale image is more or less solid black. So, if we were to convert this to a halftone bitmap, it would look the same because in order for the halftone to appear as black, or 100% of the color, there would be no space between the lines.

Quick ways to lighten the black

Here are a few efficient methods to create a uniform, gray color from the solid black areas in the image.

1 Choose Image>Adjustments>Levels from the menu. When the Levels dialog box appears, never mind the input levels or the histogram itself. Simply drag the left output levels slider to the right and you'll notice the effect immediately.

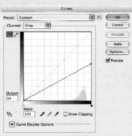

2 Choose Image>Adjustments>Curves from the menu. When the Curves dialog box appears, click on the little black square at the upper right of the curve and begin to drag it straight down. This lightens the output just like when using Levels. An output box will appear at the left when you drag. There, you can enter a numeric value if you're after a precise gray value.

3 Choose Image>Adjustments>Exposure from the menu. When the Exposure dialog box appears, simply begin to drag the offset slider to the right and you'll notice that the black lightens and the result is a very even gray value within the image.

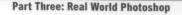

8 Use any method mentioned on the previous page to lighten the black within the image. The resulting grayscale value is up to you. If you wish to closely replicate what I'm doing, shoot for around 50%. Next, choose Image>Mode>Bitmap from the menu. When the Bitmap dialog box appears, leave the resolution set to 150 ppi, or higher if you've decided to use your own images. Basically, leave it set to the same resolution as your file. From the Method menu, choose Halftone Screen. When you click OK, the Halftone options will appear. Set the frequency to a value of around 20. Set the angle to 135°, and choose the Line option from the Shape menu.

Variations in halftone

As mentioned earlier, the density of your halftone screen is directly linked to the grayscale value, or density of your black. If you perform a bitmap conversion and then decide afterward that the screen is too sparse or too dense, you can fix it. Start by undoing the conversion, and then step back in the History palette to the state before you lightened the black. Once you're back to the original black art, lighten to the desired degree and try the conversion again.

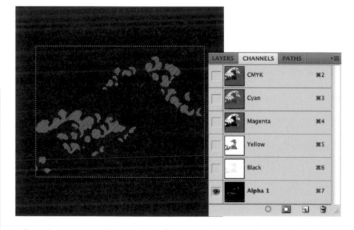

9 I'm going to assume that your Alpha Channels options are left at their default settings; color within a channel indicates a masked area. If that is the case, invert your image by typing Command(PC)/Control(Mac)-I. If your Channel options are set up so that color indicates selected areas, you can ignore this inversion and further inversions performed in this chapter. Select all, copy, and return to your working file. In the Channels palette, click on the Create New Channel button at the bottom of the palette. Target the new channel and paste your copied art into it.

10 In the Channels palette, click in the column to the left of the CMYK composite channel. This enables visibility, and your channel is previewed against the image as a red overlay. Choose the Move tool, or if you're using a selection tool currently, hold down the Command(PC)/Control(Mac) key to temporarily switch to the Move tool. Click and drag within the selected area and move the halftone pattern into place. Use the visible CMYK composite channel as your guide to place the halftone pattern in the appropriate area of the canvas. Position it so that the lines act as shadows beneath the raised portions of the top of the wave.

11 Command(PC)/Control(Mac)-click on the alpha channel thumbnail in the Channels palette to load it as a selection. With the selection active, return to the Layers palette and create a new layer. Drag the layer to the top of the stack within the palette. Then change the foreground color to purple by using the Eyedropper tool to click somewhere in the background. Fill the active selection with the new foreground color on the new layer and then deselect.

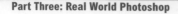

12 Open up the wave3.jpg file. Use a method of your choice to lighten the black within the image. Try to keep it a little darker than the previous image so that the resulting halftone pattern is denser. Convert it to grayscale and then to bitmap mode. Leave the resolution setting the same as the document. This will remain a constant throughout the chapter. In the Halftone Screen options, set the frequency to 10 so that the lines are thicker. Set the angle to 45° instead of 135° and click OK. When the image is converted, invert it. Select all and copy.

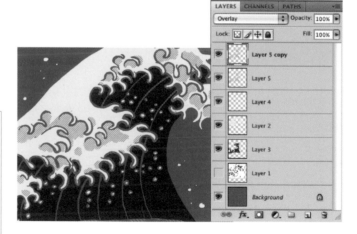

 Nudging layers

If you decide after the fact that you'd like your layer contents in a slightly different position, you can remedy this at any point. Simply target the desired layer in the Layers palette. Then, while holding down the Control(PC)/ Command(Mac) key use the arrow keys to nudge the content of the layer in the desired direction. The amount you nudge depends upon what percentage you're viewing at. For instance, if you nudge while viewing at 25%, the movement is much greater than it would have been if you were viewing at 100%.

13 Return to the working file. Create a new alpha channel and paste the copied art into it. Use the visible composite channel as your guide to position the art properly within the channel. Try to position it in a way that some areas of the halftone overlap onto the light areas of the wave a little, so that it looks slightly off-register. Load the new channel as a selection and then create a new layer in the Layers palette. With the selection active, click on the Foreground Color swatch and select a light blue foreground color from the picker. Fill the active selection with the new color. Deselect and change the blending mode of the layer to multiply. Duplicate the layer by Alt(PC)/Option(Mac)-dragging it to the space above itself in the Layers palette. Change the blending mode of the duplicate to overlay.

PART THREE: Organize and repeat

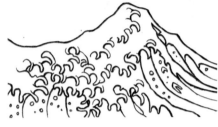

14 With the top layer targeted, Shift-click on the invisible wave drawing layer in the Layers palette. This will target all of the layers that make up the wave. Type Control(PC)/Command(Mac)-G to group them. Go ahead and name the group and then open up the wave4.jpg file. Select all and then copy. Paste the wave into the working file as a new layer. Position it so that it sits against the bottom and the left edge of the canvas.

Altering color

Now, you may be wondering what happens if you decide to change your mind about a certain color within the image. Had we built this file with masked solid color layers, you'd simply double-click the layer to change the color. In this case, because we're using standard layers, a different approach is required. And don't worry; you don't need to create a selection. Simply enable the transparency lock for the layer that you'd like to alter. Then, choose a new foreground color and use the Alt(PC)/Option(Mac)-Delete keyboard shortcut to fill the layer with the new color. Because the transparency lock is enabled, only areas of pre-existing color will be affected.

15 Now, you are going to essentially repeat the process you used to create the solid-colored regions of the previous wave. Use the Magic Wand tool to select all of the white regions that make up the top of this wave and the bubbles too. Create a new layer and fill the selection with the same light blue you used for the previous wave. Repeat this procedure again to select the lower regions of the wave and fill them with the same dark plum color that was used before, on a new layer. Reduce the opacity of the light blue layer slightly so that you can see a bit of the underlying wave through it. Disable the visibility of the wave drawing layer.

16 Open up the wave5.jpg file. Lighten the black to a similar gray value that you used for the top areas of the first wave. Convert the image to grayscale, then to a bitmap. Again, specify in the halftone settings, set the frequency to around 20 and the angle to 135°. Select the Line option from the Shape menu. In fact, you'll be selecting the line method for every conversion you perform throughout this chapter. Invert the image, select all, and copy it. Return to the working file and paste it into a new channel. Position the art in the channel accordingly, using the composite channel as your visual guide. Then load a selection from the channel. Target the light blue layer, the top of the wave. Press the Delete key to erase the selected area from the layer and deselect.

17 Open up the wave6.jpg file and repeat the process again. Lighten, convert to bitmap, enter the halftone settings, paste into a new channel in the working file, position the art in channel, load it as a selection, and create a new layer. Fill the active selection on the new layer with the same blue that you used on this section of the previous wave. Deselect and change the blending mode of the layer to vivid light. Duplicate the layer and change the blending mode of the duplicate to hard light. Reduce the opacity of the duplicate layer to 25%. This will result in a similar looking wave, which has a slightly lighter presence within the composition. Add all of these wave layers to a group and name it.

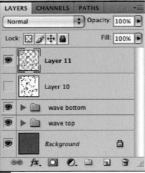

PART FOUR: Create the main squid

18 Open up the squid1.jpg file. Select all, copy, and then paste the copied art into the working file as a new layer. Select the Magic Wand tool and this time, disable the Contiguous option. Leave all other Magic Wand settings as they were and click on a black region of the squid layer. This will select all black regions within the layer. Disable the visibility and, with the selection active, create a new layer. Select a lighter plum foreground color from the picker and fill the active selection with it on the new layer. Deactivate the selection and now enable the Magic Wand's Contiguous option in the Tool Options bar once again.

19 Double-check the Tool Options bar to ensure that the Sample All Layers option is disabled. Click in the sclera, or what should be the white part, of the creature's eyeball to select this area. Create a new layer and, while the selection is still active, drag it below the plum outline layer in the Layers palette. Specify a white foreground color and fill the active selection with it on the new layer. Reduce the opacity of the layer to 90%. Take a moment to reflect upon how the composition is coming together.

Perhaps this is premature, but I think it would balance better if the squid were slightly to the left. If you agree, target the squid outline layer and the sclera layer and use the Move tool to drag the contents of both to the left until the plum outlines touch the left edge of the canvas.

20 Target just the squid's plum outlines layer in the Layers palette. Use the Magic Wand to click inside the main body area of the squid. Shift-click on any remaining unselected areas of the main body and tentacles to add them to the selection. Create a new layer and drag it beneath the plum outline layer in the Layers palette. Select a lime green foreground color from the picker and fill the active selection with it on the new layer. Deactivate the selection and use the Move tool to drag the layer slightly, so that it is no longer aligned nicely with the plum outlines. The goal is to create a noticeable gap between colors. Reduce the opacity of the layer to 95%.

21 Open up the squid2.jpg file and lighten it slightly. We don't want it too light because we want the resulting halftone to be quite dense. Convert to grayscale and then to bitmap mode. In the halftone settings, set the frequency to 20 and the angle to 135°. Invert the image, select all, and copy. Return to the working file and paste it into a new channel. Load the channel as a selection and create a new layer. Fill the active selection on the new layer with a mint green foreground color chosen from the picker. Deactivate the selection and use the Move tool to position the layer on the canvas so that it appears offset slightly.

22 Open up the squid3.jpg file. Again, lighten it, convert to grayscale, and then convert to bitmap mode. This time use a line frequency of 10 and an angle of 45° in the halftone settings. Invert the image. Select all, copy, and paste it into a new channel in the image. Load it as a selection, fill it with white on a new layer. Use the Move tool to alter the position and create an offset effect.

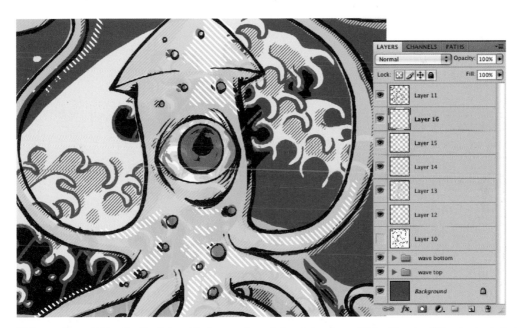

23 Open up the squid4.jpg file. Simply invert the image and copy it. Do not close the squid4.jpg file yet, we'll be returning to it shortly. Create a new channel in your working file and paste the copied art into it. Load a selection from the channel and create a new layer. Fill the selection on the new layer with a new pink foreground color. Deselect and position the art as carefully as you can with the Move tool. Type Control(PC)/Command(Mac)-T to enable Free-Transform. When the bounding box appears, click and drag outside of it to rotate the artwork slightly, refine the positioning by clicking and dragging inside the bounding box. The goal is to line this up nicely within the purple outlines, with a very slight offset still present. Press Enter to apply the transformation.

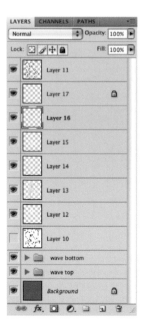

24 Use the Lasso tool to draw a selection around the pink areas on each side of the eye. Leave the iris alone, just focus on the areas at the sides. When they are selected, press the Delete key to remove them and then deactivate the selection. Now use the Lasso tool to draw a selection around a single pink dot on this layer. Type Control(PC)/Command(Mac)-J to copy the selected area to a new layer. Use the Move tool to position the contents of this layer just above, and to the right of, the pupil. Enable the transparency lock for this layer and fill it with white.

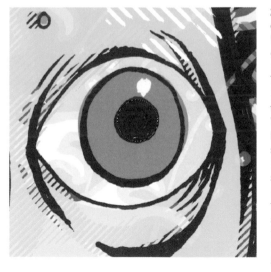

25 Now, just by looking at the effect of the pink iris and dots, I can see that although it looks good on the squid's spots, the iris area looks a little rough. To remedy this, target the pink iris and spots layer. Now, select the Elliptical Marquee tool. While holding down the Shift key, draw a circular marquee selection that surrounds the iris. Click and drag within the selection to reposition it if necessary. Use the Eyedropper to sample pink from another area on the layer and then fill the active selection with it. Deselect and then draw a smaller, circular selection that covers the pupil area. Delete the contents of this smaller selection and then deactivate it.

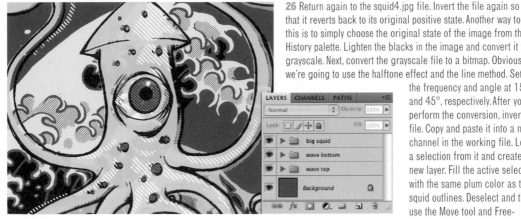

26 Return again to the squid4.jpg file. Invert the file again so that it reverts back to its original positive state. Another way to do this is to simply choose the original state of the image from the History palette. Lighten the blacks in the image and convert it to grayscale. Next, convert the grayscale file to a bitmap. Obviously we're going to use the halftone effect and the line method. Set the frequency and angle at 15° and 45°, respectively. After you perform the conversion, invert the file. Copy and paste it into a new channel in the working file. Load a selection from it and create a new layer. Fill the active selection with the same plum color as the squid outlines. Deselect and then use the Move tool and Free-Transform to rotate and position it over the pink regions. Select all of the squid layers in the Layers palette and group them.

PART FIVE: Add the smaller creatures

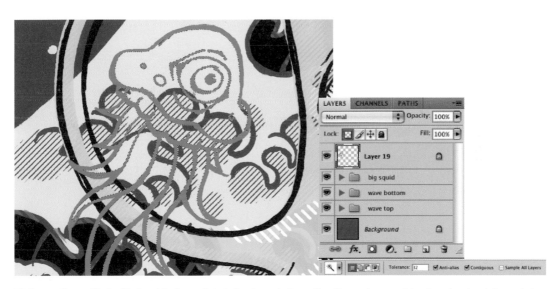

27 Open up the small1a.jpg file. Invert the image. Select all and copy. In the working file, create a new alpha channel and paste the copied art into it. Enable the visibility of the composite channel to aid in placement and position it at the upper left area of the canvas. Load the channel as a selection and create a new layer in the Layers palette. Select a cyan-blue foreground color from the picker and fill the active selection with it on the new layer. Deselect and choose the Magic Wand tool. Ensure that the Contiguous option is enabled and the Sample All Layers option is disabled in the Tool Options bar. Use the Magic Wand to select all of the areas inside of the blue outlines on the current layer.

28 Create a new layer and drag it beneath the blue outlines layer. Select a pink foreground color from the picker and fill the active selection with it on the new layer. Deselect, and offset the layer contents by moving them with the Move tool or nudging with the arrow keys. Feel free to rotate the contents of this layer while offsetting with the Free-Transform tool if you like. Open up the small1b.jpg file. Lighten the black, convert to grayscale, and then convert it to a bitmap. Perform what is now becoming a familiar operation to create the bitmap halftone screen effect. Angle and frequency settings can be left the same as they were the last time. When you have completed the conversion, invert the image. Select all and copy.

29 Return to the working file and create a new alpha channel. Paste the copied art into it and position the art over the small squid with the aid of a visible composite channel. Load the channel as a selection and create a new layer. Set the foreground color to white and fill the active selection with it on the new layer. Deactivate the selection and nudge or move the layer contents if necessary. Open up the small1c.jpg file. Invert the image, copy it, and paste it into a new alpha channel in the working file. Move the channel contents into position and load the channel as a selection. Create a new layer and fill the active selection with light green on the new layer.

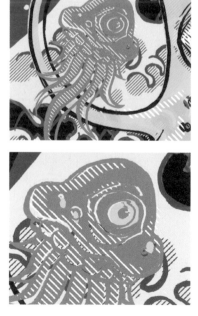

30 Select all of the layers that make up this smaller squid creature and group them. Open up the small2a.jpg file. Invert the image and copy it. Paste it into a new alpha channel in the image. Position the art so that the creature's tail extends beyond the right side of the channel and then load the channel as a selection. Create a new layer and fill the active selection with the same light green foreground color you just used. Now use the Magic Wand to select the inner area of the creature on this layer; a single click should do it. Create a new layer. Drag it beneath the green outlines layer, fill the active selection with pink, and then deselect. Use the Move tool to Shift-drag the layer down slightly to offset it.

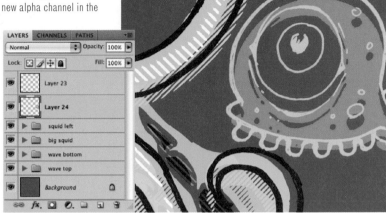

31 Target the layer that contains the green outlines and use the Magic Wand to select the iris area of the creature. Create a new layer and fill this selection with cyan-blue. Deselect and move the contents upward a little. Then drag the layer beneath the outlines layer in the Layers palette. Target the three layers that make up this creature and group them.

32 Open up the small3a.jpg file and invert it. Copy the artwork and paste it into a new alpha channel in your working file. Position the art over the big squid's tentacles, a little to the left of the center of the canvas. Load the channel as a selection and create a new layer. Fill the active selection on the new layer with a dark blue foreground color. Deactivate the selection and use Free-Transform to rotate the layer contents a little. Select the Magic Wand, but don't select anything with it yet, I'm going to show you a shortcut.

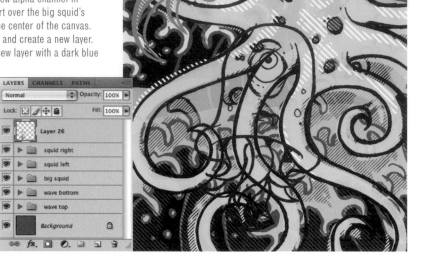

Quickly selecting interior regions

Previously, we selected all regions within a creature manually. However, this alternative method is just as effective and perhaps a little quicker.

1 First, load a selection from the contents of the entire layer. In the Layers palette, Control(PC)/Command(Mac)-click on the layer thumbnail that contains the squid's blue outlines in the Layers palette.

2 Now that the areas of the layer content are selected, invert the selection. Type Control(PC)/Command(Mac)-Shift-I on the keyboard to invert the selection, so that all of the transparent areas of the layer are selected.

3 Now, select the Magic Wand tool and ensure that the Contiguous option is enabled and the Sample All Layers option is disabled. Hold down the Alt(PC)/Option(Mac) key and then click in the selected transparent area that surrounds the creature. This will effectively remove this region from the selection, leaving only the areas inside the creature selected.

33 Create a new layer and fill the active selection with a cyan-blue foreground color. Deactivate the selection and drag the layer beneath the dark blue outlines layer in the Layers palette. Use the Move tool or arrow keys to offset the cyan-blue fill slightly. Reduce the opacity of the layer to 95% so that a little of the underlying layers show through. Target the dark blue outlines layer in the Layers palette. Select the sclera of the eye and the inside of the tooth. Create a new layer and fill these selected regions with white. Drag the layer beneath the blue outlines layer in the Layers palette and offset it slightly with the arrow keys or the Move tool.

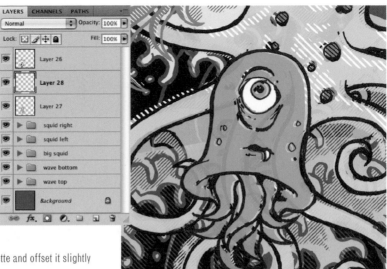

34 Open up the small3b.jpg file. Lighten the black. Convert to grayscale and then to bitmap mode. Use the halftone effect to create a line pattern and then invert the results. Select the inverted halftone art and copy it. Return to the working file and paste the copied art into a new channel. Move that art in the channel into position and then load a selection from the channel. Create a new layer and fill the active selection with a very light green foreground color on the new layer. Deselect and alter the position and/or angle of the contents of this layer if necessary.

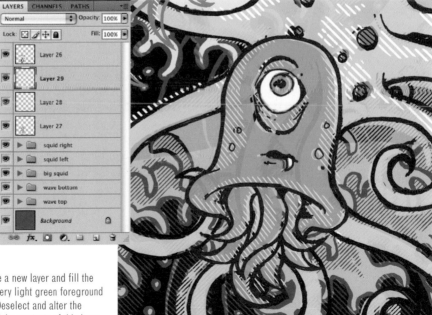

35 Open the small3c.jpg file now. Invert the image and copy it. In the working file, paste the copied art into a new channel. Align the art with the current squid and then load the channel as a selection. Create a new layer and fill the active selection with a pink foreground color. Deactivate the selection and use Free-Transform to rotate and resize the contents of the layer as necessary. Target all of the layers that make up this squid in the Layers palette and group them. Select the Gradient tool. Enable the linear method and the Foreground to Background Color Gradient preset in the Tool Options bar. Press the "D" key to set the foreground color to black and the background color to white.

The finishing touch

Use the Gradient tool and everything you've learned thus far to add shading into the background, completing the illustration.

1 Create a new image file in grayscale mode, which has the identical size and resolution as the working file. Set the gradient opacity to 50%. Use the Gradient tool to click and drag from the upper right corner to the center of the canvas, creating a diagonal, linear gradient in the corner.

2 Convert the image to a bitmap. This time set the line frequency to around 15 and the angle to 135°. Invert the image, copy it, and return to the working file. In the working file, create another alpha channel and paste the copied art into it.

3 Load the channel as a selection and create a new layer. Drag the layer down in the Layers palette so that it resides beneath all layers except for the background layer. Fill the selection with a blue foreground color and then deselect. Offset the layer content with the Move tool or the arrow keys.

Practical uses of this technique

This technique lends itself nicely to works that are meant to convey an organic, nostalgic, or friendly feeling, like the coffee cup illustration shown here. Also, the compositions can be less complicated than the featured image, yet still convey the desired feeling. Sometimes a real-world element, like a desktop scan or a photograph in the background, can also help to convey the feeling. Generally, the success lies in the style of the illustration itself, which is a direct result of the halftone effect, not the intricacy of the design.

Chapter 14

Real World Collage

Flexibility and functionality make Photoshop the ultimate digital collage tool. If you're holding this book in your hands, it's likely that you're more than familiar with this concept. The downside to all of these is that we, digital artists, are only human and unfortunately, more often that not, we'll tend to follow the path of least resistance. We get locked in front of our computers and through convenience, whether conscious of it or not, we tend to get into the habit of creating only on the screen. The unfortunate byproduct of this is a vast array of uninspired digital collages everywhere you look. You'll notice a lot of softly blended imagery, sleek stock photos and royalty-free textures, and in the case of something really innovative, you might just see a desktop scan used.

My goal in this chapter is to offer you an alternative to uninspired collage conformity. Hopefully, getting a bit of paint on your hands will help you snap out of the convenient and predictable. Let's make a bit of a mess and combine some real-world materials to give your collage a distinctly non-digital look. I want to encourage you to bridge the gap between the tactile and the digital, allowing you to create strange hybrid works of art that look like something new altogether.

DIFFICULTY 2.5/5

Although you'll be expected to have a basic understanding of selection tools, layers, paths, and file creation, the actual Photoshop methods for compositing this piece are rather rudimentary. Anyone who has a basic understanding of Photoshop should be able to pull this off.

What you'll learn in this chapter

Prior planning and observation

Planning and forethought is an integral part of the creative process. Unfortunately, the habits of digital artists tend to gravitate away from this preliminary and crucial phase. It seems to be common practice to open a new file and jump right to the stage of creating finished art digitally. The early portions of this chapter discuss the planning stage, and that is what I want to draw your attention to. Take a look at what is around you. Find interesting items that lend themselves to a composition and will work together. Devise a plan and work to that plan. The results of your efforts will certainly benefit from this.

Imperfection

Looking at the opening image of this chapter, it is hard to ignore the fact that a large part of the appeal is the imperfect, distressed, and choppy execution. In this chapter, quick and dirty compositing methods will prevail. You won't be asked to produce precise selections or masks. You'll focus more on what goes where and intentionally leave things a little rough. Roughness is a key component in this image's unique quality.

Photoshop Tools, Features, and Functions

Inverted Wand selections

The Magic Wand isolates solid areas of color easily. But you can use it to quickly select complicated surrounding areas just as easily. Simply generate a selection of the solid areas, in this case black, and then invert the selection to capture the multicolored area that surrounds them.

Layer blending modes

Planning your project with blending modes in mind will save you time in the long run. By photographing certain elements against black, they can be easily placed over the top of dark regions, and the lighten blending mode will make them appear to be close-cut, saving you the trouble.

Color range to isolate texture

A lot of people think of this tool as a photography retouching device, allowing you to generate complex selections like the perimeter of a person's hair. However, a simple approach proves that this is part of an efficient method for capturing ranges of color and using them to create surface textures.

◉ Selection ○ Image

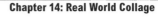
PART ONE: Planning and gathering

1 When creating a collage like this, the first step is to get your idea down on paper. It doesn't have to be exact in terms of proportion, just something to use as reference. Adding brief notes will assist you in planning as well as aid you in gathering up the different props and materials that you'll need. You don't have to be an accomplished illustrator by any means. The goal of sketching is to get you to devise a plan that consists of a basic image composition while considering the resources at your disposal. If you are going to follow this chapter exactly, using the supplied images, there is no need for a sketch as the concept is already provided for you.

Project files

All of the files needed to follow along with this chapter and create the featured image are available for download on the accompanying Web site in the project files section. Visit www.creativephotoshopthebook.com.

Skipping ahead

The first two parts of this chapter describe the process of preparing and creating art before entering Photoshop. If you aren't interested in this aspect and just want to get busy creating the featured image, go ahead and skip forward to Part Three of this chapter. However, those of you interested in using these methods to generate original works of your own will likely find the entire chapter of interest.

2 The next step is to source props and gather up all of the items you'll need. The finished image in this chapter contains a mixture of real-world paintings as well as photographed items. To create the painted components, I needed to set up a paint station. I also needed to set up a camera, lights, and backgrounds to capture elements photographically. Again, if you're following along using the supplied files then you needn't worry about this part. This is only a consideration if you're creating and using your own resources.

PART TWO: Prepare and create the traditional components

3 On an illustration board, I carefully drew the image border in pencil so that the painting would be proportionately accurate later, when it comes back into Photoshop. Flat black paint was used to paint the dark areas indicated by the original sketch. The paint was then allowed to dry thoroughly. Flat black was used because solid black is easy to work with. If a gloss or semigloss paint was used, the lights could cause irritating specular highlights on raised areas of the paint, regardless of the angle of the lights, when photographing the result.

 Photographing paintings

When you're ready to shoot a finished painting, proper lighting is something you need to bear in mind. Position two identical light sources in front of the painting on either side of the camera. Position the light sources apart evenly and try to aim them so that the light hits the painting at a 45° angle. Move the light sources back far enough so that there are no sharp specular highlights appearing on the paint.

4 After creating the black areas I mixed up a variety of colors. Then a second illustration board was used to paint bold, paint laden brush strokes upon. The paint was kept thick, so there would be noticeable raised and recessed areas within each stroke. I am yet to see a digital tool that replicates this raised paint effect randomly and convincingly enough for it to look as realistic as possible.

5 After the finished painting was photographed, I peeled the top layer of the illustration board off the backing. This effectively removes the painting from the board as a thin layer. The next step is to tear up and cut the painting into smaller pieces. Then the little pieces are glued onto the unpainted areas of the first painting.

6 After gluing down enough pieces to cover the white areas and create an overlap effect, I went back to my paint station and mixed up some more colors. Using colors that were similar to those used in the existing pieces, I painted over the glued on pieces in certain areas. This is a good way to sort of tie things together. Think of it as a blending technique, much like you would blend layers together in Photoshop with masking techniques. When the paint dried, I photographed the results.

Board versus canvas

You'll notice that the actual paintings created for this tutorial were done on illustration board instead of canvas. This is because one of the paintings needed to be torn and cut apart. Illustration board allows you to peel off the surface as a thin layer, whereas canvas does not. However, canvas is a fine material for surfaces that are destined to remain intact.

7 Bear in mind that painting doesn't have to be restricted to flat surfaces. As you can see here, the masks were painted so that they'll blend into the composition better. Once the paint dried, the lower mask was photographed on a white background and the other mask was photographed on a black background.

Photography preparation
Combining things in the tactile realm can add a unique look as well as improve efficiency.

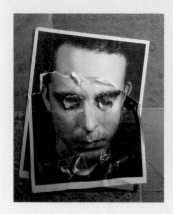

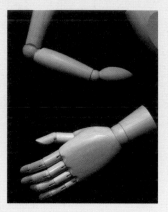

1 Here, a face photo was printed out twice, the first printout had holes poked in the eyes and was torn, revealing another printout below. Both the printouts were slightly crumpled to emphasize the tactile feel.

2 Here, an empty frame was placed on a printout, then a torn printout was added on top of the frame, and finally the composition was photographed as is, shadows and all. Combining items before you enter Photoshop provides a natural feel.

3 Combining items can also save you time. Since both of these elements were to be photographed against black, there was no reason why they couldn't be ganged up in the same shot, then quickly isolated later.

PART THREE: Building the background

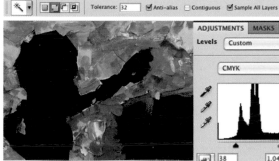

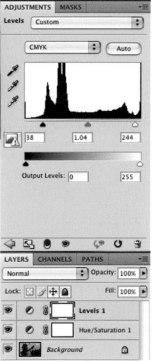

8 Start by opening up the background.jpg file. In the adjustments panel, click on the Hue/Saturation button to create a new hue/saturation adjustment layer. Adjust the hue to 130 and then increase the saturation by 16. When you're finished, click on the Return to Adjustment List arrow in the bottom left corner of the adjustments panel. When the adjustment list reappears, create a new levels adjustment layer by clicking on the Levels button in the adjustments panel. Drag the left and right input levels sliders toward the center of the histogram to increase the contrast.

Adjustment layers in CS3

The adjustments panel is new to CS4. Those of you who are still using CS3 will notice its absence very quickly when you begin to work through the steps on this page. So, if you are still using CS3, you'll need to create your adjustments layers via the Layer menu or the pop-up menu at the bottom of the Layers palette. You'll need to edit your adjustments in the pop-up dialog boxes that appear, and you'll need to press OK to apply your edits. To perform further edits to your adjustment layers after the fact, you'll need to double-click their thumbnails in the Layers palette.

9 Select the Magic Wand tool. Ensure that the Contiguous option is disabled and that the Select All Layers option is enabled in the Tool Options bar. You can leave the tolerance set at the default value of 32. Click within the black area to select all of the black areas. Then type Control(PC)/Command(Mac)-Shift-I to invert the selection. The selection doesn't have to be precise or anywhere near perfect; we want this image to have a rough and rugged feel. Open up the sky.jpg file.

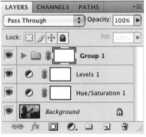

10 Select the contents of the sky file by typing Control(PC)/Command(Mac)-A and copy by typing Control(PC)/Command(Mac)-C. Return to your working file and, with the selection still active, paste into the active selection by typing Control(PC)/Command(Mac)-Shift-V. This pastes your copied art into the working file as a masked layer. Use the Move tool to move the layer contents to the upper right within the mask. Ensure that the layer is targeted in the Layers palette and not the mask or you will accidentally move the mask instead.

11 Change the blending mode of the layer to luminosity and reduce the opacity to 71% in the Layers palette. Duplicate the layer by dragging it onto the Create a New Layer button at the bottom of the Layers palette. Return the opacity of the duplicate layer to 100% and then change its blending mode to hard light. Now hold down the Shift key and click on the original layer in the Layers palette. This will select both layers. Add both of these layers to a group by typing Control(PC)/Command(Mac)-G. Click the Add Layer Mask button at the bottom of the Layers palette to add a mask to the group. Select the Gradient tool.

12 In the Tool Options bar, select the radial gradient method and the Foreground to Transparent preset. Set the foreground color to black. A quick way to do this when a mask is targeted is to first hit the "d" key to set the foreground and background colors to white and black, respectively. Then, press the "x" key to invert them, setting the foreground color to black. Now, with the group's mask targeted, create a series of small, black to transparent gradients with the mask to reveal subtle blends of imagery on the underlying layers.

13 Open up the tree.jpg file. Select the entire image and copy it. Then return to your working file. As you've done previously, use the Magic Wand to select the black areas of the image and then invert the selection. Paste the copied tree image into the selection as a new layer and move it to the left within the mask. This is exactly the same procedure, using the same keyboard shortcuts, that you used to paste the sky into a masked layer moments ago. Duplicate the layer and change the blending mode to overlay.

⚠ Foreground to transparent

You'll notice throughout this tutorial that in every instance where a gradient is used to edit a layer mask, the same Gradient preset is used. Foreground to transparent is the Gradient preset of choice because it doesn't fill the entire area surrounding your gradient with color, allowing you to create multiple gradients within your mask. Be very careful to ensure that you are not using the Foreground to Background preset. Many people make this mistake because it is the default preset. Using Foreground to Background will always fill the entire area; so if there is an existing gradient within a mask, it will be replaced each time you create a new gradient.

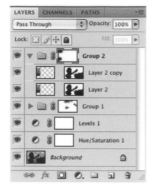

14 Shift-click on the original tree layer, below the currently targeted duplicate layer in the Layers palette, so that both the tree layers are selected and then group them. Add a mask to the new group. Target the mask and again use the same radial gradient methods that you used previously with the sky group to mask areas of the tree group, blending it into the background. Ensure that you are using the Foreground to Transparent preset and a black foreground color as you create gradients within the mask.

PART FOUR: Create the body of the figure

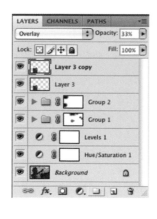

15 Open up the suit.psd file. Select the contents of the image layer in that file by typing Control(PC)/Command(Mac)-A. Then paste it into your working file as a new layer by typing Control(PC)/Command(Mac)-V. Use the Move tool to position it over the black area that defines the figure's body at the left. Reduce the opacity of the layer to 33%. Duplicate the layer and change the layer blending of the new duplicate layer mode to overlay.

16 Open up the arm1.jpg file. Use the Polygonal Lasso tool to draw a rough selection border that contains the arm and a bit of the shoulder of the wooden figure; it is fine to have some black within the rough selection. Copy the selected contents. Paste the copied arm into the working file as a new layer. Use Edit>Free-Transform to resize it. Simply drag a corner handle of the bounding box while holding down the Shift key to scale it proportionately. Then press Enter to apply the transformation. Change the blending mode to lighten, then place it over the black area where it belongs. Add a mask to the layer and create black to transparent, radial gradients within the mask to blend it into the background.

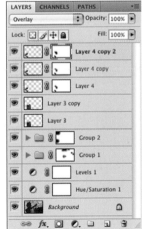

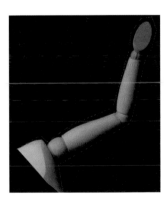

17 Duplicate the arm layer and change the blending mode to overlay. Then duplicate the newly duplicated layer as well. The result of building up layers like this is a colorful and intense image component. Now open up the arm2.jpg file. Again, use the Polygonal Lasso tool to draw a very rough, polygonal selection around the arm and copy it. Again, black within the selection area is fine.

18 Paste the copied arm into your working file as a new layer. Resize with Free-Transform and reposition the arm to the other side of the suit. Add a mask to the layer and then, while the layer mask is targeted, draw a rough polygonal selection around the forearm and hand. Fill the current selection within the layer mask with black to hide it. Deactivate the selection by typing Control(PC)/Command(Mac)-D. Create radial, black to transparent gradients within the mask to gently mask the shoulder. Duplicate the layer and change the blending mode to overlay.

Adding hands
Use what are now becoming familiar methods to add some disproportionate hands to the ends of your mannequin arms.

1 Open up the hand1.jpg file. Select all and copy. Then paste the copied image into your working file as a new layer. Use Free-Transform to rotate, size, and position it. Change the layer blending mode to lighten and add a layer mask.

2 Create gradients within the mask to hide the visible sharp edges that remain. Duplicate the layer and change the blending mode of the duplicate layer to soft light. Now open up the hand2.jpg file. Again, copy the image and paste it into the working file as a new layer.

3 Use the Move tool to position it at the end of his other arm. Change the blending mode to lighten. Duplicate the layer and change the blending mode to overlay. There is no need to mask these layers, the subtle hard edges add to the choppy feel of the composition.

PART FIVE: Create the main facial components

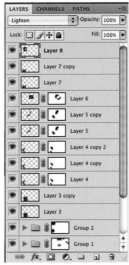

19 Open up the mask1.jpg file. Select all and then copy. Return to your working file and paste the copied mask into it as a new layer. Use the Move tool to position it over the black area that defines the region for the figure's head. Change the layer blending mode to lighten so that any dark areas that overlap the painted sky will disappear. Use the Pen tool to carefully draw a closed path around the mask.

20 When you have finished drawing the path, load the path as a selection by Control(PC)/Command(Mac)-clicking on the path thumbnail in the Paths palette. With the new selection active, choose Layer>New>Layer Via Copy from the menu to create a new layer containing only the selection contents. Add a mask to the layer and create gradients within the mask to softly mask areas, like the bridge of the nose. While editing the mask, remember to use the radial gradient method, a black foreground color, and the Foreground to Transparent Gradient preset. Basically, you're just repeating the methods you used previously to edit other masks. Reduce the layer opacity to 41% and then duplicate it. Change the blending mode of the duplicate layer to soft light and increase this layer's opacity to 100%.

21 Open up the face.psd file. Select the contents of the file and copy. Return to your working file and paste the copied contents into your file as a new layer. Use the Move tool to position it in the face area on the canvas and then drag it beneath all of the mask layers in the Layers palette. Duplicate the layer and change the blending mode to hard light. Now duplicate the newly duplicate layer and change the blending mode to soft light. Add a mask to each layer, one at a time, and edit each mask independently. Use the Gradient tool with the same method, foreground color, and preset to replicate the same soft layer blending effect you've achieved previously with other components.

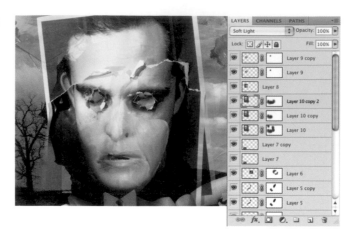

PART SIX: Place strange items in the figure's hands

 Floating windows

In Photoshop CS4, by default, new files are opened as tabbed image files within your currently active window. This makes for a well-organized workspace, but it makes dragging and dropping between files difficult. If you want to have two files open in separate image windows at the same time, you'll need to direct your attention to the Application bar or the Window menu. In the Application bar, there is an Arrange Documents pull-down menu. Simply choose the Float All in Windows option from this menu to give each open file a window of its own. In the Window menu, navigate to the Arrange submenu and then choose the Float All in Windows option.

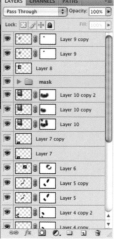

22 Open up the mask2.psd file. Arrange your open files in your workspace so that you can clearly see both of the open image windows. In the mask2.psd file, click on the group in the Layers palette and then drag it into the working file's image window. This drag-and-drop approach allows you to quickly move a group from one file to another and you can also use this method to expedite the process of cutting and pasting. Use the Move tool to position the masks group at the end of the outstretched arm on the working file's canvas. This group contains a shadow layer, a mask layer, and a layer to enhance the mask's colors. The group, when you drag it into the file, will be placed directly above the currently targeted layer in the Layers palette. This will vary depending upon which layer mask you edit before you drag, but the exact positioning of the group within the stack is not crucial.

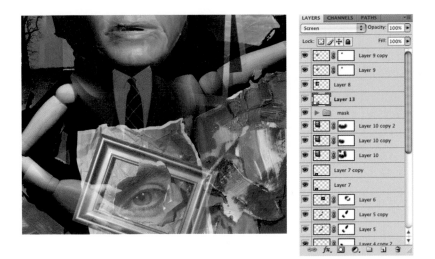

23 Open up the framed.psd file. You can either copy the contents of the image and paste them into the working file as a new layer or drag and drop from file to file via the Move tool as described on the previous page. Once the new layer is in the working file, use the Move tool to position the layer content so that it overlaps the stomach area of the figure at the left. When you are satisfied with the position, change the blending mode of the layer to screen.

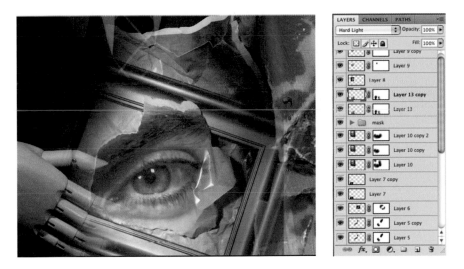

24 Add a layer mask to the layer and select the Gradient tool. Create a series of radial, black to transparent gradients within the layer mask to gently blend the layer contents into the background and reveal parts of the image on the underlying layers. By now, you're certainly getting the hang of editing masks using this method. Also, note that if you accidentally mask something that you want to reveal, you can gently reintroduce it by using the same method. Simply change the foreground color to white and then create white to transparent gradients within the mask over areas that you wish to softly reveal again. When editing the mask, bear in mind that we want to reveal the fingers on the wooden hand. Duplicate the layer and change the blending mode to hard light.

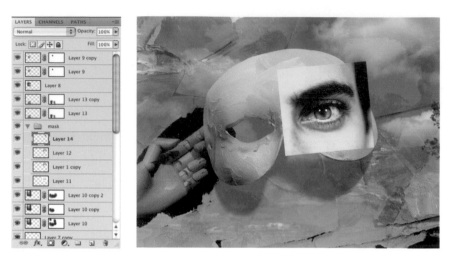

25 Open up the eye.psd file. Drag it into the working file as a new layer or copy and paste it into the working file as a new layer. Use the Move tool to position it over the eye-shaped hole at the right of the mask in the figure's hand. Choose Edit>Free-Transform from the menu. When the bounding box appears, Shift-click on a corner point of the bounding box to proportionately resize the contents. Click and drag just outside of the bounding box to rotate the contents. When you are happy with the size and rotation of the eye, press the Return or Enter key to apply the transformation. For the sake of establishing a hint of order in the Layers palette, let's place this layer into the mask group. Expand the group so that you can see the layers within and drag the current eye layer into the group, above the other layers within.

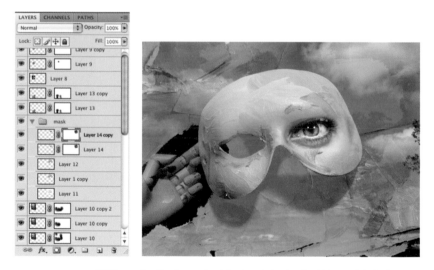

26 Change the blending mode of the layer to luminosity. Add a mask to the layer and add a series of black to transparent radial gradients into the mask, blending the hard edges into the imagery on the layers below. Duplicate the layer and change the blending mode of the duplicate layer back to normal. Target the mask of the duplicate layer and add more black to transparent radial gradients around the perimeter, masking almost all of the skin on this layer.

PART SEVEN: Take a moment to organize your layers

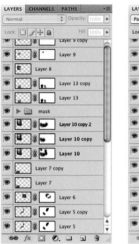

27 You'll notice that the Layers palette is quickly filling up with layers and duplicates and because you're working at different places within the hierarchy when adding layers, new layers aren't always added at the top either. Obviously, this can cause confusion. Things can get a little chaotic; so let's take a moment to establish some order here. Select layers that go together logically and add them to groups. For instance, click on one of the torn face layers, and then Control(PC)/Command(Mac)-click on the others so that all three are selected. Then, with all of the layers selected, type Control(PC)/Command(Mac)-g to group them. To name the group, double-click on the name to highlight the text. When the text is highlighted, enter a new and relevant name for the group.

28 Repeat this process to group all clusters of layers that belong together, and name the groups appropriately. Immediately after you do this, the Layers palette will make more sense at a glance. However, you will notice that you cannot add an actual background layer to a group. To remedy this, you can quickly convert the background layer to a normal layer by double-clicking it in the Layers palette. When the New Layer options appear, all that you need to do is click OK to complete the conversion. Once the layer is converted, it can then be grouped in the same manner as the rest. Also, you will have some unnamed groups that were created previously; go ahead and name them now. Taking a few moments to do this will make it much easier for you to make sense of your file if you decide to perform alterations at a later date.

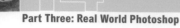
PART EIGHT: Add some painted surface texture

29 Open up the painting.psd file. This is a photograph of the original color painting before it was torn and cut up. A hue adjustment was applied to the original image, altering the overall color. Choose Select>Color Range from the menu. Color Range allows you to target a range of color from within the painting. When the Color Range dialog box opens, simply click on a color in the image window that you wish to isolate. The black-and-white preview will show you, in white, how the selected areas will be generated. You can add other ranges of color to your selected regions by Shift-clicking on them. Alternatively, you can remove ranges of color from the selected area by Alt(PC)/Option(Mac)-clicking on them. The fuzziness slider allows you to quickly control how particular the Color Range function is when selecting regions of color. When you're satisfied with the preview of the selected regions, click OK to generate a selection.

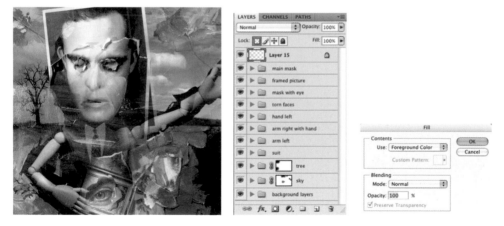

30 With the new selection active, choose Edit>Copy from the menu. Return to your working file and paste the copied selection into it as a new layer. Drag the layer to the top of the stack in the Layers palette if necessary. Position the layer so that it overlaps the image in a pleasing manner. Now, just because we copied a specific range of color, it doesn't mean we can't alter the color now in our working file. In the Layers palette, enable the transparency lock for this new layer. Choose Edit>Fill from the menu. In the Fill dialog box, select the Color option from the Contents menu to open the picker. Select a new color from the picker and click OK. In the Blending options, leave the blending mode set to normal and the opacity set to 100%. Click OK to fill the layer with your new color. Use Free-Transform to resize and position the layer further if you like.

31 Return to the painting.psd file and select another range of color with the Color Range command. Again, copy the selected region and paste it into the working file as a new layer. Feel free to enable the transparency lock of this layer and fill it with a different color. Use Free-Transform to alter the size and positioning as required. Repeat this process over and over again to build up a number of different layers that add painted and tactile feeling to the surface of your image. Feel free to duplicate the layers and resize or reposition them as well, varying layer opacity and blending modes along the way. When you're satisfied with the results, add these new textural layers to a named group.

32 The results of this textured stage of the project will vary greatly from individual to individual. However, if you feel that the surface texture is too strong in any specific area, you can remedy this by adding a mask to the group. Simply target your new group in the Layers palette and click on the Add Layer Mask button at the bottom of the palette. Target the mask and select the Gradient tool. Specify a black foreground color and set up the Gradient tool like you've been doing all along. Introduce some radial gradients into the mask in areas that you wish to fade. This is the same process that you've been using all along and even at this final stage, it proves quite useful.

This compositing style can be used in moderation as well. It doesn't always need to dominate the composition. In this instance, it was used to create just the background of the illustration. Something as subtle as a tactile background can alter the feeling of the illustration, making it a little more human feeling when the majority of the composition is so obviously digital.

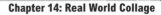

This method of working really lends itself to expressing something ominous. The torn painting can contribute to an unsettled feeling, which is only helped by a large, black, primary image component like the ravens shown here. These illustrations, which accompanied an article about Internet-pedophiles stalking children, were an ideal subject for this very expressive style.

Chapter 15

In and Out of Photoshop

Sometimes we get locked into routines that keep us complacent and uninspired. To break free of visual monotony, try breaking free from your computer for a while. By beginning with photos in Photoshop, we can manipulate them to lend themselves to tracing. After printing them out, we can use traditional drawing techniques to create natural, personalized art. This artwork is then scanned back in and used alongside other elements as the basis for a stunning and original composition. Working this way is a breath of fresh air and provides a nice break from the usual routine.

Traditional thinkers are often under the misconception that the incorporation of tactile elements into digital art means they'll be using scanned textures as backgrounds, or creating distressed, scratchy effects. This chapter will get you thinking beyond that. There's so much more you can do when you incorporate the tactile into the middle of the workflow. A willingness to go in and out of the digital realm is required. And I think you'll agree that not only is the process interesting, but also the results are a unique combination of both worlds, blurring the lines of distinction in-between.

DIFFICULTY 3.5/5

You'll need to have a bit of experience with shape layers and paths to make your way through the chapter with ease. All is explained, but a little know-how will make things less confusing. It is also beneficial to know your way around the Layers palette, the Tool Options bar, and understand how black and white is used within layer masks.

What you'll learn in this chapter

Creative Techniques and Working Methods

Analysis and adjustment

You'll learn to analyze images and adjust them in order to enhance the details. Your analysis will deviate from the analysis of photography in the classic sense. You are not concerned with the end product of each photographic image. The initial photography is merely seen as a means to an end. You will look for regions of detail that you can enhance via Adjustment tools and regardless of the color balance and tonal perfection of the final image, you'll concentrate on creating something that you can use for the specific task of tracing traditionally.

Stripping things down

In addition to preparing images for tracing purposes, you'll also learn to perform drastic adjustments to strip images down to the core, or essence, of the image. The result of this is a stark, black-and-white version of the photograph that clearly divides positive and negative space, removing anything in-between.

Photoshop Tools, Features, and Functions

Solid color layer masks

Many people work with solid color layers, but rarely do I see people editing the masks to realize their vision. In this chapter, editing the masks of solid color layers is the key to creating the main components within the image shown here.

Smart objects

Groups of layers will be stored within smart objects further along in the chapter. Because numerous instances of these objects are scattered around, the timesaving benefit of editing all instances of an object at once becomes invaluable.

Quick targeting

It may seem like a small thing, but the method of targeting layers by Control-clicking with the Move tool will help you navigate the clutter of the Layers palette with ease.

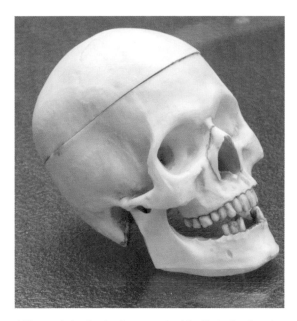

Project files

All of the files needed to follow along with this chapter and create the featured image are available for download on the accompanying Web site in the project files section. Visit www.creativephotoshopthebook.com.

1 When capturing the visual components of the illustration, there is no need for perfect lighting, focus, or exposure. The resulting images are for tracing purposes only, so your photography doesn't need to be technically perfect. This skull was quickly photographed outdoors on an overcast day, which provided nice, even lighting.

Skipping ahead

The first two parts of this chapter describe the process of preparing and creating art before entering Photoshop. If you aren't interested in this aspect and just want to get busy creating the featured image, go ahead and skip forward to Part Three of this chapter.

2 The octopus and flower were photographed outdoors on the same day. The background of the image isn't a concern at all because we'll be tracing the subject only. The tree and hydro tower images will be incorporated as manipulated photos, not hand-drawn reproductions. Shooting these against a clear sky makes it easier to isolate them later on.

PART TWO: Adjust, print, trace, and scan

3 The next step, after photographing the image components, is to drastically alter the images that we'll be tracing by hand. Open up the skull.jpg file. Choose Image>Adjustments>Black and White from the menu. The goal now is to enhance contrast while preserving detail. Choose the High Contrast Blue Filter preset from the Preset menu.

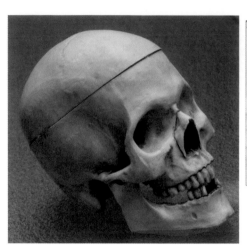

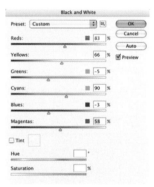

4 Open up the flower.jpg. Again, use the black-and-white adjustment from the Image>Adjustments menu. This time, select the darker preset to begin with. Then, you'll need to tweak individual sliders to enhance the contrast while preserving the detail. Repeat this process with the octopus.jpg image as well. The Blue Contrast preset does a sufficient job of converting the image to high contrast black and white, while preserving the necessary details.

270

5 Print each image as large as you can on a single sheet of paper. A black-and-white printout on cheap paper is fine. There is no need to waste color toner or inks on this part of the process. Take each printout and tape a translucent sheet on top of it. Something like tracing paper, onionskin paper, or drafting vellum will suffice. You may wish to use two or three sheets if the underlying image on the printout appears too prominent. It should serve as a guide, not a distraction as you draw.

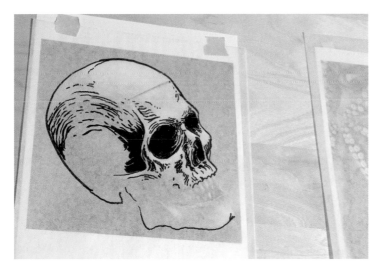

6 Use a black marker or felt-tipped pen to trace the photograph. The goal when tracing is to create solid areas of black, alongside thick and thin line work, to represent the shading in the image. Keep in mind that although you are tracing, the way in which you approach the shading and create your line work will express your personal style.

7 Continue on in this manner until you've traced each printout. You may wish to use a combination of markers and felt-tipped pens to introduce lines of varying thickness. Take your time and ensure that you don't overdo it when it comes to creating shaded areas. Areas of negative space must be present in your drawing to represent highlights.

8 Peel each sheet away from the printout it is taped to, and then carefully remove the tape. Scan each drawing at a resolution of at least 300 ppi in grayscale mode. Perform any tonal adjustments necessary to brighten the whites to 0% and darken the blacks to 100% gray. Use Levels, Curves, Brightness/Contrast, or whatever feature you're most comfortable with. Make sure that you have the Info palette visible. If it isn't visible, choose Window>Info from the menu. Ensure that you check the density of the blacks and whites with the Eyedropper and pay attention to the readouts that appear in the info window. As shown here, my dark areas are 100% black.

PART THREE: Prepare the photographs

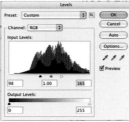

9 Open up the hydro.jpg file. Type Control(PC)/Command(Mac)-L to open up levels. We are going to use levels to begin stripping midtones out of the image. Drag the left input levels sliders toward the center to darken the shadows. Next, drag the right input levels slider toward the middle to lighten the highlights. By increasing the range consumed by highlights and shadows, you are reducing the range of midtones, thereby effectively increasing the contrast.

Using selective color

Stripping color out of separate ranges selectively allows us to enhance the effect.

1 Choose Image>Adjustments>Select-ive Color from the menu. Choose cyans from the Colors menu and then strip all of the color out of the cyans by pulling all of the sliders to the far left. You'll immediately notice the whitening of cyan areas in the image.

2 You'll notice, however, that areas of darker blue in the image are unaffected. To remedy this, select blues from the Colors menu. Perform the same operation of dragging all of the sliders to the left. This will remove much of the lingering darker blue colors from the image.

3 Now choose the Neutrals option from the Colors menu. Go ahead and strip all of the cyan, magenta, and yellow out of the neutral areas using the same method. In the end, you'll be left with what looks like black hydro towers set against a white sky. Click OK and leave the file open for the time being.

273

10 Open up the tree.jpg file and repeat the same procedure you used to strip color out of the hydro.jpg image. First use levels to increase the contrast, and then use selective color to strip color out of the sky so that all that remains is a black tree and horizon set against a white sky. Click OK and leave this file open as well.

 Varying results

Because we're relying on an intuitive approach to performing levels adjustments, the results of these conversions will vary from person to person. What you do in the Levels dialog box will directly affect how selective color adjustments will be made. If you find that areas that should be dark are being stripped away when you perform selective color adjustments, use the History palette to go back to the state previous to your levels adjustment. Perform the levels adjustment again, but concentrate on creating darker shadows this time. Then perform your selective color adjustment and you'll likely notice an improvement.

11 Now open up the tree2.jpg file. Again, perform a levels adjustment first. Because of the exposure of this image, you won't need to darken the shadows as much as you'll need to increase the range of highlights. After applying the levels adjustment, launch selective color. Depending upon how you adjusted the levels, it is likely that with selective color you'll need to concentrate on whites and neutrals only, stripping cyan, magenta, and yellow out of each. Click OK and leave this file open as well.

PART FOUR: Incorporating the altered photographs

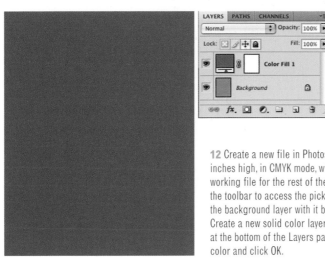

12 Create a new file in Photoshop that is approximately 7.5 inches wide and 9.5 inches high, in CMYK mode, with a resolution of 300 ppi. This will act as your working file for the rest of the chapter. Click on the Foreground Color swatch in the toolbar to access the picker. Select a cool gray color from the picker and fill the background layer with it by typing Alt(PC)/Option(Mac)-Delete on the keyboard. Create a new solid color layer from the Create New Fill or Adjustment Layer menu at the bottom of the Layers palette. When the picker appears, select a darker gray color and click OK.

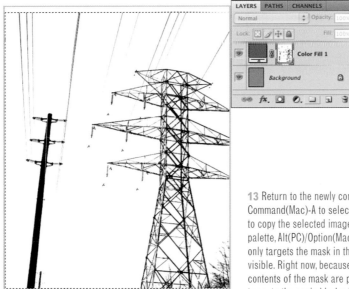

13 Return to the newly converted hydro.jpg file. Type Control(PC)/Command(Mac)-A to select all. Then type Control(PC)/Command(Mac)-C to copy the selected image. Return to the working file. In the Layers palette, Alt(PC)/Option(Mac)-click on the solid color's mask. This not only targets the mask in the Layers palette but also makes the contents visible. Right now, because no areas of the layer are masked, the contents of the mask are pure white. Type Control(PC)/Command(Mac)-V to paste the copied hydro image into the visible mask.

14 Type Control(PC)/Command(Mac)-T to access Free-Transform. When the bounding box appears around your selection, Shift-drag a corner point outward to increase the size proportionately. Drag within the box to reposition the art on the canvas. When you're happy with the new size and position, press the Enter key to apply the transformation. Alt(PC)/Option(Mac)-click on the layer mask in the Layers palette to hide it. Now you can see the effect of editing the solid color layer's mask. However, what we're after is the inverse of what you see here. To invert the mask, simply ensure that it is targeted in the Layers palette (it doesn't need to be visible, just targeted). You can either click the Invert button in the Masks palette or opt for the keyboard shortcut, which is Control(PC)/Command(Mac)-I.

15 Now, duplicate the layer by dragging it onto the Create a New Layer button at the bottom of the Layers palette. With the duplicate layer's mask targeted, type Control(PC)/Command(Mac)-T to access Free-Transform again. When the bounding box surrounds the image, right-click(PC)/Control-click(Mac) inside of it. A pop-up menu will appear. Choose flip horizontal from the pop-up menu. After the flip is complete, press Enter to apply the transformation.

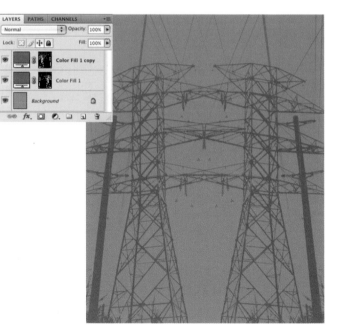

16 Select gradient from the Create New Fill or Adjustment Layer menu at the bottom of the Layers palette. Click on the arrow to the right of the gradient thumbnail to access the list of presets. Select the Black, White Linear Gradient preset from the list. Change the style to radial and enable the Reverse option. Click OK and then change the blending mode of this new gradient layer to overlay in the Layers palette. This will nicely enhance the silhouetted towers in the sky effect we've just created.

17 Create another solid color layer. This time, choose a darker gray than the one you used previously. Don't be alarmed by the fact that it completely obscures your composition, we'll remedy that soon enough. Return to the tree2.jpg file. Select all and copy. Now, go back to your working file and Alt(PC)/Option(Mac)-click on the new solid color layer's mask in the Layers palette to make it visible. Paste your copied art into the visible mask. Use Free-Transform to alter the size and position of the pasted art so that it sits near the bottom right corner within the layer mask. Invert the mask by typing Control(PC)/Command(Mac)-I.

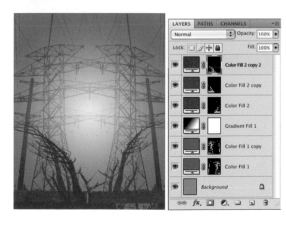

18 Alt(PC)/Option(Mac)-click on the layer mask thumbnail in the Layers palette to remove it from view and return to the normal workspace. Duplicate this layer, and then use Free-Transform to horizontally flip it. After you flip it horizontally, duplicate this newly duplicated layer. Select a foreground color from the picker that is darker and contains more blue than the current gray of the layer. Ensure that your newly duplicated layer is targeted in the Layers palette (not the mask, but the layer itself), and then type Alt(PC)/Option(Mac)-Delete to replace the fill color of the layer. Target the layer's mask in the Layers palette and use Free-Transform to increase the size, considerably stretching the layer to the right and downward. Do not allow the left edge to move toward the right, or you'll see an unmasked region creep into the canvas area. Apply the transformation.

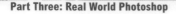

Returning to the workspace

You already know that when you're working on a visible mask, you can Alt(PC)/Option(Mac)-click on its thumbnail to return to the normal workspace. However, you can also achieve this by simply clicking on any layer thumbnail in the Layers palette. However, do not click on another mask thumbnail, or it won't work. It must be a layer thumbnail.

19 Duplicate this layer also and then flip it horizontally via Free-Transform. You'll notice that you'll need to click inside the bounding box and Shift-drag to the left to properly position the flipped contents on the layer mask on the canvas area. This is due to the fact that the mask contents were stretched beyond the edge of the canvas. Apply the transformation, then target both of these new, darker blue layers in the Layers palette and group them by typing Control(PC)/Command(Mac)-G. Name the group and then group the other two, lighter gray layers that contain the same tree. After that, group the gradient and fill layers that reside below the two groups you just created.

20 Create a new solid color layer. Specify a deep red fill color when the picker appears and then drag it beneath the top group in the Layers palette. Return to the tree.jpg file and copy it. Now, return to the working file and Alt(PC)/Option(Mac)-click on the new solid color layer's mask to make it visible. Paste the copied tree image into the mask and then use Free-Transform to proportionately increase the size of the tree and position it centrally within the mask. After you apply the transformation, invert the image within the mask and then hide the visible mask by Alt(PC)/Option(Mac)-clicking on it in the Layers palette.

PART FIVE: Incorporate the scanned drawings

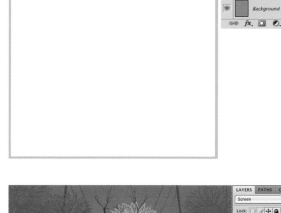

21 Duplicate the red tree layer and flip the duplicated layer horizontally. Group these two red tree layers and name the group. As of now, we're moving on from photographs to drawings. From here on, I'll be referring to the drawings that are available for download by their file names. However, if you created drawings of your own, simply substitute them as necessary as we make our way through the chapter. Open up the flower sketch.jpg file. Copy the artwork. Return to the working file and use the Eyedropper to click on one of the lighter gray trees in the image, setting the current foreground color to that color. Create a new solid color layer. Adjust nothing in the picker and simply click OK. Make the layer's mask visible and then paste the copied flower into it. Use Free-Transform to reduce the size of the flower and position it in the upper left.

22 Invert the mask and then Alt(PC)/Option(Mac)-click on its thumbnail to return to the normal workspace. Select the Move tool. Hold down the Alt(PC)/Option(Mac) key and then click on the flower on the canvas. Drag while continuing to hold down the Alt(PC)/Option(Mac) key to create a duplicate of the flower layer in a different region on the canvas. Repeat this process a couple more times until you have a number of gray flowers scattered across the top of the image. Create another duplicate layer and double-click on the solid color layer icon in the Layers palette to open the picker. Select a lighter gray fill color and click OK. Change the blending mode of the layer to screen and reduce the opacity to 59%.

Seldon Hunt

My inspiration for this style of artwork, especially for the incomplete state of the illustration on this particular page, is the work of Seldon Hunt. His otherworldly digital Rorschach tests have always proved compelling and inspiring. So take a look at the state of the image on this page because after this page it will begin to look a little more like my own again as I add the main visual components. Remember that Rorschach effect, then head over to his Web site and see how it's really done. Visit www.seldonhunt.com

23 Use this same method to Alt(PC)/Option(Mac)-drag with the Move tool to make numerous copies of the layer throughout the top of the canvas. Target the layer masks for individual layers and use Free-Transform to resize the contents of the mask as you see fit. This will likely result in a lot of flower layers in the Layers palette. Target all of them and then type Control(PC)/Command(Mac)-G to group them.

24 Open up the octo-sketch.jpg file. Select all and copy. Return to the working file and create a new solid color layer. Choose a light yellow color from the picker and click OK. Alt(PC)/Option(Mac)-click on the layer's mask thumbnail to target it and make it visible. Paste the copied art into the visible mask. Use Free-Transform to resize it and position it quite low on the canvas area, just to the left of the center. Invert the mask and then Alt(PC)/Option(Mac)-click on it again to return to the normal workspace.

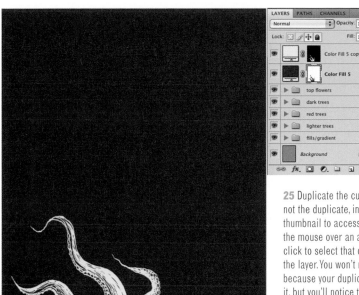

25 Duplicate the current layer and then target the original, not the duplicate, in the Layers palette. Double-click the layer's thumbnail to access the picker. When the picker appears, move the mouse over an area of red trees in the image window and click to select that color. Click OK to change the fill color of the layer. You won't notice it immediately in the image window because your duplicate layer is still sitting directly on top of it, but you'll notice the change in the Layers palette. Target the layer's mask and type Control(PC)/Command(Mac)-I to invert the mask. You'll see the effects immediately as all of the visible areas of the underlying image are covered with red.

26 Alt(PC)/Option(Mac)-click on the layer's mask thumbnail to make it visible. Select the Magic Wand tool and in the Tool Options bar, ensure that the Contiguous option is enabled. Leave the tolerance set at its default value of 32 and use the Wand to click on the white area surrounding the tentacles. Once the area is selected, choose Select>Modify>Expand from the menu and expand the selection by 1 pixel. If your current background color is not set to black, press the "d" key. After expanding, type Control(PC)/Command(Mac)-Delete to fill the area with black. Type Control(PC)/Command(Mac)-D to deactivate the selection and then Alt(PC)/Option(Mac)-click on the layer's mask thumbnail again to hide it.

27 Target both tentacles layers and group them. Duplicate the group the same way that you would duplicate a layer. With the duplicate group targeted, flip it horizontally via Free-Transform. Select the Move tool. Use the Move tool to right-click(PC)/Control-click(Mac) on one of the larger flowers at the top of the canvas. A pop-up menu will appear. The menu will list every layer in the file that has content in the area of the canvas that you just clicked on. We want to select the flower layer from the list. Although we didn't name it, it is easy to pick out from the contents of the list. We know that it is a solid color layer and it is a copy, so both of those details will be contained in the name of the layer. Select the appropriate layer from the list and you'll notice that the layer is targeted in the Layers palette. The group that it resides within will expand to show it.

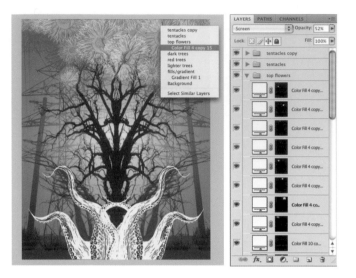

Targeting layers

Using the Move tool to right-click(PC)/Control-click(Mac) on layers and select them from the pop-up menu is quick and easy. However, you don't need to select the Move tool before you do this. While using any tool, you can access this pop-up menu by holding down the Control(PC)/Command(Mac) key while you right-click(PC)/Control-click(Mac) on an area of the canvas. Introducing the Control(PC)/Command(Mac) key temporarily switches your current tool to the Move tool.

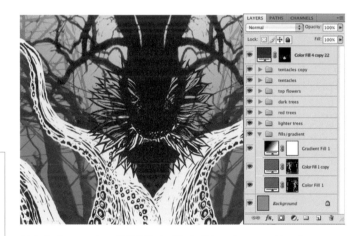

28 In the Layers palette, Alt(PC)/Option(Mac)-click on the targeted layer's thumbnail and drag it upward in the Layers palette to the top of the stack. When you see a dark horizontal line appear above the top group, it is safe to release the mouse button. A copy of your layer will appear. The black line indicates the copied layer's destination, so watch for it carefully. If you don't pay attention to the destination it might end up nested within a group. Increase the opacity of the copied layer to 100% and change the blending mode to normal. Double-click on the layer's thumbnail to access the picker. When the picker appears, move the mouse over a red region of the canvas and click. When the red color is sampled, click OK. Use the Move tool to reposition the flower to the center of the canvas, just above where the tentacles cross over each other.

29 In the Layers palette, Alt(PC)/Option(Mac)-click on the flower layer and drag just below it in the Layers palette to copy it. You'll see that familiar dark horizontal line appearing directly below your layer. When the line appears in this position, release the mouse button. A copy of your red flower layer is now directly beneath the original at the top of the Layers palette. Double-click the layer's thumbnail to access the picker. Sample a light yellow color from within the image and click OK to change the layer's fill color. Target the layer's mask in the Layers palette and type Control(PC)/Command(Mac)-I to invert the mask. Again, this process of inverting the mask will hide underlying layers.

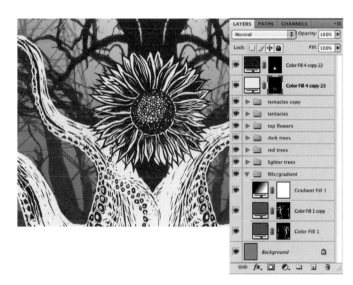

30 Alt(PC)/Option(Mac)-click on the layer's mask to make it visible. Select the Magic Wand tool and use the same tool options settings that you used previously. Leave the tolerance set at 32 and ensure that the Contiguous option is enabled. Click on the white area surrounding the flower to select it. Choose Select>Modify>Expand from the menu and expand the selection by 1 pixel. Fill the expanded selection with black. Deselect and Alt(PC)/Option(Mac)-click on the layer's mask to hide it.

Why expand?

You'll notice that I am using black to fill selected areas within masks, hiding them as a result. You'll also notice that before I fill each selection, I expand the selection slightly. This is an insurance policy against the appearance of a hairline edge at the end of the procedure. The wand selection doesn't quite make it all the way into the black because of the anti-aliased edge where the black and white meet. If you don't expand, there will be a very thin, light, halo between the pre-existing black and the newly filled area. The unwanted effect of this will be visible in the illustration. However, a simple expansion quickly prevents this from happening at all.

31 Group these two flower layers and then use the Rectangular Marquee to draw a small rectangular selection around the outside of the flower area. With this selection active, and your group targeted, click on the Add Layer Mask button at the bottom of the Layers palette. This will mask the area surrounding the flower. I know there is nothing visible here at the moment, but the logic for masking this group will reveal itself soon enough. Create copies of the group and strategically place flowers within the lower region of the canvas as shown here. Now, expand some of your duplicated flower groups and have a look at some of the yellow solid color layer masks. You will see that because we filled the selected outer area with black, there is an edge where the black fill ends. When you move that layer, the region on the outside of this area is white, meaning that the color would be visible. Masking the group ensures that this region is not visible.

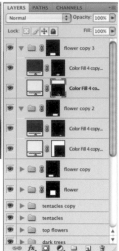

32 Open up the skull-sketch.jpg file. Copy it and then create a new, black, solid color layer at the top of the stack in the Layers palette. Alt(PC)/ Option(Mac)-click on the layer's mask to make it visible. Paste the copied skull drawing into the visible layer mask. Deselect and then invert the mask so that the skull drawing becomes white and everything else becomes black. Alt(PC)/Option(Mac)- click on the layer's mask to return to the normal workspace. With the layer mask targeted, enable Free-Transform. A bounding box will appear around the skull. Move the mouse outside of the bounding box and then click and drag to rotate the skull. Shift-drag the corners to adjust the size proportionately. Flip it horizontally and position it on the canvas as shown here.

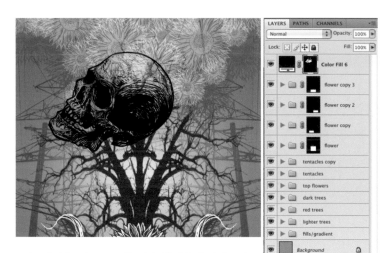

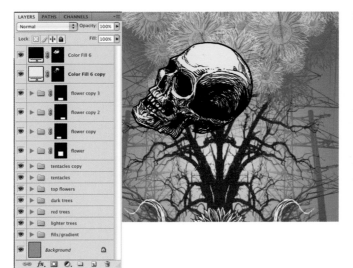

33 Alt(PC)/Option(Mac) drag to create a copy of this layer below the original in the Layers palette. Change the fill color of the duplicate layer to the same light yellow that you see in the image in other areas. Target the layer's mask and then invert it so that all of the visible areas on the underlying layers are hidden by the light yellow fill color. Alt(PC)/Option(Mac)-click on the duplicate layer's mask to make it visible. Use the wand to select the region that surrounds the skull. Shift-click in the empty white space between the two jaws to add it to the selection. Expand the selection and fill it with black. Deselect and return to the normal workspace.

PART SIX: Working with smart objects

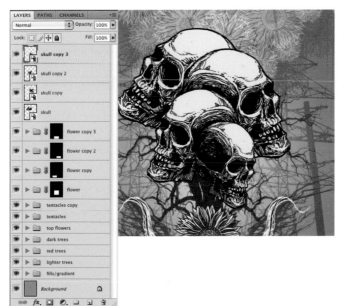

34 Add both of the skull layers to a group. Draw a selection around the skull with the Rectangular Marquee tool. While the selection is active, click the Add Layer Mask button at the bottom of the Layers palette to mask the group. Target the group in the Layers palette and then choose Layer>Smart Objects>Convert to Smart Object from the menu. Duplicate the smart object in the same way you would an ordinary layer. Make several duplicates and use Free-Transform to rotate, resize, reposition, and flip them as necessary. The goal is to create a small cluster of skulls that overlap the main area of the red trees.

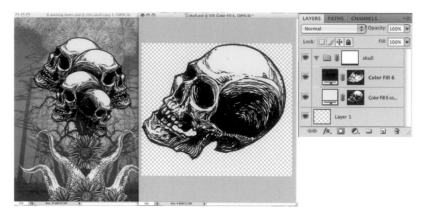

35 The initial idea here was to give the skull a black outline to make it stand out within the composition. However, upon further reflection, this really just causes it to look disconnected from the rest of the image. To re-integrate the skulls into the image, double-click on one of the skull smart objects in the Layers palette. This opens a version of the smart object as a layered file, allowing you to edit the content. Expand the group in the Layers palette and ensure that you are floating the windows so that you can see red areas of your working file in the background.

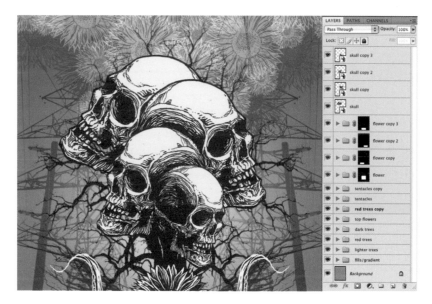

36 Double-click the black solid color layer in the Layers palette. When the picker appears, move the mouse over a visible red area of the working file in behind the current window, and click to sample the color. Click OK to close the picker, making the skull outlines red instead of black. Close this window. Save changes when prompted. When you return to the working file, you'll immediately notice that all instances of your smart object are updated to reflect the change. Now, although the translucent flowers at the top of the canvas add a nice effect, they obscure the tree branches at the top. To remedy this, duplicate the group that contains the red trees and place it just above the group that contains the translucent flowers in the Layers palette.

PART SEVEN: Juxtaposition via shape layers

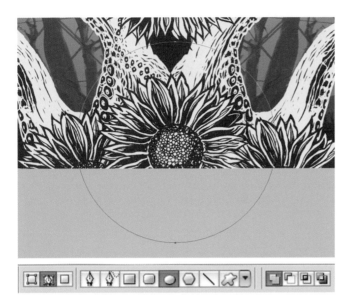

37 Now that the composition is beginning to take shape, we can see that the hand-drawn art is taking prominence, giving the composition a very organic feel. Let's add a bit of interest, introducing some juxtaposition in the overall feel by adding some sharp, vector-based elements. Select the Ellipse tool in the toolbar. In the Tool Options bar, ensure that the Ellipse tool is set to create paths and not shape layers by clicking on the button second from the left. Also ensure that the Add to Path Area option is enabled. Hold down the Shift key, then click and drag to draw a circular path at the bottom center, which extends below the bottom edge of the canvas.

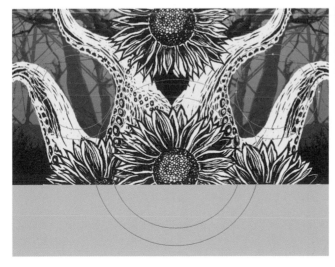

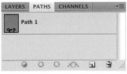

38 Draw another, smaller circle inside of this one. Use the Path Selection tool to select the path and then click on the Subtract from Path Area button in the Tool Options bar. Hold down the Shift key and select the outer path as well. In the Tool Options bar, click on the Align Vertical Centers and the Align Horizontal Centers buttons to align the two paths. With both paths selected, hold down the Alt(PC)/Option(Mac)-key and drag to copy both selected paths to another area of the canvas. Use Free-Transform to reduce the size of these paths and then, once reduced in size, copy them again.

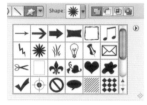

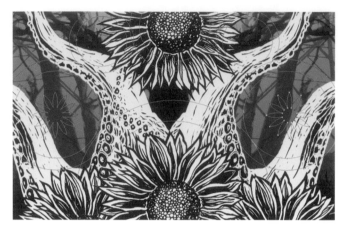

39 Duplicate the newly reduced, copied, pair of paths again. Reduce them in size and place them so that they surround the center of the flower in the center of the image. Next, make a couple more reduced copies of the paths and place them on either side of this central pair, creating a nice cluster of circular paths. Press the "U" key to access the Ellipse tool. In the Tool Options bar, select the Custom Shape option. And then, in the Custom Shape Preset picker, choose the Flower 5 Shape preset. Hold down the Shift key, then click and drag to create a flower shape within one of the circular paths as shown here. You can use the Path Selection tool to adjust the placement of the new shape. Then, Alt(PC)/Option(Mac)-drag the shape to the inside of the opposite circular path to copy it.

 Do your paths look different?

For the gradient map layer to appear as it does here, you must pay careful attention to path area operations. For instance, if you did not set an inner circle path to subtract, you might see a solid circle rather than a hoop. If you did something wrong, don't worry about it. You can use the Path Selection tool to select any path with an incorrect path area setting and simply reset it in the Tool Options bar as necessary.

40 Target the top smart object in the Layers palette. Choose the Gradient Map option from the Create New Fill or Adjustment Layer menu at the bottom of the Layers palette. This will create a new gradient map layer at the top of the layer stack. Your current path will be used to add a vector mask to the layer. In the Adjustments palette, click on the gradient to access the gradient editor. In the gradient editor, click on the stop at the lower left to select it. Click on the Color swatch below to access the picker. When the picker appears, run the mouse over an area of dark gray-blue in the image and click to select that color. Press OK to exit the picker, and then click on the stop at the lower right. When the picker appears, choose a taupe color and click OK. Again, click OK to close the gradient editor.

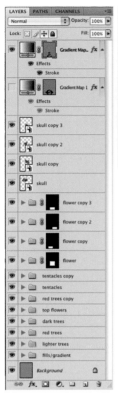

41 Now select the Stroke option from the Add a Layer Style menu at the bottom of the Layers palette. When the Stroke options appear, click on the Color swatch and then choose a white color from the picker. Set the size at 3 pixels and click OK to add a thin white stroke around the visible areas of your gradient map layer. Duplicate the layer and disable the visibility of the original layer in the Layers palette—this will avoid confusion. Ensure that your duplicate layer is targeted in the Layers palette, not the original. Use the Path Selection tool to select the flowers and all other path components except for those that make up the two central circles. Press the Delete key to remove all selected path components from this layer's mask.

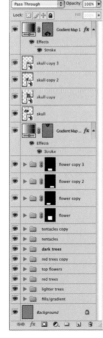

42 Select all of the remaining path components on the layer's mask and then click on the Align Vertical Centers and the Align Horizontal Centers buttons in the Tool Options bar. Then drag all of the selected, aligned path components up to the top area of the canvas. Now, drag the current layer beneath all of the skull smart objects in the Layers palette. Enable the visibility of your original gradient map layer once again. Moving things up and down within the Layers palette is essential when it comes to building a composition like this. However, you need to pay attention to everything on the canvas as you do this. Remember, not too long ago, when we duplicated the red trees group and moved it up in the Layers hierarchy, one thing that went unnoticed as a result of this procedure was that it obscured the dark blue grass along the bottom of the canvas. To remedy this, select the dark trees group in the Layers palette and drag it above the red trees group copy.

289

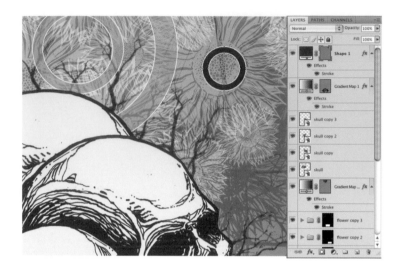

43 Use the Eyedropper to click on an area of red within the image, sampling it as the current foreground color. Select the Ellipse tool from the toolbar. In the Tool Options bar, click the button at the left to ensure that you'll be creating a shape layer with this tool. Target the top layer in the Layers palette to ensure that your new layer appears above it in the hierarchy. Hold down the Shift key, then click and drag to create a circular shape layer. You'll immediately notice that the stroke effect we used previously is automatically added to the new layer as well. This saves us the trouble of copying the effect to our new layer. Hold down the Alt(PC)/ Option(Mac) and Shift keys while you draw a smaller circle inside the original circle on this layer. Select both shape components with the Path Selection tool and then align the centers vertically in the Tool Options bar.

44 While the two shape components are selected, click on the Combine button in the Tool Options bar to combine them into a single shape. The advantage of this is that we can select the entire shape by clicking on any line segment. We don't need to click on one component and then Shift-click on the other now that the components are combined. Use the Path Selection tool to click on the shape and then Alt(PC)/Option(Mac)-drag it to another region of the canvas to duplicate it within the same shape layer. Repeat this a number of times to scatter red hoops around the top of the canvas. Select individual shape instances and alter the size of them via Free-Transform.

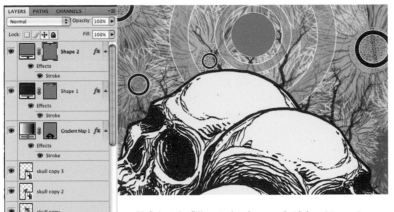

45 Select the Ellipse tool and ensure that it is set to create a new shape layer in the Tool Options bar. Create a new shape layer that contains a single circle. Position it within the center of the gradient map hoops at the top of the composition. Use the Eyedropper to sample a dark gray color from the image and then type Alt(PC)/Option(Mac)-Delete to fill the shape layer with the new foreground color.

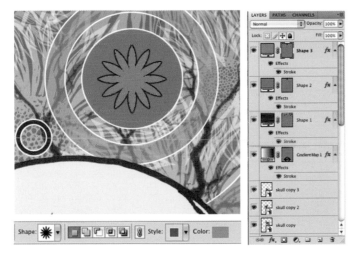

46 Select the Custom Shape tool. Unless you've changed something since you used the tool last, the Flower 5 preset will be selected in the Custom Shape picker in the Tool Options bar. Ensure that the tool is set to create a new shape layer. The Chain-Link button will be enabled in the Tool Options bar; click on it to disable it. This ensures that any changes you make will affect your new layer, not the layer currently targeted in the Layers palette. Click on the Color swatch in the Tool Options bar and select a desaturated gray color from the picker. After that, click and drag on the canvas to create a new shape layer with a flower on it. Press the Shift key while you're dragging to constrain the flower's aspect ratio. Ensure that you do not press the Shift key before you drag or your flower shape will be added to the previous shape layer. We want this flower to be on a separate shape layer. Use the Move tool to place the flower on top of the circle you created previously. Use Free-Transform to adjust the size of the shape if necessary. In the Layers palette, double-click on the stroke effect attached to this layer. Change the stroke color to the same red you've been using in the image all along.

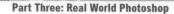

47 Create a couple of duplicates of your flower shape within the same layer. Place them lower down, and on either side of the central elements of the image. Select the Ellipse tool and create another new shape layer that contains a small circle. Change the color of this layer to the same light yellow color used within the skulls. Create numerous duplicates of this shape within the layer and scatter them around the top half of the canvas and on the background regions on either side of the skulls. Use Free-Transform to adjust the individual shapes as required.

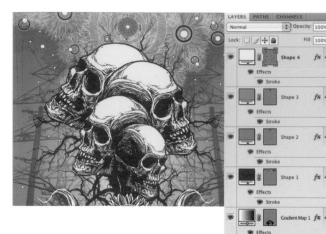

48 Now, depending upon the colors you've been using, you may or may not feel that the image needs a bit of tonal enhancement. I thought that my version needed a slight tweak, so I created a new levels adjustment layer and dragged the left and right input levels sliders toward the center of the histogram. This increased the contrast a little overall, giving the image more impact when printed. Take a moment to organize the contents of the Layers palette into logical groups wherever you can. This file is constructed in a way that lends itself to further editing. Feel free to tweak color fills, gradient, or alter smart objects at will. A well-organized Layers palette will make it much easier to perform desired edits at a later date.

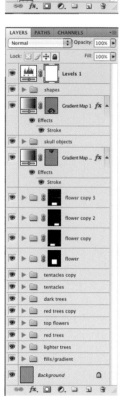

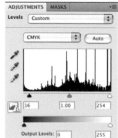

Other things to consider

If drawing isn't your thing, there is certainly no end to the resources out there that lend themselves to this technique. In this image, I used an existing ancient anatomical drawing instead of creating my own skeleton. As you can see, the overall feel remains quite similar. Also, shape layers can be used to create main visual components. Here, I created some more elaborate shapes via the Pen tool to represent wings. And finally, solid color layers are very useful; however, if you alter the blending mode and then use a real-world material like a watercolor painting in behind, it can give the image a more organic feel.

PART FOUR
Illustrative Photography

16

Chapter 16

Creature Architecture

Looking at this beautiful creature before you, it is difficult to imagine that it is nothing more than a simple model shot combined with various photographs of stone textures and architectural details. In a composition like this, the images provide the raw materials, but it is the Photoshop process that allows you to dissolve the boundary between photographic collage and stunning illustration. Things as basic as blending modes, layer masks, and layer groups are much more powerful than they seem. When features are used together as a means to an end rather than on their own, the resulting imagery is always much more than the sum of its parts.

The process of creating an image like this may seem daunting at first, but once you get started, the logic reveals itself and you will find yourself perfecting this stacking technique until it comes naturally. Here, I've decided to make a beautiful stone alien by adding snapshots of architectural details to her face. However, as is evident in the showcase images at the end of this chapter, this illustrative effect can be achieved with anything, it doesn't have to be stone details, it can be leaves, or whatever you like.

With the exception of channel usage, there is a bit of everything in this chapter. In places you'll be required to create paths. In others you'll perform a number of layer creation, masking, and grouping tactics. You will duplicate things, flip them around, place groups within groups, and so on. No single aspect of this project is extremely complicated; however, it is the abundance of things you must do that may prove taxing to inexperienced users.

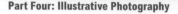

What you'll learn in this chapter

Creative Techniques and Working Methods

Stacking and duplication

As is often the case in Photoshop, something vast and complicated in appearance is merely the result of repeating an integral procedure over and over again. In this chapter, you'll learn how to stack up duplicate layers, alter the blending modes of each, and place them in masked groups. It is very important to remember that groups, like layers, can be duplicated as well. Duplicated groups, like individual layers, can be horizontally flipped and this will allow you to duplicate portions of the image so that you can create both sides of the face with mirror-like precision. And although in this chapter I'll explain in detail, numerous ways to finesse your imagery as well as work with color and texture, layer stacking and duplication is essentially the nuts and bolts of what we're doing here.

Visualization and implementation

Apart from the instructional benefits of this chapter, it is also my hope that you will walk away from this with a heightened awareness of your environment. And by that I mean that you will begin to view everything around you as a resource for your artwork. Ideally, you'll develop a feel for which sections of imagery are useful for specific tasks in future projects. Also, it is my hope that you'll be able to visually dissect the world around you at the planning and gathering stages for further projects. Once you have an idea of what you want to achieve, you'll be well equipped to spot the potential in anything. Use my methods here as your guide while photographing, isolating components within the images, and then finally incorporating those components in a natural way into your composition. Here, you'll notice that the piece used over the eyebrow is a shape suited to this area. The same principle applies to the cheek detail and even the crown on her head. Knowing just what to capture, and where to put it, is a skill that will come effortlessly with experience.

Photoshop Tools, Features, and Functions

Lighten mode

Using this layer blending mode is immensely beneficial while you paint over areas of skin to smooth them out. It prevents accidentally sampled dark colors from appearing against the background image.

Flip horizontal

This Transform option is an essential tool in saving time as well as providing perfect symmetry.

Fill layers

A subtle combination of fill layers near the end has a dramatic impact on the overall feel of the image.

When you look at this group of photographs, you may find it difficult to envision the results. But rest assured, the stunning image at the beginning of this chapter is nothing more than the product of very basic photographs. Be warned however, as you read through the following pages and develop an understanding of the process, it may change the way you view the world surrounding you. One hazardous side effect of producing photographic illustrations is that you'll tend to always be scanning everything you see, trying to find something useful for your next composition. So proceed at your own risk, and don't say I didn't warn you first.

PART ONE: Preparing the face

1 The first thing you need to do is open up the face.jpg file. This file provides the basic starting point for the photographic illustration. In the Layers palette, click on the background layer and drag it onto the Create a New Layer button at the bottom of the palette to duplicate it. Target the duplicate layer in the Layers palette and then choose Edit>Transform>Flip Horizontal from the menu to flip the contents of the duplicate layer. Use the Rectangular Marquee tool to draw a selection around the left half of her face on this layer.

Project files

All of the files needed to follow along with this chapter and create the featured image are available for download on the accompanying Web site in the project files section. Visit www.creativephotoshopthebook.com.

Duplicating layers

There is more than one way to duplicate a layer in Photoshop. You already know that you can drag a layer onto the Create a New Layer button at the bottom of the palette, but there are a few other ways to do it. With your layer targeted, simply choose the Duplicate Layer option from either the Layers Palette menu or the Layer menu in the Menu bar. Another method is to hold down the Control key(Mac), or right-click(PC) on your targeted layer in the Layers palette. A pop-up menu will appear that offers up the Duplicate Layer command here as well.

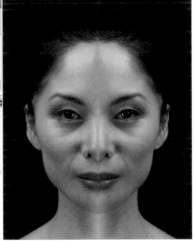

2 Press the Delete key to remove the selected area from the duplicate layer. Already, things are beginning to appear a little strange as a result of reflecting half of her face. Deactivate the current selection and then click on the Add Layer Mask button at the bottom of the Layers palette to add a mask to the duplicate layer. Select the Gradient tool, and in the Tool Options bar, choose the Radial Gradient option. From the list of Gradient presets, choose the Foreground to Transparent Gradient preset. Click on your layer mask in the Layers palette to ensure that it is targeted.

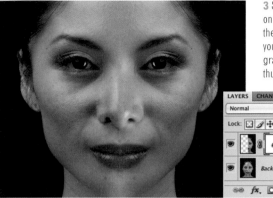

3 Set the current foreground color to black, then click and drag on the canvas to add a gradient within the layer mask. Start with the nose area, you'll immediately see the hard line disappear as you introduce a gradient over the top of it. Also, as you introduce gradients into the mask, you'll see them appear on the layer mask thumbnail in the Layers palette.

Using the Gradient tool within your new layer mask

You need to think beyond a single gradient when it comes to creating a gentle mask effect for an image like this.

1 If you find that you have masked out areas by accident because you have created a gradient that is too large within your mask, worry not, there is a way to remedy this. First, set the foreground color to white.

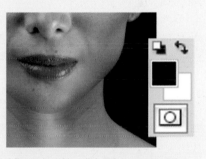

2 Now, using white, click and drag to unmask areas of the layer, blending them back into visibility. The key to successful masking is to add and remove as needed, drawing gradients and switching back and forth between black and white as required.

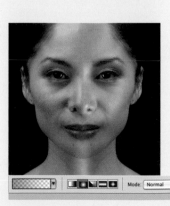

3 Create large and small gradients as required, masking and unmasking, until you've removed the hard line dividing the two halves of her face. Also, for gentle results, try reducing the opacity of the gradient in the Tool Options bar as you use it.

PART TWO: Creating luminous eyes

4 When you're happy with the results of the mask, choose Layer>Flatten Image from the menu to merge the layers. Now we're going to add a blur effect around the edges. Duplicate the newly merged background layer in the Layers palette using the layer duplication method of your choice. With the duplicate layer targeted in the Layers palette, choose Filter>Blur>Gaussian Blur from the menu. Enter a radius value that has a significant impact. This will vary depending upon the resolution you're working at. Click OK to apply the blur effect to your duplicate layer.

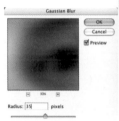

 Setting and swapping colors

When editing the content of a layer mask, you'll generally want to use either black or white, if your foreground and background colors are showing up as shades of gray you can quickly set them to their default black-and-white state by pressing the "d" key on your keyboard. By default, white is the foreground color and black is the background color when a mask is active. However, if you want to switch them quickly, just press the "x" key on your keyboard. You can swap the foreground and background colors as often as you like by simply hitting the "x" key.

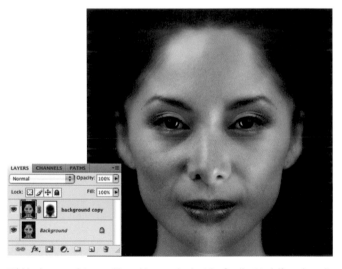

5 Add a layer mask to your blurred layer and select the Gradient tool. If you haven't altered any of the tool settings, they will remain the same way you left them. With the foreground color set to black, the Gradient preset set to foreground to transparent, and the Radial option enabled, click and drag from the center of her face outward to reveal the image underneath the layer that remains in focus. Add gradients to the mask, in black and white as required, masking and unmasking the contents of the layer, until her face is in focus and the surrounding areas are not.

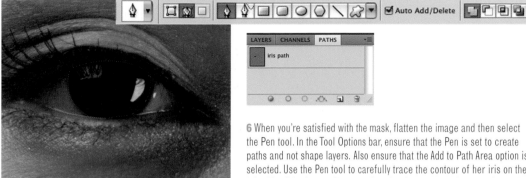

6 When you're satisfied with the mask, flatten the image and then select the Pen tool. In the Tool Options bar, ensure that the Pen is set to create paths and not shape layers. Also ensure that the Add to Path Area option is selected. Use the Pen tool to carefully trace the contour of her iris on the left side of the image. Create a closed path component by returning to the starting point. Now, in the Paths palette, generate a selection from the path by Control-clicking(PC)/Command-clicking(Mac) on the path thumbnail.

Building up luminous eye effects

Use a series of different layers to begin stacking up the luminous eye effect that gives our alien her otherworldly stare.

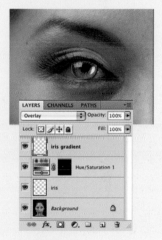

1 Choose Layer>New>Layer Via Copy from the menu to create a new layer containing the selection contents. Choose Image>Adjustments>Levels from the menu and drag the center input slider to the left to lighten the iris midtones. Drag the left slider toward the right a little.

2 Control(PC)/Command(Mac)-click your layer thumbnail to generate a selection from it. Then click on the Hue/Saturation button in the Adjustments palette to create a new hue/saturation adjustment layer. Enable the Colorize option and then manipulate the sliders to give the iris a bright blue hue. Select the Magic Wand tool when finished.

3 Click on a blue area of the iris to generate a selection from it. Create a new layer and then add a white to transparent radial gradient inside the active selection on your new layer. Change the layer blending mode to overlay.

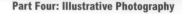

7 Duplicate the top layer and change the blending mode to screen; this adds some white into the iris. Reduce the opacity of the top layer to 40% or so. Now, go ahead and add layer masks to the top two layers and use the aforementioned gradient methods to blend any hard edges or mask out any unwanted areas from the individual layers. Target the top layer and then, while holding down the Shift key, click on the iris layer that sits just above the background layer. This targets both layers as well as all layers in-between within the Layers palette.

 Smoothing

Leaving the Smoothing option enabled in the Brushes palette will allow you to produce smoother curves while you paint. It is very useful to those of you who are painting quickly with a stylus instead of a mouse, but if you are painting very quickly you may notice a slight delay while your finished strokes are rendered on the screen.

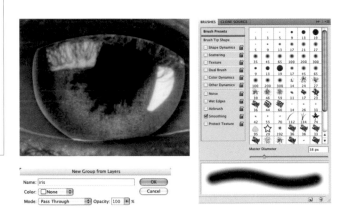

8 With multiple layers targeted in the Layers palette, choose Layer>New>Group From Layers from the menu. This creates a new group containing all of the layers. Go ahead and name it "iris." Deselect any currently active selections and click the Add Layer Mask button in the Layers palette to add a mask to your group. Select the Brush tool. In the Brushes palette, choose a soft, round Brush Tip preset. Disable all of the brush dynamics from the column at the left with the exception of smoothing. Zoom in close on the iris.

9 Adjust the master diameter of your brush in the Brushes palette so that it is about half as wide as her pupil. Target the iris group mask in the Layers palette and then, while using a black foreground color, paint over all of the hard edges around the perimeter of the iris. Next, in the Tool Options bar, reduce the opacity of the brush considerably, and paint over areas of the iris within the layer mask that you want to soften. Try working with a variety of opacity settings to get the best results.

ⓘ Duplicating groups

Duplicating a group is done exactly the same way as duplicating a layer. You still have a number of options when it comes to exactly how you create your duplicate. You already know that you can drag the group onto the Create a New Layer button in the Layers palette, but the other duplication methods will work as well. You can target your group and then choose Duplicate Group from the Layer menu in the main menu or from the Layers Palette menu. Also, you can Control-click(Mac)/right-click(PC) on the layer in the Layers palette and then choose the Duplicate Group option from the resulting pop-up menu. In every case, the procedure is exactly the same as duplicating a single layer, except for the fact that Duplicate Layer is replaced with Duplicate Group within any menu you decide to use.

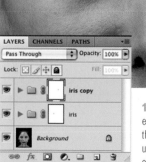

10 In the Layers palette, drag the iris group onto the Create a New Layer button to duplicate the entire group. With the duplicate group targeted, choose Edit>Transform>Flip Horizontal from the menu to flip the duplicated iris group. Select the Move tool. While holding down the Shift key, use the Move tool to drag the duplicate group across the canvas so that it rests perfectly on top of the other eye.

PART THREE: Incorporate architectural details

11 Now that you've completed the iris effects, we'll begin to add some of the stone details to her face. Start by opening up the piece1.psd file. Use the Move tool to click on the stone detail and drag it into your working file as a new layer. Position the contents of the new layer on the canvas so that the stone detail overlaps her cheek at the right. Next, duplicate the layer, change the blending mode of the duplicate layer to screen, and reduce the opacity to 10%.

 Precise dragging

When you are dragging layers from one file to another, it is likely that you'll need to reposition the layer on the canvas once it is in your destination file. However, if your source and destination files have exactly the same pixel dimensions, try holding down the Shift key while dragging your layer from file to file. This will place the layer in your destination file, exactly in the same position on the canvas area as it was in your source file.

 Dragging multiple layers

You can drag more than one layer at a time from file to file. First, ensure that your windows are floating and not tabbed. Second, simply target more than one layer in the Layers palette. Next, click on any one of the targeted layers and drag it into the image window of any other open file. The layer you dragged will be added to the destination file, as well as all of the additional layers that were targeted in the Layers palette of the source file.

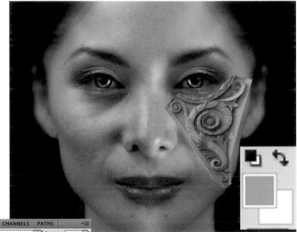

12 Control(PC)/Command(Mac)-click on the top layer's thumbnail to generate a selection from the contents of the layer. Now, with the new selection active, select the Eyedropper tool and click on an area of her skin to sample it. This will set the foreground color to the new sampled color. Create a new layer and then fill the contents of the selection on the new layer by typing Alt(PC)/Option(Mac)-Delete. And finally, change the blending mode of this new layer to color and deactivate the current selection.

13 At the moment, your top layer should be targeted in the Layers palette. Hold down the Control(PC)/Command(Mac) key and then click on the two layers beneath it that contain the stone detail, to target them as well. Now that the top three layers are targeted, choose Layer>New>Group From Layers from the menu to add them to a group. Once they are grouped, add a layer mask to the group and ensure that the mask remains targeted in the Layers palette.

Merging groups

As is true with many Photoshop functions, you can access the Merge Group function in a number of different places. First, target your group in the Layers palette, and then you can either choose Merge Group from the Layer menu or from the Layers Palette menu. In addition to these methods, you can always right-click(PC)/Control-click(Mac) on the group itself within the Layers palette. A pop-up menu will appear and you can choose the Merge Group option from the list. However, the quickest method, and the one you should familiarize yourself with, is the keyboard shortcut. Simply target your group in the Layers palette and then type Control(PC)/Command(Mac)-E on the keyboard.

14 Use the Lasso tool to draw a rough selection on the layer mask that traces the contour of the stone detail. Then invert the selection by choosing Select>Inverse from the menu. Fill the inverted selection on the targeted layer mask with black and then deactivate the selection. This will remove the straight edges contained within the original file. Next, with your group targeted in the Layers palette, choose Layer>Merge Group from the menu to merge the entire group into a single masked layer. Now, drag your layer mask into the trash in the Layers palette to remove it. When prompted, click the Apply button.

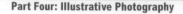

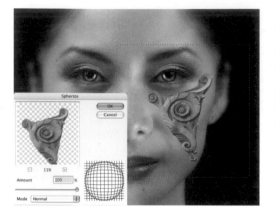

15 Next, select the Rectangular Marquee tool and draw a rectangular marquee that contains the stone detail as well as a fair amount of the background image within the selection border. You need an ample amount of space between the stone detail and the selection border for this effect to work out properly. Once you've made your selection, ensure that your newly merged layer is targeted in the Layers palette. Then choose Filter>Distort>Spherize from the menu. Increase the amount considerably to add the necessary contour to the stone detail and then click OK.

Completing the spherize effect

Before moving on to masking or another piece of stone detail, this piece still needs a little bit of finesse to make it work

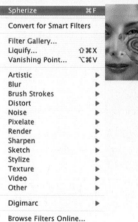

1 Deactivate the selection and then choose Edit>Free-Transform from the menu. Hold down the Control(PC)/ Command(Mac) key while dragging the corner points of the bounding box to freely distort the contents of the layer, making it fit her cheek area better.

2 Press Enter on your keyboard to apply your transformation. Draw another rectangular selection around your stone detail like you did before using the Spherize filter. Next, just choose Filter>Spherize from the menu to repeat the previous spherize effect.

3 Deselect and again, use the same Free-Transform method while holding down the Control(PC)/Command(Mac) key to adjust the shape, making it fit her face better. Sometimes a bit of repetition is necessary to get the effect you're after. Press Enter and add a layer mask.

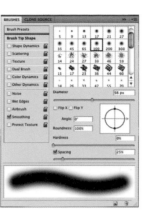

16 Target your layer mask in the Layers palette and then select the Brush tool. Choose a soft, round Brush Tip preset and disable any brush dynamics in the Brushes palette. Use the brush, with a foreground color of black, to paint within the mask. Vary the brush diameter in the Brushes palette as well as the opacity in the Tool Options bar. Varying the size and opacity will allow you perform large, gentle mask effects, as well as more drastic, smaller, and precise effects. Continue masking until the stone detail begins to look like what you see here.

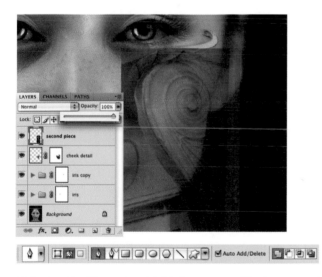

17 Now, to add a different stone detail to the same area of her face, open up the piece2.jpg file. Use the Move tool to drag the image into your working file as a new layer. Reduce the opacity of your layer in the Layers palette so that you can see the underlying image and position it so that it fits nicely within the composition, overlapping her existing cheek detail. Next, return the layer to full opacity and select the Pen tool. Ensure that the Paths option and the Add to Path Area option are both enabled in the Tool Options bar.

Choosing details

The process described here will definitely have you producing impressive results when it comes to blending different photographic elements into people. However, one of the most important, and often overlooked, parts of the process is selecting just what to use. I took over seventy photos of various architectural details with this image in mind. Before I began the process of compositing within Photoshop, I spent a lot of time looking at all the detail of the photos. Rotating them, flipping them, assessing which particular detail was appropriate for which portion of her face, etc. It is necessary to spend the time planning what to use ahead of time so that you don't spend hours adding various elements into your image, only to find that at the end of it all they don't work. Whether you're adding architectural details or something else entirely, a little forethought goes a long way in the end.

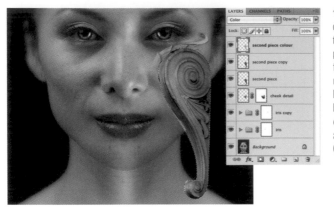

18 Draw a closed path that surrounds the piece of detail. Generate a selection from the new path in the Paths palette using the same methods as you did previously with the iris path. Choose Select>Inverse from the menu and then press the Delete key to remove the unwanted portions from this layer. Duplicate the layer. Change the duplicate layer's blending mode to screen to lighten the detail. Now, create a new layer and fill the active selection with a color sampled from her skin via the Eyedropper. Change the blending mode of the layer to color.

Reshaping the stone detail

You'll notice this fundamental process begins to repeat itself as we use Free-Transform and Spherize to customize this piece of detail too.

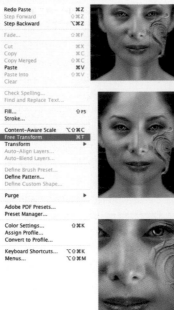

1 Deselect, then target all three layers that make up this new piece of detail and merge them by choosing Layer>Merge Layers from the menu. Select Edit>Free-Transform from the menu. Hold down the Control(PC)/Command(Mac) key while dragging the corner points of the box to reshape the detail.

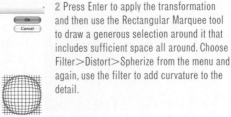

2 Press Enter to apply the transformation and then use the Rectangular Marquee tool to draw a generous selection around it that includes sufficient space all around. Choose Filter>Distort>Spherize from the menu and again, use the filter to add curvature to the detail.

3 After you apply the filter, like last time, you'll need to tweak the detail by transforming and possibly spherizing again. When you're happy with the results, add a layer mask. Again, use a soft brush, with varying size and opacity, to paint within the mask, gently blending the detail.

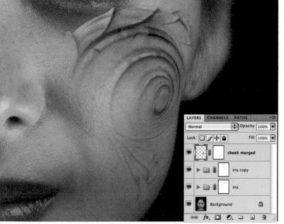

19 Target the two layers that contain stone details in the Layers palette and merge them into one. Target the new, merged layer and repeat the process of spherizing within a large rectangular selection border to add some curvature to the newly merged details together. Next, add a layer mask and use the paintbrush method employed previously to gently fade areas of this layer into the background by painting within the mask using various opacity and size settings.

Why screen?

You've probably noticed by now that when I want to lighten a layer by placing a duplicate of that layer on top of it, the blending mode I reach for is screen. People often think literally when it comes to lightening one layer with another and tend to reach for the lighten blending mode instead. That is fine if your top layer contains lighter colors. However, if it is an exact duplicate, like we're using here, there will be no visible effect. Choosing the screen blending mode is excellent for this because it multiplies the inverse of the blended colors, resulting in a bleach effect, lightening the base layer with an exact duplicate on an overlaying layer.

20 Open up the detail.psd file. Use the Move tool to drag the layer into your working file as a new layer. Use Free-Transform to resize, reshape, and position the new detail to the side of her face by her eyebrow. Duplicate the layer and change the blending mode of the layer to screen. Generate a selection from the contents of this layer. Now, create a new layer and fill the selection with a pink color sampled from her skin. Change the layer blending mode to color.

21 As you've done previously in this chapter, create a new group containing the three newest layers. Add a mask to the group and select the Brush tool. Paint with varying opacity settings and a soft, round tip, to gently fade the layers within the group into the background by painting black into the mask. Remember to vary the size of the Brush Tip as required. Don't bother with the top of the detail or the right-hand side. Open up the detail1.psd file.

 Layer destinations

When you drag the detail1.psd file into the working file, you'll probably notice that it goes into your existing layer group in the Layers palette. This is because the layer group was targeted in your working file when you dragged the layer from the detail1.psd file into it. Obviously you don't want this layer to reside within the existing group; so to move it out, begin by clicking on your layer in the Layers palette and dragging it upward. Drag it above the current group until you see a dark horizontal line appear just above the set in the Layers palette. When you see this line, let go of the mouse button, and your layer will be placed above the group, outside of it, in the Layers palette.

22 Use the Move tool to drag the layer from the detail1.psd file into your working file as a new layer. This stone detail is light enough that we don't require a duplicate layer with a different mode to lighten it. This time, simply generate a selection from the contents of the layer and then create a new layer. As you've done previously, fill the selection with skin color on the new layer and change the layer blending mode to color. Add both layers to a group. Mask the group and then edit the mask like you've done previously with the Brush tool.

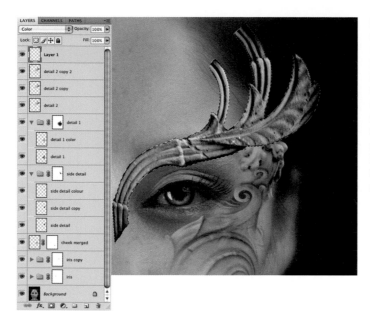

23 Open up the detail2.psd file and drag the image into the working file as a new layer. Move the layer out of any groups it may have fallen into and drag it to the top of the Layers palette. Use Free-Transform to resize and place it just above her eye. Duplicate the layer, change the mode to screen, and reduce the opacity to 56%. Duplicate this layer and then change the blending mode to soft light, adding contrast. Reduce the opacity of this layer a little more. Generate a selection from the layer and create a new layer while the selection is active.

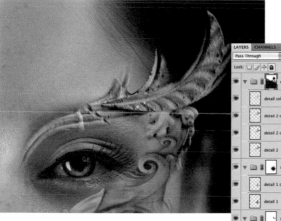

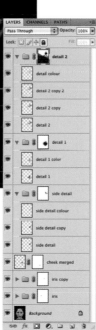

24 Again, as you've done previously with the other detail layer stacks, fill the selection on the current layer with skin color and change the blending mode to color. Deselect and then create a new group that contains all of the detail2 layers. Add a mask to the group and then edit the mask with the Brush tool, painting with black, like you've done previously to blend the detail into the underlying face. Vary the brush size and opacity as required and even use the Gradient tool to create larger, sweeping blend effects.

Group advantages

When you've created a stack of layers, grouping the layers is always a much better option than merging if at all possible. By keeping layers separated within the groups you can edit things at any point later on. You can increase or decrease layer opacity, alter a blending mode, or even add and edit individual layer masks. So by keeping things separate, you are affording yourself the luxury of changing your mind later on. Now, in some cases, like when you want to add a spherize effect to a stack of layers, you'll need to merge the layers first. But whenever possible, you should try to keep everything within your file as separate as you can for further editing.

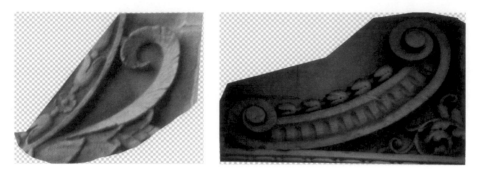

25 It is safe to assume that at this point that you can't ignore the repeating pattern that is emerging here. Every time you add a new element you place it as a layer in the image, resize, and position it exactly where you want it. Then you duplicate it, alter the blending mode to enhance it, and repeat if necessary. Finally, you generate a selection from your layer contents, fill the selection with skin color on a new layer, and change the blending mode of the new layer to color. Open up the detail3.psd and detail4.psd files.

 Groups within groups

At this point you're well aware of the advantages of grouping layers. However, it is important that you don't forget that you can group groups as well. This adds another level of organization to your files. Again, grouping rather than merging affords you the luxury of editing individual groups later on. In addition to this, grouping a number of groups allows you to move, duplicate, and transform large numbers of layers together at the same time. In this particular case, all of the stone detail groups are now neatly contained within a single group, making it easy to duplicate and flip them to the other side of the face, preserving all blending operations as well as their special relationships to each other within the image.

26 Use all the methods we've used so far to introduce each element into the image. Bring them in as layers, use duplication, blending modes, color fills, and masked sets. It is unlikely that you aren't familiar with the process at this point as we've gone through it a few times already. Position each of these new detail groups above the large eyebrow detail. Collapse all of your groups in the Layers palette to conserve space. Target every group except the two iris groups and the background layer. Choose Layer>New>Group From Layers from the menu. Then choose Layer>Duplicate Group from the menu to copy the new group.

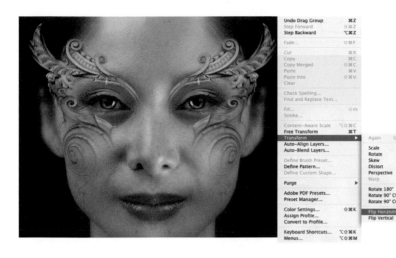

27 With the duplicate group targeted in the Layers palette, choose Edit>Transform>Flip Horizontal from the menu. It may take a moment to perform this operation as Photoshop has a lot to think about here, but just like that, you'll see the duplicate detail flip over and position itself on the other side of her face. You can move it a little with the Move tool; just be certain that you're holding down the Shift key while you click and drag sideways to avoid any unwanted vertical movements.

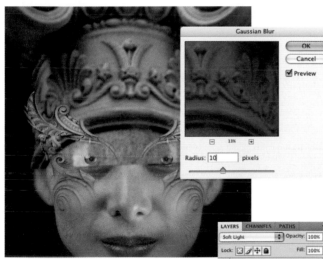

28 Open up the column.psd file. Use the Move tool to drag the layer into your working file as a new layer and position it at the top of the canvas. In the Layers palette, drag the new layer down so that it sits above the background but underneath all of the other layers and groups. Use the Gaussian Blur filter to add a slight blur to the contents of the layer. Duplicate the new layer and change the blending mode of the duplicate layer to screen. Then, duplicate the duplicate layer and change the blending mode to soft light.

Further masking

Now that you have the face details separated into two groups, you may notice visible layer artifacts here and there that you don't want to see in your image. To remedy this, go ahead and add a mask to either or both of your stone detail groups. Use the Brush tool or a series of gradients to gently mask out any areas you don't want to be visible. Try editing the masks of the two halves a little differently here and there, so that they don't look exactly the same as each other. You still want a mirror image effect across her face, but mask editing allows you to introduce a little bit of subtle individuality to each side.

29 Generate a selection from the contents of your newest duplicate layer and, with the selection active, create a new layer on top of it in the Layers palette. Fill the active selection on the new layer with skin color, change the layer blending mode to color, and deselect. Add a new group containing all of your column layers and add a mask to it. Edit the mask with the Brush and Gradient tools to gently blend the column group of layers into her forehead.

PART FOUR: Refine, adjust, and add texture

Adding lighter areas

Now that the details are in place, it is time to begin smoothing out her skin with some lighter colors.

1 Create a new layer that sits above your column group in the Layers palette. With this layer targeted, use the Pen tool to draw a closed path that surrounds her forehead. Ensure that the path overlaps, but does not extend below, her eyebrow details.

3 Deselect and use the Brush tool, with varying opacity settings and a soft, round tip, to paint over dark blemishes and unwanted areas on this layer with colors sampled from neighboring areas. Hold down Alt(PC)/Option(Mac) while using the brush to sample colors as you work.

2 Generate a selection from the path and then change the layer blending mode to lighten. Use the Radial Gradient tool, set at foreground to transparent, to create gradients within the selection at varying opacities; sample various skin colors as you go.

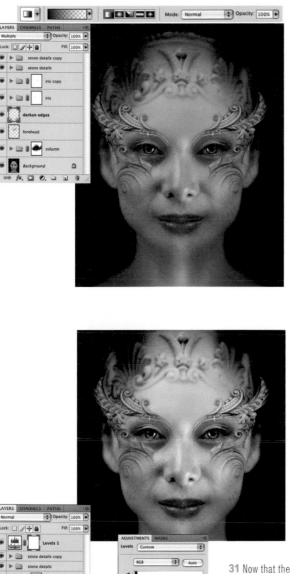

30 Next, create another new layer; ensure that it sits above the previous "lighten" layer you were just working on in the Layers palette. Change the blending mode of this layer to multiply and then select the Gradient tool. This time, select the linear gradient method but leave the preset set at foreground to transparent. Sample a dark background color from the image and then draw a gradient from each corner inward slightly to darken the edges of the image.

(i) Multiply versus darken

In order to add the burn or darkening effect around the edges, I created a number of dark-colored gradients, extending from the corners inward, on a layer with the blending mode set to multiply. Because the desired effect is to darken, you might wonder why I did not use the darken blending mode instead. The darken blending mode looks at the color on the active layer and the color on the underlying layers and displays whichever is darkest. However, multiply blending mode does not compare colors, it simply multiplies the underlying color by the color on the layer, resulting in a much darker color than the color on either layer. Because of this, the multiply blending mode gives a more drastic darken effect than the darken blending mode.

31 Now that the illustrative portion of the image is complete, the next stage is to alter the color. The first step in achieving this ghostly gray look is to increase the contrast. Target the top layer in your Layers palette so that any new layers we create will automatically reside above all of the others in the Layers palette. Click on the Levels button in the Adjustments palette to create a new levels adjustment layer. Drag the input level sliders from the left- and right-hand sides toward the center until you see the overall contrast increase. If the midtones get too dark, drag the center input level slider to the left until they improve.

32 Click on the Hue/Saturation button in the Adjustments palette to create a new hue/saturation adjustment layer. Adjust the hue to 211, and decrease the saturation to almost nothing. This will remove a great deal of color from the image. Change the blending mode of the hue/saturation layer to color and reduce the opacity considerably in the Layers palette. She still needs a bit of color in her complexion to work with. Now, we want to make things appear a little more blue, so choose Layer>New Fill Color>Solid Color from the menu.

Undoing adjustments

When you add an adjustment or fill layer, you'll notice that the underlying image is affected in its entirety. However, you may notice specific details in the image, like her iris and lip areas in this case, that you want to remain unaffected by one or all of the adjustment layers. If this is what you're after, simply target an adjustment or fill layer's mask in the Layers palette. You can edit an adjustment or fill layer mask exactly like you edit any other layer mask. Adding black to the mask will hide the effect of the layer in that area; so if you want her iris areas to be unaffected by one of your adjustment or fill layer, simply paint over that area within the specific layer's mask.

33 In the New Layer options, set the blending mode to color and reduce the opacity to 80%. Once you click OK, the picker will appear. Select a nice, bright blue color from the picker and click OK. You'll immediately notice that the effect is much too strong. To remedy this, drag the fill slider down to 10% in the Layers palette. Now you'll notice the effect is a little too soft. Remedy this by simply duplicating the solid color fill layer.

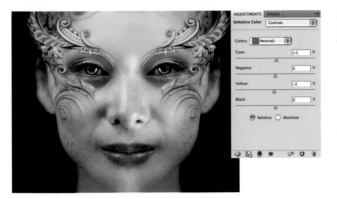

34 The effect is almost complete. However, achieving a very desaturated color cast can be tricky. Sometimes your images can look too warm or too cool. In this case, it looks a touch too warm. In order to remedy this, click on the Selective Color button in the Adjustments palette to create a new selective color adjustment layer. Choose neutrals from the Color menu. Increase the amount of cyan slightly, while equally reducing the amount of yellow. The result will be subtle, but it helps cool the image overall.

Adding surface texture

Now that the color adjustments are complete, the final stage is to add a textured effect.

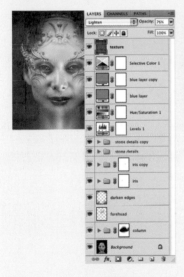

1 Open up the texture.psd file. Use the Move tool to drag it, while holding down the Shift key, into the working file as a new layer at the top of the Layers palette. Change the blending mode to lighten and reduce the opacity to 76%.

2 Duplicate the layer and change the blending mode of the duplicate to soft light. Add both of these layers to a new group and then add a layer mask to the group. Select the Gradient tool and target the group's mask in the Layers palette.

3 Choose the radial gradient method and the Foreground to Transparent preset in the Tool Options bar. Using a black foreground color, click and drag within the mask to create a variety of gradients, masking the texture overlapping the center of her face.

35 Now, duplicate the topmost texture layer within the group. Click on it and drag it out of the group within the Layers palette. Ensure that it is on top of the group and at the top of the entire layer stack within the Layers palette. Increase the opacity of the layer to 100% and ensure that the blending mode is set to soft light. Add a mask to this layer. Use the Gradient tool, set up exactly the way it is, with varying opacity settings to edit the layer mask, adding gradients to reveal the underlying face.

Final inspection

Let's take one last look at the image and examine which techniques will prove useful later on, when you're creating other images on your own.

a This cheek detail was made perfect by transforming and spherizing and then repeating the process. It is important to be willing to repeat a process as many times as it takes until things look just right.

b Adding a blur effect not only to this crown, but also to the outer edges of her face and neck, adds a nice depth of field effect, while removing amateurish hard edges.

c Painting and adding gradients on a layer with a lighten blending mode allows you to smooth out her forehead nicely. It also preserves any highlights underneath that are lighter than the colors on your layer.

d Creating details on half of her face and then duplicating them not only provides a sense of surrealistic symmetry, it also saves a massive amount of time.

e Adding a rough surface texture to the entire image not only helps to bring it all together, but it also creates an illustrated feeling that helps the image to transcend that of the basic photographic collage.

Don't limit yourself to stone details

Once you master the technique of building up layer stacks and working with groups, you're only limited by your imagination. This image was created using the same techniques, but instead of stone details, I decided to create a mythical green woman by incorporating desktop scans of leaves.

This method works with anything

Again, here is another fine example of the same techniques, using different photographic resources. You can blend almost anything into a human face and make the result look convincing if you abide by the methods explained previously in this chapter.

Try the same approach with subtle differences

The same model was used here, as was the general approach outlined on the previous pages. What sets this image apart is not only the use o-f tentacles, but also the fact that the tentacles were the only things that were duplicated and flipped. The result is less surreal in this image because I didn't create false symmetry by mirroring half of her face as well.

Chapter 17

The Third Dimension

As an artist who works digitally, when I hear the words 3d I think of software. Programs like Maya, SoftImage, and Cinema 4d come to my mind. I think of building objects in 3d space, adding light, texture, and rendering. The right software package can certainly assist in creating amazing works of 3d art; however, those who are accustomed to working in 2d may find the steep learning curve a little daunting. As someone who grew up drawing and painting, I have found that working in a 3d program is just never as intuitive as working on a flat canvas. For years I have been working with a variety of 3d programs, but I always find myself struggling against the software at some stage in the process. I have the idea in my head or on paper, and it generally seems to be a battle to get it the way I want it within the software. In short, no 3d method was ever as effortless or intuitive as painting and image editing within Photoshop.

Now, with the advent of Photoshop CS4 extended, we see a new and impressive list of tools for working with models and applying texture and lighting in 3d space. Granted, these tools are powerful and there will certainly be no shortage of books that cover this aspect of the program. However, in this chapter we're going to focus on creating the illusion of 3d with 2d tools. We'll use Photoshop's paint tools and a series of photographs to realize our vision. We're going to create something that looks 3d, yet remains a 2d work of art. This allows us to remove any software handicaps or 3d learning curves. We don't need to build elaborate models; we can simply illustrate a picture with believable depth

It was the work of traditional artists, especially M.C. Escher, that got me thinking of just illustrating my 3d effects the old-fashioned way. These artists never had any 3d software; they just sat in their studios and drew or painted what was in their heads. I finally decided that there was no reason why I, as an illustrator armed with Photoshop, couldn't do the same thing digitally, and the image you see here is my most successful attempt so far. As you work through the process of re-creating this image on the following pages, you see that although we're using Photoshop instead of a pencil or Paintbrush, the fundamental process of creating art with depth is quite similar to traditional methods of drawing or painting in perspective.

This chapter runs through a massive amount of operations, tools, and features. Many stages of the process are quite labor intensive and the files will get quite complicated. Perhaps the most challenging part will be the artwork that is created with paths. Experience with the Pen tool will be massively beneficial for creating the 3d ribbon effect and especially useful while creating the facial grid work. You'll have to carefully create regions of even thickness to make the effect appear genuine. This can take some time.

What you'll learn in this chapter

Creative Techniques and Working Methods

Work intuitively

Because we aren't working with 3d software to create this effect, you'll learn to rely on your intuition as you work. Basic analysis of the world around you will assist you in creating a natural and realistic result. By simply observing how objects appear in the real-world 3d realm, and making mental notes regarding perspective, depth, and appearance, you'll gain an understanding of how to create a convincing 3d effect. If you have ever studied drafting or Southern European Renaissance art, you're already aware of mathematically perfect methods for creating linear perspective. However, in this case we aren't going to rely on vanishing points or mathematical accuracy. We're going to take our cue from Northern European Renaissance artists. Northern European Renaissance artists took a more naturalistic approach to perspective and relied on

intuition as opposed to calculation. That is exactly what we're going to do here. Based on your observation of the world around you, you'll create a sense of depth and thickness in the image based on your own perception and intuition.

Visualize planar divisions

Another visualization method that you'll be required to exercise is an observational dissection of surface regions. In this illustration, lines are used to divide the face into a 3d grid. You will carefully create this meticulous grid as a series of separate lines with the Pen tool. As you create each line, you'll observe the curves within the face and the contour of the curling ribbon. You'll create all of the lines so that they work together to behave as if they were originally there in the first place—a remnant of the face's initial construction. Examining how lines would surround, and emanate from individual features, coupled with contour based on 3d space is what makes this effect believable.

Photoshop Tools, Features, and Functions

Stroke path

After you've created the facial grid with paths, the stroke path operation is your key to incorporating the paths into the image. The Pen tool automatically traces everything you've created, using current Brush tool settings and color.

Vanishing point

Perfect perspective is achieved within this powerful native filter. Create planes in 3d space and paste artwork onto them with ease.

Smart objects

By placing the finished head artwork into the background composition as a smart object, it can be edited at any point independent of the rest of the contents of the final layered file.

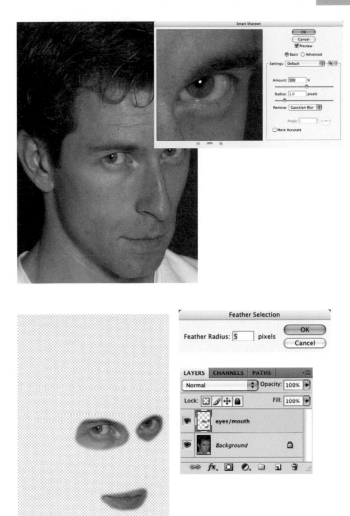

1 Open up the face.psd file from the CD. Initially you'll notice that this image appears a little soft; so the first thing we need to do is sharpen it. Choose Filter>Sharpen>Smart Sharpen from the menu. Basic mode is fine for this simple task. Increase the amount to around 100 and set the pixel radius to 1. Leave the Remove option set to Gaussian Blur. Although we're going to drastically alter this image before it's finished, a little sharpening will help in areas that will remain largely untouched, like his eyes.

Project files

All of the files needed to follow along with this chapter and create the featured image are available for download on the accompanying Web site in the project files section. Visit www.creativephotoshopthebook.com.

Feathering selections

In this instance, I created a selection and then feathered it to soften the edges after the fact. However, when you choose a selection tool like the Lasso or Marquee tool, take a look in the Tool Options bar and you'll see a feather function there. You can enter a pixel radius and then every time you create a selection with that tool, your selection will be feathered instantly. This value remains set until you change it, even when switching back and forth between tools.

2 Select the Lasso tool and draw a rough selection that surrounds one of his eyes. Then, while holding down the Shift key, draw another rough selection that surrounds his other eye, and then draw another that surrounds his lips. With both eyes and his lips surrounded by selections, choose Select>Modify>Feather from the menu. Here I decided to use a radius of 5 pixels to create a gentle soft edge; however, depending upon the resolution you're working at, this number may vary. With the feathered selection active, choose Layer>New>Layer Via Copy from the menu. Temporarily disable the visibility of the background layer to view the new layer you've created from the selected contents.

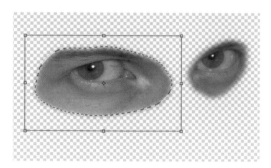

3 With your new layer targeted, use the Lasso tool to draw a selection that completely surrounds one of the eyes. Once selected, choose Edit>Free-Transform from the menu. Use the corners and midpoint handles of the bounding box to increase the eye in size and alter the proportion so that it is larger and wider than the original. Press Enter on the keyboard and then repeat the process with the other eye and the lips until all elements on this layer have been edited individually with the Free-Transform tool. Enable the visibility of the background layer when finished.

 Checking position

When you alter the eyes and mouth on the new layer, you may find it difficult to visualize how they will appear against the face in the background because, at this stage, the background layer's visibility is disabled. The best way to see if things are working out is to enable the background layer visibility after each Free-Transform operation. Then you can see how the transformed facial feature fits within the face on the underlying layer. If you don't like the result, you can always undo the transformation and try it again, bearing in mind what not to do the second time around.

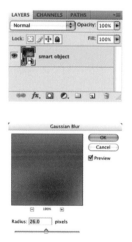

4 With your top layer targeted in the Layers palette, hold down the Shift key and then click on the background layer. This will allow you to target both of your layers at the same time. Now, with both layers targeted, choose Layer>Smart Objects>Convert to Smart Object. This converts your layers into an editable smart object. With the smart object targeted in the Layers palette, choose Filter>Blur>Gaussian Blur from the menu. Enter a substantial radius value to blur the smart object considerably and click OK.

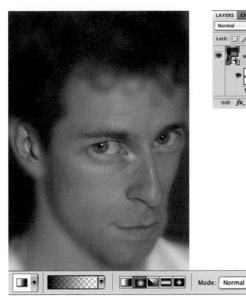

5 When you apply a filter to a smart object, it shows up in the Layers palette as a smart filter, complete with a mask. A smart filter mask works just like a layer mask, except that it allows you to mask filter effects instead of layer contents. Target the smart filter mask and select the Gradient tool. In the Tool Options bar, choose the radial method and the Foreground to Transparent Gradient preset. Set your foreground color to black. Use the Gradient tool to click and drag within the smart filter mask. Create a series of gradients, both large and small, that mask the blur effect in key areas of his face.

6 Create a new hue/saturation adjustment layer by clicking the Hue/Saturation button in the Adjustments palette. Adjust the hue to 24 and decrease the saturation by 14. This removes a bit of pink from his skin. Now create a new curves adjustment layer by clicking the Curves button in the Adjustments palette. Adjust the curve of all the CMYK channels to increase the contrast and then adjust the magenta curve only to reduce a bit more of the pinkish hue.

PART TWO: Creating the ribbon effect

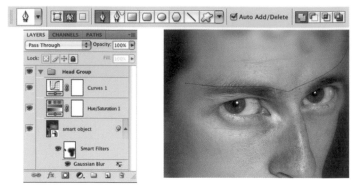

7 Target all of the contents of the Layers palette and then choose Layer>New> Group From Layers from the menu. We are adding the layers and the smart object to a group so that everything can be masked together with a single vector mask. Select the Pen tool, and in the Tool Options bar ensure that the Pen tool is set to create paths and not shape layers. Click the Add to Path Area option and then begin to draw a horizontal line that follows the contour of his face.

A 3d spiral

Visualize, draw path components, and create a vector mask to create the 3d spiraling ribbon effect.

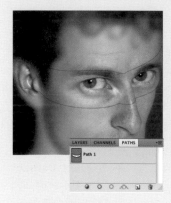

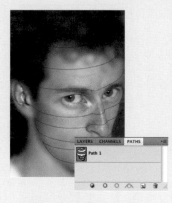

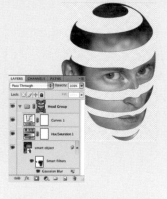

1 Give some thought to your viewing angle and how the face would look as a spiral ribbon. Continue your line and use it as the basis for a closed path component that looks like a strip across his eyes and his ear.

2 Draw more closed path components across his face, paying attention to the contour of his features. Feel free to alter the sides as you see fit, including background into the shape or removing skin, to get the head shape you're after.

3 When you're finished, ensure that your new path is targeted in the Paths palette and return to the Layers palette. Target your group and choose Layer>Vector Mask>Current Path from the menu. This masks areas that lie outside of your path components.

PART THREE: Smooth and embellish visible regions

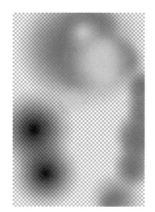

8 To add to the surreal feel, we'll remove his hair and smooth his complexion, so create a new layer. Because you have the group targeted, it will automatically be added to the group at the top of the stack. Select the Gradient tool. Leave the Gradient tool options set as they were previously and begin to click and drag, creating different colored gradients on the new layer. Hold down Alt(PC)/ Option(Mac) to sample colors from the underlying layers for your new gradients. Shown here is the gradient layer by itself; yours should look something like this when you're finished.

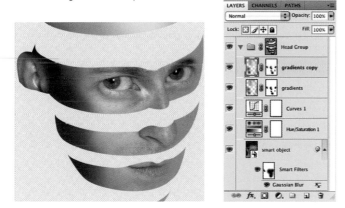

9 Add dark gradients in areas of shadow and light gradients where there should be highlights. If some of your gradients accidentally cover features and details like his eyes or his inner ear, worry not, we'll remedy this now. Add a layer mask to the layer by clicking on the Add a Layer Mask button at the bottom of the Layers palette. Then, with the layer mask targeted, use black to create gradients within the mask to mask the stray gradients. Duplicate the layer by dragging it onto the Create a New Layer button in the Layers palette to strengthen the overall gradient effect.

ⓘ Editing your vector mask

Should you decide at any point that you're not happy with the shape of the bands you've created across the face, you can fix them by editing the vector mask. As soon as you click on your group, the path components that make up the vector mask will become visible on the canvas. The visible paths can be edited by using the Direct Selection tool. Simply click and drag any of the anchor points, line segments, or Bezier handles to edit the path. When you edit a path, you'll instantly see the results of altering your vector mask.

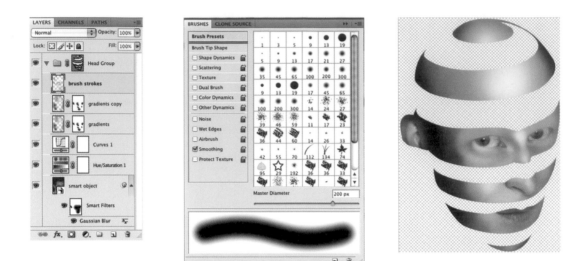

10 Create a new layer at the top of the stack in your group. Target the new layer and select the Brush tool. In the Brushes palette, choose a large, soft, round brush tip, and disable all brush dynamics except for smoothing. Choose a diameter that is large in relation to your image. Set the brush opacity to about 25%, then Alt(PC)/Option(Mac)-click on an area of skin to sample the color. Gently paint with this color over areas of similar color that require a smoother blended appearance. Use this method to blend areas of color together on the new layer, sampling different colors as you go.

 Keeping things separate

You'll notice here that I've instructed you to create another new layer to use before you paint. You may wonder what the point of this is, as both the new layer and the underlying layer have a normal blending mode and an opacity setting of 100. The main reason, apart from the fact that the previous layer is already masked, is to keep things separate for flexibility. Often when painting on a layer, I find that I want to decrease the opacity of the layer later on, to lessen the effect. This usually happens a number of steps later, and if I had painted on the same layer that the gradients were on, I wouldn't be able to reduce the brush stroke opacity without affecting the gradients. Ensuring that the brush strokes are on their own layer also allows me to mask them separately from the gradients.

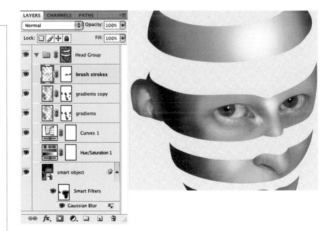

11 Continue to paint in this manner, varying color, brush tip size, and opacity as you go. Keep painting until you've created a nice, soft feel overall. It is fine to stray over areas like his eyes because again, we can mask unwanted areas from this layer. Add a layer mask, ensure that it is targeted, and set the foreground color to black. Use your brush to paint over brush stroke areas within the mask that you want to hide, specifically going over his eye areas so that there is no skin color straying into the whites of his eyes.

12 Use the Pen tool to draw a closed path in the shape of his lips. Ensure that the Add to Path Area option is selected in the Tool Options bar. This is your chance to alter the shape of his lips, so feel free to deviate from the original photo. Generate a selection from your new path by Control(PC)/Command(Mac)-clicking on it in the Paths palette. With the selection active, return to the Layers palette and create a new layer at the top of the layer stack within the group.

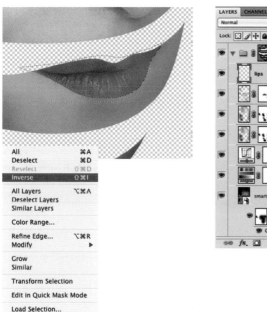

Painting within selections

The method of painting within a path-based selection can be used for things other than reshaping lips. As you've noticed by now, creating gradients and soft brush strokes on a series of layers can tend to hide sharp details contained in the original image underneath. By carefully creating closed paths and generating selections from them, like we've done here with the lips, you can paint within sharp-edged selection borders. In areas like the side of his nose, you can introduce slightly darker colors into the selection right next to the edge, creating sharp contrast with adjacent pixels that are on the other side of the selection border, making certain features like his nose stand out better.

13 Use the Eyedropper to sample a pink color from his lips and then paint over any areas within the selection on the new layer that need to be pink. Ensure that you paint within all of the selection edges that contain regular skin color. This will help to define the edge of his lips. When you're finished choose Select>Inverse from the menu to invert the selection. Paint over any areas that should be skin colored within the inverted selection using colors sampled from his skin. When you have achieved a nice defined lip shape choose Select>Deselect to deactivate the selection.

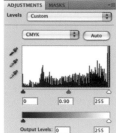

14 Create a new brightness/contrast adjustment layer by clicking the Brightness/Contrast button in the Adjustments palette. Now that we're finished painting, it is time to bump up the color and contrast on the underlying layers a little. Increase the brightness slightly, but greatly increase the contrast. After clicking OK, create a new levels adjustment layer. Select the black channel and drag the left input levels slider to the right to darken the shadows. Then drag the middle input levels slider to the right too, to darken the midtones. Finally, create a new hue/saturation adjustment layer and increase the saturation by 16.

Changing his eye color

Build a set of virtual contact lenses by combining path-based selection with adjustment layers.

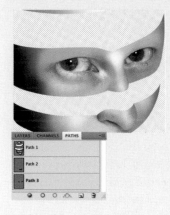
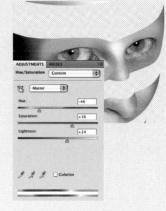
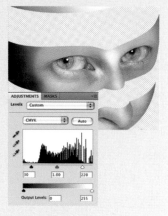

1 Use the Pen tool to draw two closed path components in the image, one surrounding each iris. Ensure that the Add to Path Area function is enabled when you do this. Generate a selection from your new path in the Paths palette.

2 With the selection active, create a new hue/saturation adjustment layer. The active selection will automatically mask the new layer. Move the hue slider until the blue changes to a greener blue. Increase the saturation and the lightness and click OK.

3 Generate a selection from the same path one more time. With the selection active, create a new levels adjustment layer. Drag the left and right sliders for the CMYK input levels to the center of the histogram to increase the overall contrast.

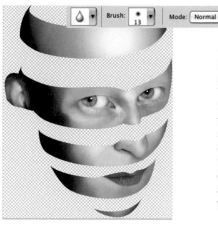

15 Create a new layer. Ensure that this new layer is targeted in the Layers palette and select the Blur tool. Choose a soft, round Brush Tip preset and enable the Sample All Layers function in the Tool Options bar. Set the strength to 100 and begin to paint over areas that need softening; specifically areas like the edges of his iris, which are looking rather sharp from the previous adjustments. Increase and decrease the strength and size of the brush tip as required to soften the underlying imagery to your liking.

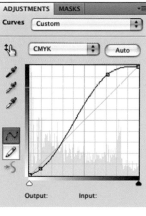

16 Alright, one more adjustment layer and then we'll get onto the intricate line work and square divisions across his face. Create a new curves adjustment layer. Alter the CMYK curve so that the shaded areas are enhanced and the highlight areas are lightened. Have a look at the curve I've created here and use it as a guide for this adjustment. When you're happy with the result, click OK and then select the Pen tool.

(i) Disabled dynamics

Often, when choosing a Brush preset, you'll notice that the Shape Dynamics option is enabled in the Brushes palette. Stylus users will frequently find this set to pen pressure and as a result, when they paint, the thickness of the stroke will vary depending upon pressure. Because the painting methods used here require a predictable and uniform stroke thickness, you are instructed to disable brush dynamics. When using the Blur tool, stroke variation is not as apparent as when painting; so disabling shape dynamics isn't that crucial. However, if you decide you want uniform stroke thickness when blurring, by all means, go ahead and disable shape dynamics when using the Blur tool as well.

PART FOUR: Planar divisions via grid work

17 Now it is time to draw all of the individual lines that break up the face into small, cubic planes. Look carefully at the face and use the existing contours as your guide to plan where each line will go. Use the Pen tool to draw a single curved line. When it is finished, hold down the Control(PC)/Command(Mac)-key and click anywhere on the canvas. By doing this, the next time you click, you'll begin a new line rather than continuing the existing one. Use this method over and over to create all of the lines. This aspect is very time consuming, but equally rewarding in the end.

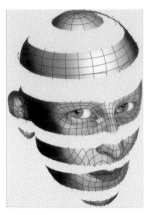

Creating the facial grid

The intricate grid across his face begins as a series of open paths and is then combined with Paint tools and layers.

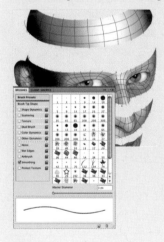

1 Your grid can overlap the edges of the face because the group vector mask will hide anything that strays beyond the edges. Select the Brush tool; choose a hard, round Brush Tip preset in the Brushes palette.

2 Specify a small diameter in the Brushes palette; this will dictate the thickness of your visible lines and will vary depending upon your image resolution. Use the Eyedropper to sample a dark brown color from the image and create a new layer.

3 Target your new layer and target your path in the Paths palette. Ensure that no single path component is selected. Choose Stroke Path from the Path Palette menu. Choose the Brush option. The grid will be stroked with your brush and current foreground color on the new layer.

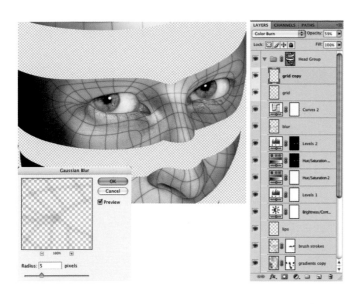

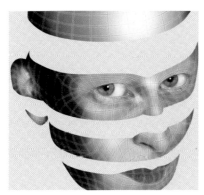

18 Change the blending mode of your new layer to color burn and reduce the opacity to 59%. This layer containing your painted grid will be one that you return to later to generate various selections from. Name it something memorable. And giving the layer thumbnail a color to make it stand out is a good idea. I have named my layer "grid" and specified a yellow color for the layer thumbnail. Duplicate the grid layer and choose Filter>Blur>Gaussian Blur from the menu. Add a slight blur, just enough to soften the grid without making it disappear.

Layer properties

You can add color to your layer thumbnails as well as change the name by accessing the layer properties. Target a layer and choose layer properties from either the Layer menu or the Layers Palette menu. You can also right-click(PC)/Control-click(Mac) on a layer thumbnail and then select layer properties from the pop-up menu.

Deselecting path components

A path can be made up of many path components. In the case of the facial grid path, each line is a path component within the path. When you stroke a path with the Brush tool like I've done here, it is very important that you do not have a single path component selected. If you stroke the path with one component selected, only that path component will be affected and the others will remain untouched. To deselect a path component, simply hold down the Control(PC)/Command(Mac)-key while using the Pen tool and click on an area of the canvas that contains no path components.

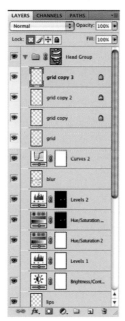

19 Enable the transparency lock for the duplicate grid layer in the Layers palette and then choose Edit>Fill from the menu. Fill the layer with 100% white. Change the blending mode of the layer to normal and increase the opacity to 100%. Keep the current layer targeted, and Control(PC)/Command(Mac)-click on the grid layer beneath it to generate a selection from the original grid layer's contents. Now, with your grid copy layer targeted, press the Delete key. Deselect. This removes the white from the grid itself, leaving behind a white outer glow around the entire grid on the current layer. Duplicate the grid copy layer a number of times to intensify the effect.

20 Add a layer mask to the original grid layer. Create radial, black to transparent gradients within the mask. Use this same method to mask one of your grid copy layers. Then, while holding down the Alt(PC)/Option(Mac) key, click on the mask and drag it onto another grid copy layer in the Layers palette to add an identical mask to that layer. Repeat this process with the remaining unmasked grid layer. Add the grid layers to a new group. Add a mask to the group and then use the same methods to edit the group's mask. Select the Magic Wand tool and deactivate the Sample All Layers function.

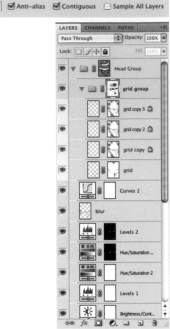

 Path editing

Because this facial grid is constructed of path components, it is entirely editable. You can use the Direct Selection tool to select and edit any point, line segment, or Bezier handle. You can fiddle until your heart's content. However, be certain that you're happy with the appearance of your grid before you go ahead and stroke the path with a brush. Once you do this, the pixels on your targeted layer are painted with the brush and editing the path from this point on won't do you any good. So be certain that you're satisfied before you select the Stroke option.

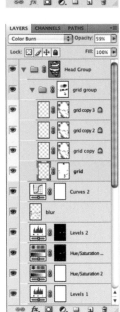

21 Ensure that the Contiguous and Anti-alias options are enabled and leave the tolerance set to the default value of 32. Target your original grid layer in the Layers palette. Use the Magic Wand tool to click on an area that is enclosed on all sides by grid lines. Hold down the Shift key and click on other enclosed areas on this layer to add them to the selection. Be careful not to click on areas that are not completely contained within grid lines or you'll end up selecting the entire background.

22 Open up the texture.jpg file. Choose Select>All and then Edit>Copy from the menu. Return to your working file and, with the new selection active, choose Edit>Paste Into from the menu. This will paste the copied image into your file as a new, masked layer. The mask is dictated by the active selection. Drag the new texture layer out, and on top of, your grid group in the Layers palette. However, ensure that your layer remains within the main group. Change the layer blending mode to luminosity and reduce the opacity to 76%. Duplicate this layer and change the blending mode to overlay.

Altering the grid

Now that you know how to select squares from the grid, there's much more you can do to embellish the face.

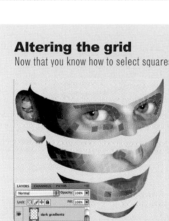

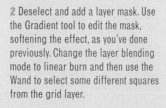

1 As you did previously, use the Magic Wand to select a number of different square areas that are contained within the grid. Create a new layer, drag it to the top within the group, and on that layer, use the Gradient tool to create a number of brown to transparent radial gradients within the selection.

2 Deselect and add a layer mask. Use the Gradient tool to edit the mask, softening the effect, as you've done previously. Change the layer blending mode to linear burn and then use the Wand to select some different squares from the grid layer.

3 Again, use the Magic Wand to select a number of random squares from the grid layer. Target the top layer in the group and then create a new hue/saturation adjustment layer. Adjust the hue and saturation, altering the color of the selected areas.

23 Repeat the process of randomly selecting squares from the grid layer; then, while the selection is active, create another hue/ saturation layer and alter the colors within those areas. Repeat this process again, but this time use a brightness/contrast adjustment layer to create some bright areas. And finally, create a levels adjustment layer while there is no current selection active. Use the CMYK input levels sliders to lighten the midtones and highlights of the underlying layers. To accentuate the line work, select your grid group in the Layers palette and drag it above all of the other layers within the main group.

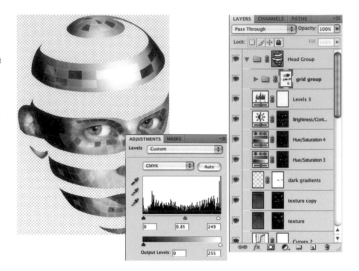

Masking the group

In addition to the existing vector mask, there are other ways to control what parts of the group are hidden and what parts are visible.

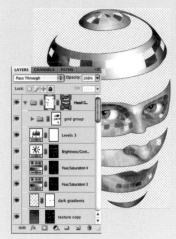

1 Finally, return to your original grid layer. Again use the Wand tool to select a number of square areas from that layer. With the selection active, target the main group in the Layers palette and choose Layer>Layer mask>Hide Selection from the menu.

2 As you can see, it is possible to use a layer mask and a vector mask at the same time. Select the Pen tool. This time, enable the Subtract from Path Area option in the Tool Options bar and target the layer mask. Zoom in close on the image.

3 Target the group's vector mask and, using the grid as a visual guide, trace over sections along the edges of the ribbons. Because the Pen is set to subtract, as you create closed shapes with the vector mask targeted, they'll be removed from visibility.

24 Collapse the layer group in the Layers palette to hide the contents as we are now finally finished with this group. Create a new layer and drag it beneath the group in the Layers palette and ensure that it remains targeted. Select the Pen tool and choose the Add to Path Area option. Draw a number of closed shapes to represent the areas of the face that we would see behind it as the ribbon effect spirals in 3d space. Now, select the Subtract from Path Area function and draw a number of squares to punch holes in your new path components.

Creating the inside

Now we'll use a number of familiar methods to add depth and texture to the inside of the spiral.

1 Generate a selection from your new path. Use the Eyedropper to sample a brownish gray color from the image and then fill the active selection with it on your new layer. Keep the selection active and open up the texture.jpg file.

2 Copy the texture image and then return to your working file. With the selection active, choose Edit>Paste Into from the menu to add it as a masked layer. Change the layer blending mode to multiply and reduce the opacity to 35%.

3 Duplicate the layer, change the mode to overlay, and increase the opacity to 100%. Use this same paste into method to add the contents of the texture1.psd file into your file as a masked layer. Change the mode to soft light, duplicate the layer, and change the duplicate layer mode to pin light.

25 Generate a selection from your newest path again and create a new layer. With this layer targeted, select the Radial Gradient tool. Use the foreground to transparent method with a black foreground color to add gradients into the active selection on the current layer. Focus on the outer edges to add shadow. Change the blending mode of the layer to multiply and reduce the opacity to 68%. With the selection still active, create another new layer, this time add some white gradients into the selection on the new layer. Create them just left of the center, near his forehead, to add highlights. Deselect and reduce the layer opacity slightly.

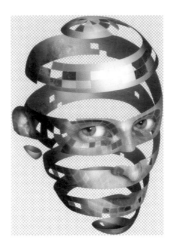 

The illusion of thickness

Again, the same methods are used, but this time to add some depth to the spiraling ribbon that makes up his face.

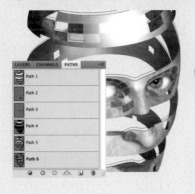

1 By now you're familiar with the process of creating paths. Use the Pen tool to draw a series of path components indicating the thickness of our spiraling ribbon. Also, add path components to create thickness within the holes in the front areas of the face.

2 Generate a selection from the path and create a new layer. Fill the active selection on the new layer with a pink color sampled via the Eyedropper tool from his skin. Deselect and enable the transparency lock for this layer.

3 Use the Radial Gradient tool with previous settings to create some brown to transparent gradients around the edges on this layer. Use the Polygonal Lasso to create sharp-edged selections over the areas where thickness was added to each square hole. This allows you to add gradients within each selection, creating the illusion of inner walls on the edges of each hole, adding depth via shading.

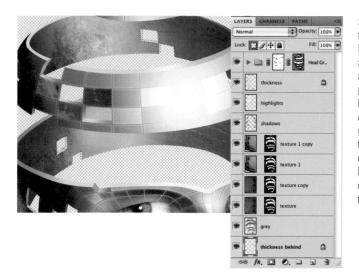

26 Now that you've created the illusion of thickness for the spiraling ribbon and the holes in the front of the face, it is time to also add some thickness to the holes in the back areas. Use the Pen tool to draw a series of path components to form the outline for the hole thicknesses. Ensure that the Add to Path Area option is enabled as you work and then generate a selection from the entire path. With the selection active, create a new layer and drag it beneath all of the other layers in the Layers palette. Fill the active selection with skin color on the new layer. Deselect, and enable the transparency lock for this layer.

ⓘ Selections, paths, and components

To generate a selection from an entire path, meaning all of the separate path components within that path, you must ensure that no components are selected. If a component or multiple components are selected, the selection you generate will be based upon the selected components only, disregarding all other path components. If you have a path component selected, you can deselect it by clicking on an area of the canvas that has no path component with either the Path Selection tool or the Direct Selection tool.

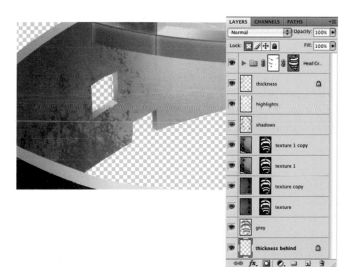

27 Again, as you did previously with the areas in the front of the face, use the Polygonal Lasso to create sharp-edged selections for each new inner wall. One by one, draw a selection in the appropriate area, add a brown to transparent gradient, deselect, and then move on to the next area. Continue in this manner until all areas of thickness have some shading on them and all the corners of interior holes are clearly indicated by shading within sharp-edged selections.

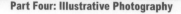

PART SEVEN: A 3d background

28 Open up the background.psd file. This file contains a background image similar to the textures we've been using so far, and it also contains a layer named "lines." This layer is included within the file to act as a template. One of the things that makes the work of Escher so powerful is his ability to create optical illusions. Here we're going to create a bit of an optical illusion of our own by creating shaded and textured planes that don't match the perspective of the imagery. Things will look normal at first glance, but upon further inspection, the viewer will notice that this is an impossibility.

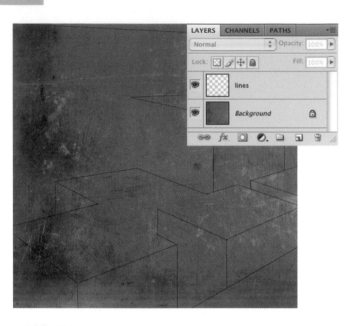

 Creating paths

When you draw a path component with the Pen tool, a path is automatically created in the Paths palette. Any components you draw while this path is targeted will be added to that path. By clicking in the empty space in the Paths palette, you are ensuring that no path is targeted. When no path is targeted, a new path is automatically created as soon as you begin to draw with the Pen tool. Another way to create a new path is to simply click on the Create New Path button at the bottom of the Paths palette. This will create an empty path and target it; then any components you create with the Pen tool will be added to that path.

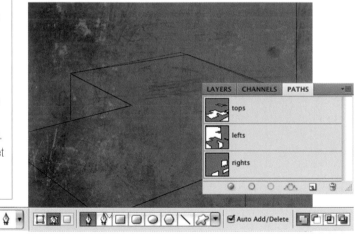

29 Select the Pen tool. Ensure that the Add to Path Area option is enabled. Using the lines layer as your guide, you're going to create three separate paths in the Paths palette. Because the shapes you need to create have no curves, this should go quick. First, trace all of the top planes that are indicated by the lines layer. Draw as many closed path components as required. Name this path "tops." Create a new path, trace all of the left-facing planes, and name it "lefts." Then do the same for the right-facing planes until you have three separate paths.

30 Open up the sky.jpg file. Use the Move tool to drag the sky into your working file as a new layer. Hold down the Shift key while you drag to ensure accurate positioning. Change the blending mode of the layer to hard light and reduce the opacity to 70%. Generate a selection from the "lefts" path in the Paths palette. With your sky layer targeted and the current selection active, choose Layer>Layer Mask>Hide Selection from the menu. Next, load the "tops" path as a selection. With your layer mask targeted, choose Edit>Fill from the menu to fill the selected area on the mask with black. Deselect.

Repeat the process

Continue to use your paths as the basis for selections, which will mask your layers as you add sky imagery to the other background planes.

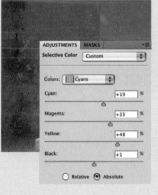

1 Disable the visibility of the "lines" layer, you don't need it anymore. Shift-drag the sky.jpg file into your working file as a new layer again. Generate a selection from your "rights" path and then click the Add Layer Mask button in the Layers palette.

2 Reduce the opacity of the layer to 70% and generate a selection from the "rights" path again. Create a new selective color adjustment layer while the selection is active. Select cyan from the Colors menu and use the sliders to alter the cyans within the selection.

3 Again, drag the sky image into the file as a new layer. Click on the "lefts" path to load it as a selection. With your new layer targeted, click on the Add Layer Mask button in the Layers palette. Change the blending mode to color burn and reduce the opacity to 73%.

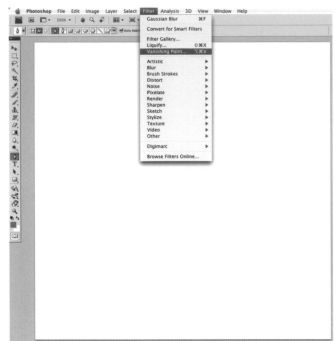

31 At the moment in Photoshop, you have two files open. There is the head file and the background file you just created. For the moment, we're going to need to create another temporary file. Create a new file in RGB mode that is approximately 3 inches high and 3 inches wide, using the same resolution as your other two files. Create a new layer in this file and with that layer targeted choose Filter>Vanishing Point from the menu.

Create a cube shape

The vanishing point filter proves useful for creating shapes in perfect perspective.

1 Use the Create Plane tool to create the first plane. Click in each of the four corners to create the plane. You can adjust the shape of your plane by moving the corner paints around with this tool.

2 While you still have the Create Plane tool selected, click on the middle handle of the left line segment and drag to create a perpendicular plane. Use the same tool to click and drag the corners to reshape this plane too.

3 Now do the same thing to create a top plane. Click on the top middle handle of both the planes and drag with the Create Plane tool to create a top plane. Once you create the top plane, your cube is complete. Click OK.

Gaussian Blur	⌘F
Convert for Smart Filters	
Filter Gallery...	
Liquify...	⇧⌘X
Vanishing Point...	⌥⌘V
Artistic	▶
Blur	▶
Brush Strokes	▶
Distort	▶
Noise	▶
Pixelate	▶
Render	▶
Sharpen	▶
Sketch	▶
Stylize	▶
Texture	▶
Video	▶
Other	▶
Digimarc	▶
Browse Filters Online...	

32 When you exit the vanishing point filter and return to your empty file, you'll notice nothing. That is because we just created the planes within the vanishing point filter, not any sort of artwork. We're now going to return to that filter a number of times to add an image to each plane that matches the perspective of the cube we just created. Open up the top.jpg file, select all, and copy. Return to your empty file and then launch the vanishing point filter again.

Adding texture to cube
Add texture by pasting a different image onto each plane within the vanishing point filter.

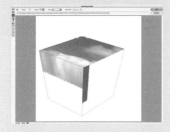

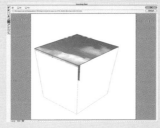

1 Inside the vanishing point filter, you'll see the planes you just created. Type Control(PC)/Command(Mac)-v to paste the copied image. Use the Marquee tool to click on your selected image and drag it onto the top of the cube.

2 You'll see a thick blue line appear around the plane to indicate that your image will be placed there. Choose the Transform tool and resize the image by dragging the corner points of the selection. Click OK and witness the results on your previously empty layer.

3 Open up the left.jpg file and use the same method to copy, launch vanishing point, and then paste onto the left plane. Exit vanishing point and then repeat the entire process with the right.jpg file. Paste it onto the right plane.

33 Use the Move tool to drag your cube layer from this file into your background image file as a new layer. Duplicate the layer a number of times and use the Move tool to scatter the cube layers around the background. Use varying opacity settings from layer to layer, making some less prominent than the others. Also try varying the layer blending modes of a few cube layers. Blending modes like pin light, hard light, and linear light produce interesting yet understated blending effects and work well with the colors in this image. Target a single cube layer and choose Edit>Free-Transform from the menu.

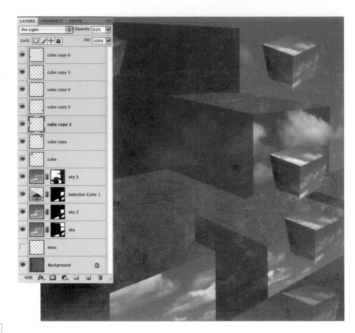

Vanishing point mode

You may be wondering why we went to the trouble of creating a new file for the cube only. Although it would have been less effort to simply create a cube on a new layer in the background file, this wasn't an option and I'll tell you why. You have probably noticed by now that for this chapter we've been working in the CMYK mode for both the head file and the background file. Vanishing point works only in the RGB mode. So in order to create the cube using vanishing point, we had to do it in a separate file using RGB mode. Once the layer is dragged from the RGB file to the CMYK file, the colors are automatically converted to CMYK.

34 Hold down the Shift key and drag the corner handle in or out, depending upon whether you wish to increase or decrease the size of the cube. To rotate, move the mouse pointer slightly outside of the box until it changes to indicate rotation. When this happens, click and drag to rotate. When you are finished rotating and/or scaling, press the Enter key. You can also alter the perspective of any cube by targeting the layer and then choosing Edit>Transform>Perspective from the menu. After doing this, dragging the corner points will allow you to alter the perspective of the targeted cube. Again, pressing the Enter key will apply the transformation.

PART EIGHT: Butterflies and clouds

35 Open the three butterfly images included with the downloaded project files. Use the Move tool to drag them into the background working file as individual layers. Scatter them around on the canvas and use the Free-Transform methods you've used previously to alter the size and rotation of different butterflies on different layers. Feel free to duplicate butterfly layers and move them around until you think there are enough of them within the scene. Go ahead and add layer masks to some of the butterfly layers. And as you've done numerous times by now, use the Gradient tool to add black to transparent gradients within individual layer masks, blending some of the butterflies into the background.

Stacking up butterflies

Create duplicate butterfly layers, alter layer blending modes and opacity, and then edit individual layer masks to gently blend your butterflies into the background.

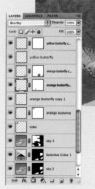  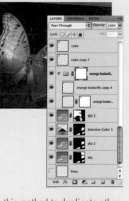 

1 Target one of your butterfly layers and convert the blending mode to luminosity; then duplicate this layer and change the blending mode to overlay. Add a mask to one of the layers and use the Gradient tool to edit the mask.

2 Use this method to duplicate other butterfly layers, building up stacks with differing blending modes and mask the layers. Remember, you can also group the layers and edit the group's mask to affect all the layers within the group.

3 Use this method to add interest to a number of the butterflies within the scene. In some instances, try simply changing the blending mode and not duplicating the layer. Vary opacity settings and blending modes as you see fit. Have a bit of fun experimenting here.

36 Open up the clouds.jpg file, select all, and copy. Return to your background file. In the Channels palette, click the Create New Channel button to create a new alpha channel. With this channel targeted, choose Edit>Paste from the menu to paste the copied clouds image into your new channel. Ensure that your new channel remains targeted in the palette and click on the Load Channel as a Selection to generate a selection from the white areas of the pasted image within the channel.

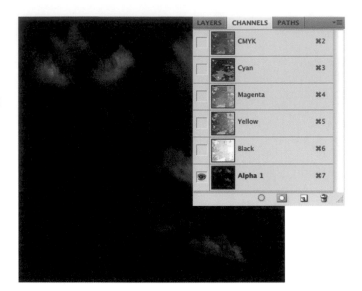

 Black sky?

When you open up the clouds.jpg image, you will notice that it is a very dark sky with a few white clouds within it. It is not exactly what you expect to see when you open up a sky image. This image was carefully prepared ahead of time and yes, it did originally start out as a nice blue sky with fluffy white clouds. Because it was destined for an alpha channel, it was altered ahead of time so that the resulting selection could be controlled before pasting into the channel. Drastic tonal adjustments were performed to ensure that the only white areas visible would remain within the cloud areas, not within the sky. Doing this ensures that when the channel is converted to a selection, the entire background will lie outside of the selection border because it is 100% black.

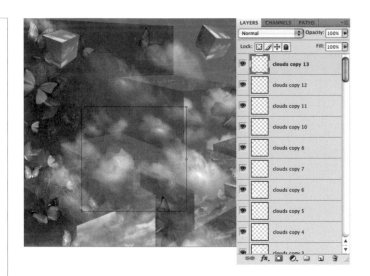

37 With your new alpha channel–based selection active, return to the Layers palette. Create a new layer and drag it to the top of the layer stack. Choose Edit>Fill from the menu to fill the active selection with white on the new layer. Deselect. Create a number of duplicates of this layer and use the Move tool to move the layers around the canvas, scattering clouds across the image. Use the Free-Transform tool to increase or decrease the contents of individual layers as you see fit. If you wish to increase the intensity of a certain layer, simply duplicate it and leave it in the same place on the canvas.

PART NINE: Putting it all together

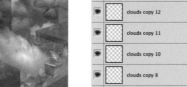

38 Return to the file that contains the head you were working on previously. Target all of the contents in the Layers palette: the groups and all the layers. Make sure that you've got everything. Choose Layer>Smart Objects>Convert to Smart Object from the menu. This will create a smart object that contains everything within the file. Now, use the Move tool to drag your smart object into the background file you've been working on. Drag it to the top of the stack in the Layers palette and use the Move tool to position it just left of the center on the canvas.

Add the floating bits
Some floating pieces of the face are all that is required to complete this scene.

1 Select the Pen tool and ensure that the Add to Path Area function is enabled in the Tool Options bar. Use the Pen tool to carefully draw a number of path components that resemble rectangles and curved rectangles. Vary the angle from component to component.

2 Create a new layer at the top of the layer stack. Generate a selection from the path and fill it with skin color. Use the Radial Gradient tool, with the Foreground to Transparent preset, to add shading to individual pieces in a variety of colors.

3 With your current selection active, open up the texture.jpg file again and copy it. Use Edit>Paste Into to paste it into your active selection. Change the layer blending mode to linear burn and reduce the opacity to 29%. Duplicate this layer and change the mode to overlay.

39 Create one final new layer and place it just above your smart object in the Layers palette so that all of the floating pieces layer sit above it. Use the Pen tool to draw a number of closed path components to add thickness to your floating pieces. Generate a selection from the path and then fill it with a sampled skin color on your new layer. Enable the transparency lock for this layer and then add some shading to the thickness you've just created. Use exactly the same methods of introducing gradients into polygonal selections that you used previously to add shading to each piece. You are now essentially finished. However, feel free to use everything you've learned so far to embellish the image further.

Head examination

Now that the composition is complete, let's take a final look at the tricks and techniques used to give the head a spiral 3d appearance.

a By working within a group that had a vector mask applied to it, we were able to concentrate on making the head itself look good, knowing that layers and paint effects weren't going to stray beyond the dictated shape and onto the background.

b Adding line work via stroked paths allowed us to give the face a 3d wire–mesh look. By dividing the face into sections, we were able to remove sections via mask editing to create the illusion of holes.

c Drawing the thickness of the spiral may be a little time consuming at first, but once you fill it with color and add shading with gradients it looks quite convincing.

d Building up texture on the inside of the spiral helps to make things look less flat. This sense of depth is aided again by adding gradients to simulate areas of highlight and shadow.

e Because his iris areas have been altered by using adjustment layers, the colors can be changed at any point by simply editing the adjustment layers. Double-click any adjustment layer to edit it.

Try a simpler approach

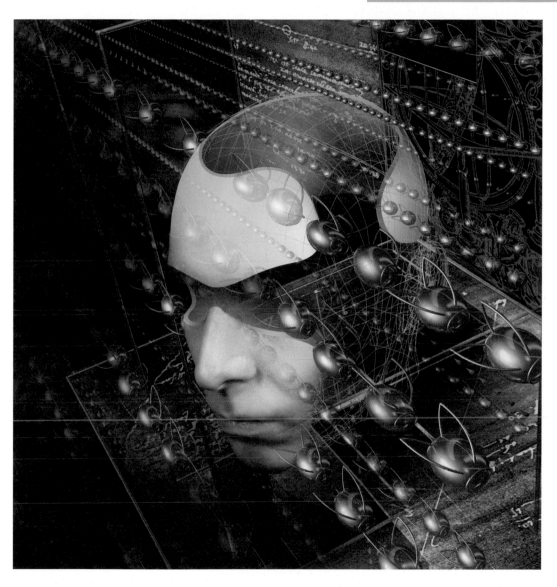

You can take a simpler approach to creating the ribbon effect in other images. It doesn't have to be a complicated spiral at all actually. Here you can see how a similar, yet simpler, effect was applied to the head. The thickness is still prevalent, yet on a whole, it is less complicated. Here you can also see how this is an ideal technique for combining photographs and rendered 3d models in a cohesive manner.

Chapter 18

Aging Effects

There is no way around it; our culture is obsessed with age and beauty. We are bombarded with advertisements and television commercials filled with young, beautiful people, and are trained to think that age is unattractive. However, if you can snap yourself out of this media-influenced tunnel vision and objectively look at the face of an older person, there is a certain majestic beauty to it. Wrinkles accentuate features, hair turns gray, and a sense of wisdom tends to come across. There is a certain beauty in the aging process that far too many people ignore.

Any photographer who has worked in advertising or magazine publishing is no stranger to battling age. When an image ends up in Photoshop, skin is often smoothed, and pores and wrinkles are removed alongside any evident gray hairs. In general, the aging process is reversed. However, it was after I received a commission from a Canadian women's magazine that I was asked to create the exact opposite as well. They wanted to show a woman both young and old. Granted, the left side of her face has all of the retouching and perfecting the Western World has come to expect, but the right side is something else entirely. It shows the same woman but many years older.

The challenge when creating something like this is authenticity; it's got to look real and the best way to achieve that is to start with the real thing. So not only did I photograph the beautiful young model you see here, but I also photographed the elderly, adjusting the lighting to accentuate every wrinkle and porous area of the skin. A method was developed for introducing sections of the aged face into the beautiful model's face, and as you can see here, the results are rather convincing.

In addition to the Photoshop face effects, the overall image needs to convey the juxtaposition between young and old. That is why one-half of the background is in full color, whereas the other half is desaturated, gray, and contains distressed, aged surface texture effects. As a result of this, the concept is evident at a glance, and after you follow along with this chapter's step-by-step instructions, the process of creating an aging effect will become just as evident.

DIFFICULTY 4.0/5 Some familiarity with all things layers, masks, and adjustment layers will be beneficial as you work your way through this chapter. We'll delve a little deeper into alpha channel editing and explore smart filters and their accompanying masks. Perhaps the most taxing part of working your way through this chapter will be the effort required to carefully incorporate each element of age into the face. This may prove time consuming.

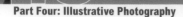

What you'll learn in this chapter

Creative Techniques and Working Methods

Blending and enhancing features

Transferring selected areas of age from one face to another is not as simple as cloning them from one image to the other or copying and pasting. In this chapter, you'll develop an understanding of what to look for in your aged faces. Then you'll learn exactly what to isolate and how to incorporate it into your youthful face. As you work your way through, you'll come to realize that each tiny piece of aged skin placed on the youthful model is carefully aligned, resized, positioned, and transformed wherever necessary. You'll smoothly blend the sections into the underlying imagery via soft-edged layer masks, and you'll learn how to use selection tools alongside layering techniques to deepen wrinkles and pores even further.

Create selections from imagery

Sometimes everything you need to create a precise selection within an image exists already in that very image. I'll show you how to paste your image into an alpha channel and then adjust and edit the results to carefully craft a custom selection that lines up perfectly with your image. You'll be amazed at the amazingly complex and accurate results that you can achieve via this method. Need proof? Simply take a look at how realistic the gray hair effect within this image is.

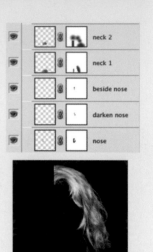

Photoshop Tools, Features, and Functions

Color range

This excellent and flexible method for generating selections based upon ranges of color is an essential tool in this chapter, especially when it comes to targeting the whites of her eyes, deepening wrinkles and pores, and isolating the figure from her photographed background.

Smart filters

By applying these nonlinear filters to smart objects within the image, we ensure maximum flexibility and future editing opportunities. At any point within the process, you can double-click a smart filter in the Layers palette and edit that filter effect. This method is much more flexible than affecting pixels directly. Smart filters also come equipped with their very own mask, allowing you to hide selected portions of the filter effect by editing the mask.

PART ONE: Create the background

1 Before we get started with the face or any aging techniques, we first need to create a background for the image, giving our model an environment to reside within. Open up the sky. jpg file. Select the Gradient tool. In the Tool Options bar, select the Foreground to Transparent option from the list of presets in the Gradient picker. Select the linear gradient method and then press the "d" key on your keyboard to set the foreground color to black.

Project files

All of the files needed to follow along with this chapter and create the featured image are available for download on the accompanying Web site in the project files section. Visit www.creativephotoshopthebook.com.

Constraining gradients

Holding down the Shift key while you create a linear gradient will constrain the resulting gradient to either 90°, 180°, or 45°. This means that it will be straight up and down, perfectly straight from left to right, or on a perfect diagonal.

2 Choose Layer>New>Layer from the menu to create a new layer. Change the blending mode of the layer to multiply in the Layers palette. Reduce the gradient opacity to 25% and then, while holding down the Shift key, click and drag from the top of the canvas down a little. Do this from the bottom up, and then in from the left and right sides so that the sky is surrounded by light gradients.

3 Click the Add Layer Mask button at the bottom of the Layers palette to mask the layer. Target the mask, then switch the gradient to the radial method and increase the opacity to 100% in the Tool Options bar. Click and drag from the center of the mask outward. Do this as many times as required to mask the gradient layer until only the corners appear quite dark. This gives the sky image the "signature look" as if it were photographed with a toy camera like a Holga or Lomo.

Add gradient effects

A series of gradients on different layers help to transform this ordinary sky image background.

1 Switch the gradient back to the linear method and create a new layer. Select a light brown foreground color from the picker by clicking the Foreground Color swatch. On a new layer, draw a gradient about half way up from the bottom.

2 Change the blending mode of the layer to color and then create another one. On this layer, use an orange foreground color to create another gradient from bottom to about halfway up. Change the blending mode of the layer to color and reduce the opacity.

3 Create a new layer and draw a black gradient from the bottom about a third of the way up. Add a layer mask to the layer and use a radial gradient within the mask to edit the layer mask like you did with your first gradient layer.

PART TWO: Add the figure

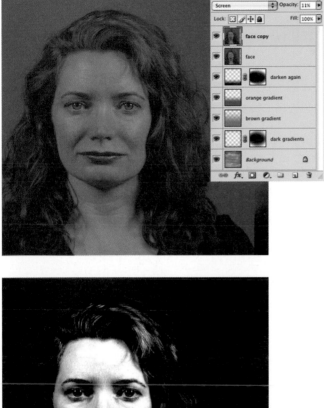

4 Open up the model.jpg file. Use the Move tool to drag the image into your working file as a new layer. Position the new layer to the left edge of the canvas. Duplicate the layer by dragging it onto the Create a New Layer button at the bottom of the Layers palette. Change the blending mode of the duplicate layer to screen and reduce the opacity to 11%. With the duplicate layer targeted, choose Select>All and then Edit>Copy from the menu. Next, Control(PC)/Command(Mac)-click on the layer thumbnail in the Layers palette to generate a selection from the contents of the layer.

Pasting with precision

When you want to paste the contents of a layer into a channel in an identical position, it is very important that you follow this process exactly. Select all and then copy the contents of the layer. Then generate a selection from the layer contents and with that selection active, paste into an alpha channel. Skipping any part of this process will result in your image being pasted into the channel in the wrong position.

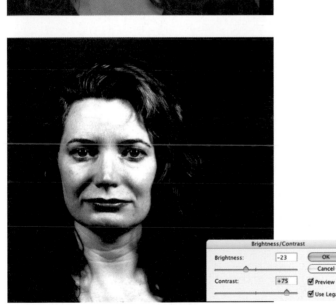

5 In the Channels palette, click on the Create New Channel button. With the new channel targeted and the current selection active, choose Edit>Paste from the menu. This will paste the copied image into your selection. Choose Select>Deselect and then choose Image>Adjustments>Brightness/Contrast from the menu. Enable the Legacy option and then perform a drastic adjustment until the image in your channel looks like what you see here. Click the Load Channel as a Selection button at the bottom of the palette and then return to the Layers palette. With the new selection active, target the top layer.

6 With your current selection active and the top layer targeted, click on the Add Layer Mask button at the bottom of the Layers palette. This will mask all areas outside of the selection, resulting in this screen layer brightening the lighter areas of her face, adding a bit of subtle contrast. Deselect and create a new levels adjustment layer by clicking on the Levels button in the Adjustments palette.

Tonal and color adjustments

It is time to alter her complexion a little. Don't worry if the background is affected, we'll remedy that next.

1 In the Adjustments palette, leave the channel set to CMYK and drag the left and right input level sliders closer to the center of the histogram. Then select the black channel and perform a similar adjustment. Click OK and target the adjustment layer's mask in the Layers palette.

2 Select the Brush tool. Choose a large, soft, round brush tip from the Preset picker in the Tool Options bar. Use black to paint over areas around the edge of her hair within the layer mask, masking the levels adjustment here.

3 In the Adjustments palette, create a new hue/saturation adjustment layer and reduce the saturation slightly. Next, create a selective color adjustment layer. Select black from the Color menu and increase the amount of cyan and black in the black component. Enable the absolute method.

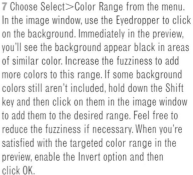

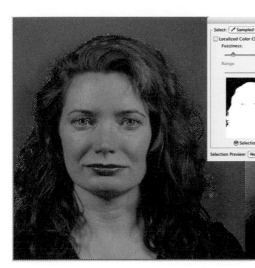

7 Choose Select>Color Range from the menu. In the image window, use the Eyedropper to click on the background. Immediately in the preview, you'll see the background appear black in areas of similar color. Increase the fuzziness to add more colors to this range. If some background colors still aren't included, hold down the Shift key and then click on them in the image window to add them to the desired range. Feel free to reduce the fuzziness if necessary. When you're satisfied with the targeted color range in the preview, enable the Invert option and then click OK.

Removing ranges

When working with the Color Range tool, you can Shift-click on colors in the image window to add that range of color to the selected range. However, if you wish to remove a range of color from the specified range within the Color Range tool, simply Alt(PC)/Option(Mac)-click on the color in the image window. You'll immediately see the range of color removed from the targeted range in the color range preview.

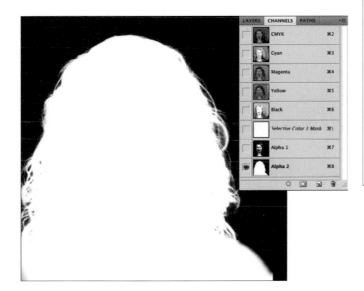

8 With your new selection active, click on the Save Selection as a Channel button in the Channels palette. Target the new alpha channel that is created and then deactivate the selection. Ideally you want all of the model, including her hair, to be white, and all of the background to be pure black. Begin with a brightness/contrast adjustment like you did in the previous channel, but less drastic. Then, select the Brush tool. Use a hard, round Brush Tip preset to paint white over unwanted black areas and black to paint over unwanted white areas. Alter brush diameter as required.

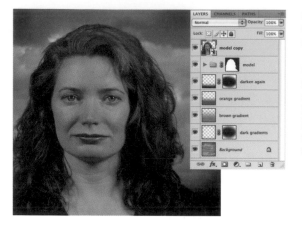

9 Load the new alpha channel as a selection and return to the Layers palette. Target the three adjustment layers and the two model image layers; then choose Layer>New>Group From Layers from the menu. Ensure that the current selection is active and that the new group is targeted in the Layers palette; then click on the Add Layer Mask button at the bottom of the Layers palette. Immediately you'll see the fruits of your labor as the original model photo background disappears. Duplicate your new group and then, with the duplicate group targeted, choose Layer>Smart Objects>Convert to Smart Object.

Adding soft focus effects

Using smart filters and smart filter masks allows us to add a blur effect around her hairline, hiding any imperfections that remain.

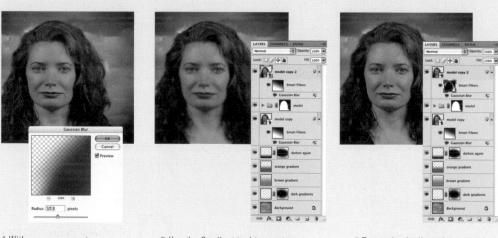

1 With your new smart object targeted, choose Filter>Blur>Gaussian Blur from the menu. Specify a generous radius, mainly to soften the edges of the hair. Click OK and drag the smart object below the group in the Layers palette. Target the smart filter mask.

2 Use the Gradient tool to create a black to transparent linear gradient within the mask from the top down, masking the top of the blur filter. Duplicate the smart object like you would any layer and drag it to the top of the layer stack.

3 Target the duplicated smart object mask and select the Brush tool. Use a large, soft brush to paint within the targeted mask. Paint with black to mask the blur effect from her face. Then paint around the edges of her hair with white to reveal the blur effect.

PART THREE: Refinements to skin and features

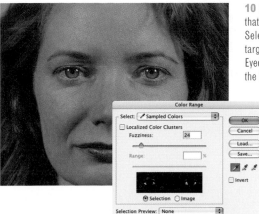

10 Use the Rectangular Marquee tool to draw a very quick selection that surrounds her two eyes only. With this selection active, choose Select>Color Range from the menu. By using a selection, you will only target ranges of color that reside within the selection border. Use the Eyedropper to click on the whites of her eyes in the image window. Adjust the fuzziness, then add and remove colors from the targeted range until only the whites of her eyes are targeted. If there is a slight overlap into other areas, that is fine. Sometimes it is very difficult targeting a range without including a few unwanted areas.

Selection previews

When you are generating a selection from a range of color while using the Color Range function, a preview of what you're going to get is absolutely essential. The preview window offers an excellent alpha channel style preview; however, if you're after something more, you need to direct your attention to the Selection Preview menu at the bottom of the color range interface. Here you can choose from a number of preview options that will allow you to see your selection previewed against the full-sized image in the background.

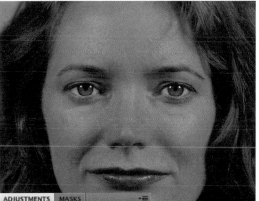

11 With the current selection active, create a new hue/saturation adjustment layer in the Adjustments palette. Leave the hue as it is. Reduce the saturation considerably and increase the lightness. This will lighten the whites of the eyes nicely. If the edges of your adjustment are too sharp, target the adjustment layer's mask in the Layers palette and then choose Filter>Blur>Gaussian Blur from the menu. Increase the radius until the edges appear soft enough. If you have unwanted areas of adjustment as a result of your color range–generated selection, paint over them within the mask.

CS4 Localized color clusters

If you enable the localized color clusters checkbox in the Color Range dialog box, a range slider appears. This range slider allows you to control how far away a color can be from the selected point and still be included within the selection.

363

12 Choose View>Show Rulers from the menu. Click on the ruler at the left and drag a new guide onto the canvas; release the mouse button when you reach the center of her nose. This guide is the reference line for the division between the young and old halves of her face. Go ahead and hide the rulers in the View menu once you've created the guide. Now create a new layer at the top of the stack in the Layers palette. Select the Brush tool and choose a soft, round Brush Tip preset.

 Painting advice

When you are smoothing skin in this manner, it is very important that you paint with a very low opacity setting and build up strokes. If you decide to save time and paint using a higher opacity, the effect won't look realistic. It is also very important to frequently sample different skin colors. Hold down Alt(PC)/Option(Mac) to temporarily access the Eyedropper tool as you go. Also remember that you can mask your layer at any point later on and gently fade things that appear too strong, introducing gradients and brush strokes into the mask.

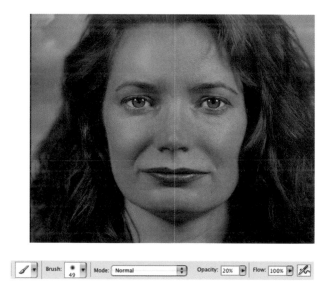

13 Set the opacity of the brush to something very low, like 15–20%. Zoom in close on the left half of her face and sample a skin color via the Eyedropper tool. Use this skin color to paint a few strokes over a porous or blemished area until it disappears. Use this method to soften the appearance of the skin on the left side of her face. Adjust brush opacity and size as required. Also, don't be afraid to frequently sample skin colors depending upon the area you're painting. Take your time and continue in this manner until her skin appears very smooth.

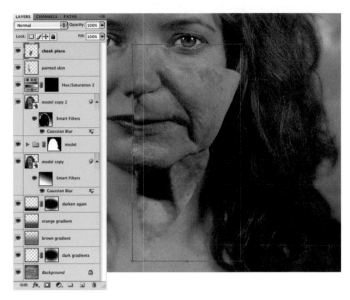

14 Open up the man.jpg file and use the Pen tool to draw a closed path that surrounds his right cheek, including quite a bit of his neck and the area under his nose. Control(PC)/ Command(Mac)-click the path thumbnail in the Paths palette to load it as a selection. Use the Move tool to drag the contents of your new selection into the working file as a new layer. Choose Edit>Free-Transform from the menu. Drag the corner handles of the bounding box to resize the new layer as required to make it fit nicely within her face.

Enhance the jowl effect

Layer masking and duplication are essential ingredients when it comes to jowl enhancements.

1 Use the Rectangular Marquee to draw a box on the left side of the guide and then choose Layer>Layer Mask>Hide Selection from the menu. Use the Brush tool with a soft tip to paint black within the mask, masking the hard edges.

2 Duplicate the layer and again choose Edit>Free-Transform. Move the contents of the box down a little and move the mouse pointer outside the box until it changes to indicate rotation. Rotate the contents a little to the right and press the Enter key.

3 Use the Brush tool to paint over any unwanted areas within the mask. Draw a Rectangular Marquee over the top of any layer content that strayed onto the left side of the guide. Fill the selection with black on the layer mask and deselect.

15 Return to the man.jpg file and this time use the Pen tool to draw a closed path around the area underneath his eye. Load the path as a selection and use the Move tool to drag the selection contents into the working file as a new layer. Again, use Free-Transform to resize and position it so that it looks as if it belongs on her face. Press Enter to apply the transformation and click on the Add Layer Mask button at the bottom of the Layers palette to add a mask to this layer. Use the same methods you used previously to edit the layer mask with a soft brush, varying diameter and opacity, blending the layer seamlessly into the background.

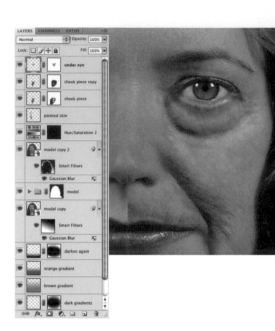

Positioning tip

When you drag a portion of the man's face into your working file as a new layer, the first thing you'll want to do is alter the size and position it properly. In some instances you may find it helpful to see underlying layers at the same time as you're doing this. To do this, simply reduce the opacity of your new layer until you can see both the new layer and the underlying imagery. Then perform your Free-Transform operation. Once finished, you can return the layer to full opacity. You cannot adjust layer opacity at the same time as performing a Free-Transform operation.

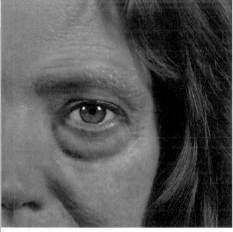

16 By now you're probably beginning to see a pattern emerge. Basically, you need to select an area of the man's face that is aged looking and bring it into your working file as a new layer. Use Free-Transform to position and resize the portion of his face until it fits nicely into the destination location in the working file. Add a mask to the layer and edit the mask with a soft brush, painting black within the mask at various opacity settings, to soften the edges and blend the layer into the background. Use this method to add the man's eyebrow to her face.

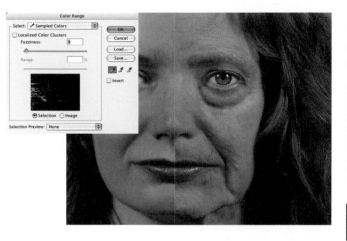

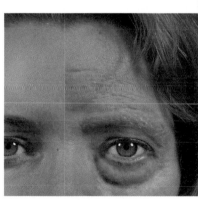

17 Return to the man's face image. Focus on areas of wrinkled or porous skin as opposed to prominent features. Bring these sections into your working file as new layers, then resize and position them. However, this time, change the blending mode of these layers to darken so that only the dark areas of his wrinkles and pores show through. Mask your layers to blend them into her face. To darken areas even more, like the added forehead wrinkles, use the Color Range tool to target only the recessed areas of the wrinkles.

Choosing the appropriate tool

Using paths to trace certain areas of the man's face is very helpful because paths allow you to create very precise selection borders. Paths are especially useful for areas that contain prominent features; however, areas like pores and wrinkles require less precision. In areas like this, you can work faster if you use the Lasso tool to draw very quick and rough selection borders. The ragged edges won't really matter because you're going to mask your layers anyway.

18 With your new selection active, create a new layer. Fill the active selection with an area of dark skin color that you sampled from the image. Change the layer blending mode to multiply. Deselect and add a layer mask. Edit the mask like you've been doing all along to blend the details of this layer into the face. If the effect is too strong, reduce the opacity of the layer. If it is not strong enough, duplicate the layer.

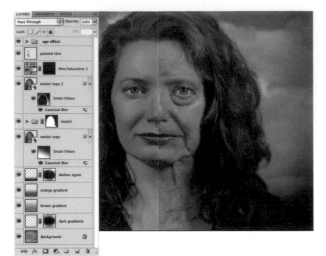

19 Use these methods repeatedly to finish adding details and signs of age to the right side of her face. Work on the nose area, and add more pores and wrinkles. Build up masked layers and remember to use color range, multiply, and the darken blending mode for certain layers to accentuate wrinkles. Open up the neck.jpg file and drag in selected portions of the neck as new layers. Again, resize and position the contents of these layers, masking them as required. When you're finished, target all of the layers that contribute to the aging effect and add them to a single group.

Create a channel-based selection

By using a pasted smart object, you can create an alpha channel that will ensure the accurate selection of her hair.

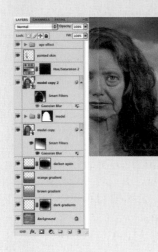

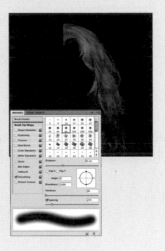

1 Target one of the smart objects in the Layers palette. Disable the smart object's Gaussian blur smart filter by clicking the visibility icon. Select all and copy. Control(PC)-Command(Mac)-click on the smart object's thumbnail in the Layers palette to generate a selection from it.

2 Re-enable the visibility of the smart filter and with the selection active, create a new channel in the Channels palette. Paste the copied contents into the new channel. Use the Rectangular Marquee to draw a selection that covers the area left of the guide.

3 Fill the active selection with black and deselect. Use the Brush tool to carefully paint black over everything white in the channel that is not hair. Take your time and fluctuate between hard and soft brush tips. Vary the size as required.

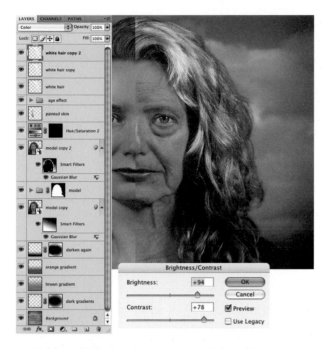

20 Use Image>Adjustments>Brightness/Contrast to increase the contrast within the channel. Load the channel as a selection and create a new layer in the Layers palette. Drag the layer to the top of the stack if it isn't there already, and then fill the active selection on the new layer with white. Deselect and duplicate the layer. Change the blending mode of the duplicate layer to color. You'll immediately notice the graying effect this has on her hair. Duplicate the newest layer with the color blending mode to enhance the graying effect.

Channel previews

When you are working within an alpha channel performing tonal adjustments, like in this case, adjusting the brightness and contrast, it can feel like a bit of a guessing game. As you increase the contrast of her hair in the channel, darker gray bits will disappear and lighter gray areas will become lighter. But how do you know when enough is enough? One handy way to see what you're doing is to enable the visibility of the color composite channel at the top of the palette. When you do this, you'll see your channel previewed against the image, similar to a traditional red rubylith overlay. Previewing your channel against your image will aid you in realizing when your adjustment has gone too far.

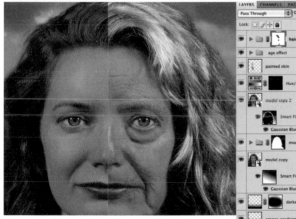

21 Chances are there will be some areas where her hair meets her face that look ragged or choppy. This is understandable regardless of your skill level. Painting around hair within a channel is a difficult thing to pull off perfectly. To remedy this, target your three hair layers and add them to a new group. Add a mask to the group and then use the Brush tool and/or the Radial Gradient tool to edit the mask. Gently paint over, or add gradients over, areas that require a smooth blend effect.

PART FIVE: Texture and color

 Hide/Show guides

While you are working your way through creating this image, there will be times when you want to view the guide that you created, and also times when you want it out of the way. You can view or show the guide via the View>Show>Guide Menu option. However, it is advantageous to learn the keyboard command for a speedier process. Hold down the Control(PC)/ Command(Mac) key and then press the ";" key on your keyboard to show or hide any guides.

22 Open up the scratches1.jpg file. Select the entire image and copy it. In your working file, create a new alpha channel and then paste the copied scratches into it. Use the Move tool, while holding down the Shift key, to drag the selection contents to the right. Move it to the right until the left side of the selection border is touching the guide. Load the new channel as a selection.

23 Create a new layer in the Layers palette. Ensure that your new layer sits above all of the other layers and then fill the active selection with white. Deselect and add a layer mask. Use the Gradient tool to mask out areas of the layer that are too strong by creating black to transparent gradients within the mask as needed. Now repeat the same process again with the scratches2.jpg. Paste it into a new channel, fill the selection on a new layer, and then mask the layer. Duplicate your second scratches layer and reduce the opacity a little, making these scratches more pronounced.

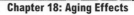

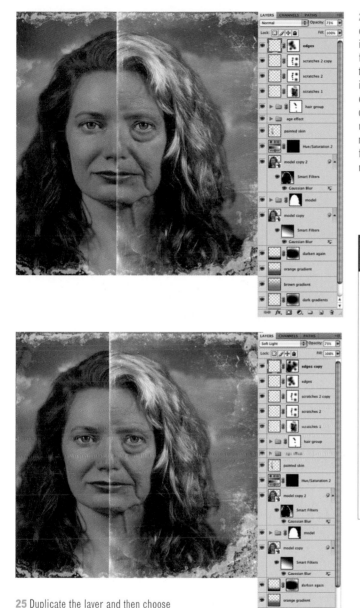

24 Open up the edges.jpg file. Copy the entire contents of the image and, you guessed it, paste it into a new alpha channel in your working file. Generate a selection from the channel and then create a new layer at the top of the stack in the Layers palette. On the new layer, fill the currently active selection with white as you've done previously with the scratches. Deselect and reduce the opacity of the layer to 73%. Add a mask to the layer and then use Radial Gradients, from black to transparent, within the mask to remove unwanted areas.

Realistic textures

Sometimes, in order for things to look genuine you simply need to use the real thing. There are loads of filters out there that claim to produce scratches and the like, but it never looks entirely real. Bearing in mind that the scratches were going to be used in an alpha channel, I printed out a solid black page on my laser printer. Then I took some very coarse sandpaper to the printout and scuffed it up. I scanned the scratched page, and just like that, I had a perfect scratches texture ideally suited for use in an alpha channel.

25 Duplicate the layer and then choose Edit>Transform>Flip Horizontal from the menu to flip the duplicate layer. Change the blending mode of the duplicate layer to color and then target the duplicate layer's mask. Use the Radial Gradient tool to create more black to transparent gradients within the mask, masking even more areas on this layer. Stand back for a moment and have a look at how simple surface textures and distressed edges can change the overall feel of the image.

26 Use the Rectangular Marquee tool to draw a rectangular selection over the right half of her face, including the background. With the selection active, choose solid color from the list under the Create New Fill or Adjustment Layer menu at the bottom of the Layers palette. Choose a gray color from the picker and click OK. Change the layer blending mode to color and then target the layer's mask. Use the Gradient tool to create black to transparent radial gradients within the mask, to mask the gray areas of this layer that cover her face.

Now examine what you've done

The accelerated aging method used here is quite successful; let's take a closer look at some of the things that make it work so well.

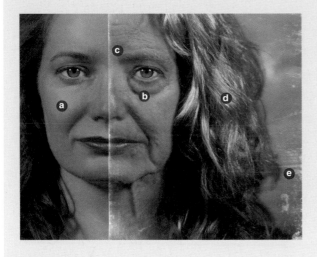

a Although this model is young and beautiful, painting over any pores on the left side creates even more contrast between the young smooth side of her face and the old, wrinkled, porous side of her face, making the result much more dramatic.

b Placing separate pieces of the aged face onto the woman allows for more flexibility and a much better result than trying fit an entire half of the old man's face in the image as a single piece.

c Some sections of the image are helped by combining selections generated from portions of the placed imagery with various layer blending modes. In the case of her forehead, a selection was generated from the deep areas of her wrinkles. Then, that selection was filled with color on a layer using a multiply blending mode, making the wrinkles appear even deeper.

d Using a section of the actual image in an alpha channel can be the perfect basis for a selection, as is evident in the gray hair effect you see here.

e Something as simple as a gray color layer and some surface scratches lend a sense of aged atmosphere to the right side of the image.

Once you master this process, you do not have to limit yourself to aging only half a face. The resulting juxtaposition can be just as powerful if you incorporate it into your imagery in other ways. In this image, the same two models were used. The face of the woman was aged extensively and then a different shot of her face was perfected and placed in her hand. The art director wanted the final result to look as if she were about to put on a mask of her former youth and beauty.

Chapter 19

Representational Surrealism

When you glance at an image like this, it becomes immediately apparent that it has a story to tell. The first thing you see is the large figure in the center being reborn. A new self bursts forth from the old self, and smaller elements on the perimeter of the image add to the narrative. The face looking through the magnifying glass represents self-analysis. The painting at the right represents a lack of focus and feelings of fragmentation. The figure with the hole in his chest represents emptiness. This image was autobiographical and all of the secondary elements represented my feelings at the time. I was due for a change and had made the decision to seriously pursue art. The figure in the center represents the cathartic relief I felt, and continue to feel to this day as a result of my decision.

Not only is the image shown here representational in terms of style, but it is also representational of my thought processes at the time of its creation. Apart from the subject matter, this image also meant change for me in terms of technique. It was the first time I decided to use photography as a resource to be heavily manipulated within an illustration. Manipulated, that is, to the point where it appears to be more painting than photography. What you'll learn in this chapter surpasses any mere collage technique.

DIFFICULTY 4.5/5   Experience with the Pen tool will be helpful as the creation of precise vector masks is important. Also, experience with the Brush, Blur, and Smudge tools will aid you in achieving smooth and painterly results. This portion of the chapter can be quite time consuming.

What you'll learn in this chapter

Creative Techniques and Working Methods

Photography as raw material

As you add the photographic resources to this image one at a time, the main thing that you'll notice is that they are not even close to a professional standard. However, something truly fantastic can be created from less than exceptional resources. This chapter's project involves a different approach to classical photography. When capturing images for compositing purposes, like those explained here, you needn't worry about perfect focus or exposure. It is more important to capture the gesture that you're after, and focus on light and shadow within the image rather than precise detail. By the time you finish this chapter, the logic of the process will become clear. You'll be well equipped to quickly capture resources with your camera, knowing fully well that this myriad of techniques is going to allow you to create something stunning from less-than-perfect resources.

A painterly approach

You will use a combination of layers, blending modes, Blur, Smudge, and Painting tools to make the main figure appear smooth and surreal. Across a series of layers, these tools are employed methodically to create a painterly version of the artwork that lies beneath. It takes a bit of time but the results are always unique, and knowing that you have created something entirely on your own is massively rewarding.

Keeping things separate and organized

An image like this can tend to fill up the Layers palette until it feels as though it will burst. Keeping everything as separate as possible is a recurring theme throughout this book and is taken to another level in this chapter. Here, in addition to groups, you'll also learn to organize key components into smart objects within your file. This allows you to access everything within the object to edit at any point, and it also keeps things tidy enough to preserve some semblance of order within the Layers palette.

main figure object

Photoshop Tools, Features, and Functions

Lighting effects

An effect as instantly recognizable as the results of lighting effects is the sort of thing that most of us will try to avoid. However, if used as a small component within the greater scheme of the composition, the result can greatly enhance the mood. The usage here will help you view this filter, and others like it, as a means to an end rather than an end in itself.

Liquify

This is another example of something generally avoided, due to the often overdone signature appearance of the result. However, if used in moderation and with clear intent in your composition, liquify can be a very useful tool indeed.

Vector masks

These wonderful masks will allow you to trim your layer content with absolute precision while retaining editability. They can be used alongside traditional masks, giving you the best of both worlds.

PART ONE: A dimly lit background

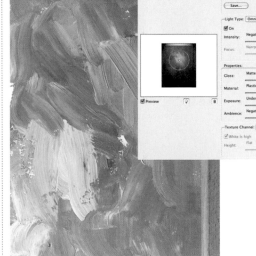

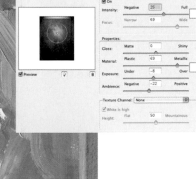

1 Open up the background.psd file. This painting will provide the background and you'll build up the finished image on a series of layers within this file. Choose Filter>Render> Lighting Effects from the menu. In the preview window, rotate the existing spotlight so that it is shining down. Decrease the intensity and the ambience until the preview is fairly dark. Drag a second light onto the preview. Make this an omni light with a relatively low intensity and ambience value.

Project files

All of the files needed to follow along with this chapter and create the featured image are available for download on the accompanying Web site in the project files section. Visit www.creativephotoshopthebook.com.

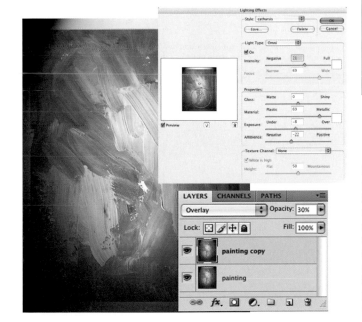

2 Alt(PC)/Option(Mac)-drag the omni light within the preview to copy it. Move it beneath the other two lights and reduce the intensity. Adjust the size and position of your lights as you see fit within the preview window. When you're happy with the result, click OK to apply the lighting effect to your painting. In the Layers palette, duplicate your layer by dragging it onto the Create a New Layer button. Change the blending mode of the duplicate layer to overlay and reduce the opacity to 30%.

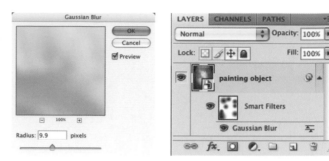

3 Target both layers in the Layers palette and then right-click(PC)/Control-click(Mac) on one of the targeted layers. Choose Convert to Smart Object from the pop-up menu. With your smart object targeted, choose Filter>Blur>Gaussian Blur from the menu. Enter a radius value that will noticeably blur the smart object. Click OK, target the smart filter mask in the Layers palette, and then select the Gradient tool. Set the foreground color to black. Use the Radial Gradient option and the Foreground to Transparent preset to create numerous black to transparent gradients within the smart filter's mask, removing the blur effect from these regions.

Setting the mood

Adjustment layers and a desktop scan help to enhance the overall mood created by this dimly lit background.

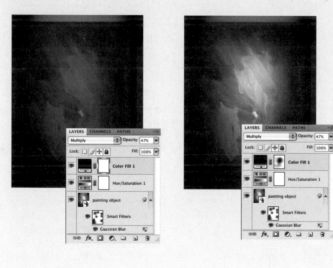

1 Create a new hue/saturation adjustment layer. Adjust the hue to −5 and decrease the saturation by 31. Next, create a new solid color layer. Choose black and then set the blending mode of the layer to multiply. Reduce the opacity to 47%.

2 Target the mask of the solid color layer and add some black to transparent radial gradients into the mask, to hide some dark areas created by this layer. Vary the gradient opacity as necessary. Open up the torn.jpg file.

3 Copy the image. Return to your working file. Create a new alpha channel and paste the copied image into it. Load the channel as a selection and then create a new layer. Use Edit>Fill to fill the selection on the new layer with white.

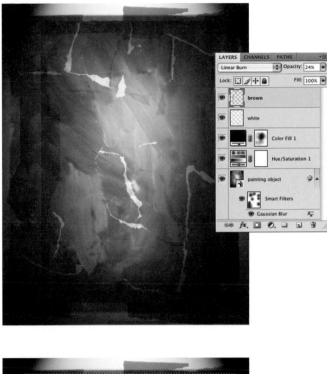

4 Change the blending mode of the current layer to overlay. With the current selection active, create a new layer. Change the blending mode of the layer to linear burn and reduce the layer opacity to 24%. Sample a brown color from the background by clicking on it with the Eyedropper tool. Type Alt(PC)/Option(Mac)-Delete to fill the selection with the new foreground color on your new layer. Type Control(PC)/Command(Mac)-d to deactivate the selection and then use the Move tool to drag the layer to the lower right slightly. Add a layer mask.

Refine edge

When you have a selection active, direct your attention to the Refine Edge button that appears in the Tool Options bar. This new feature has a number of sliders that allow you to feather your selection as well as perform a variety of other operations to modify your selection borders. One particularly useful feature when feathering is the variety of Preview options. There are a number of different image window previews similar to those included within the Select>Color Range command.

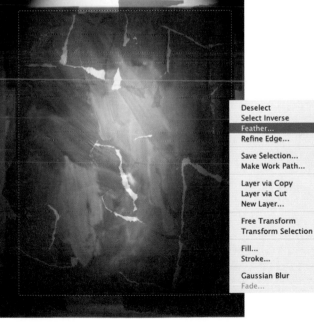

5 Use the Gradient tool to create black to transparent gradients within the mask. Create linear gradients at the top and left to mask the hard edges of the layer. Create radial gradients within the mask to hide areas that you feel are too visible. When you're finished editing the mask, select the Rectangular Marquee tool. Create a rectangular selection that lies within the white border of the original painting. Right-click(PC)/Control-click(Mac) on the canvas while the selection is active and choose the Feather option from the pop-up menu that appears. Enter a radius value that will significantly soften the edge.

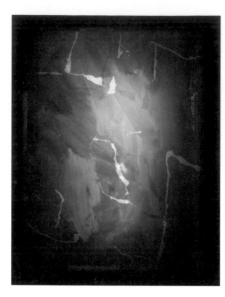

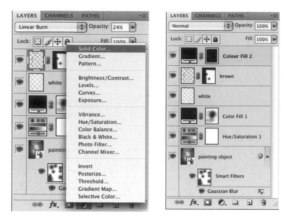

6 Type Control(PC)/Command(Mac)-Shift-i on the keyboard to invert the active selection. Now with the inverted selection active, create a new solid color adjustment layer from the menu at the bottom of the Layers palette. Areas that fall outside of the selection border will be automatically masked. Choose a black color from the picker and click OK.

PART TWO: Adding the central figure

Neatly trim the subject

Place the main figure in the scene using a vector mask to remove unwanted portions of the layer.

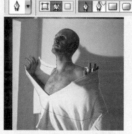

1 Open up the middle.jpg file. Use the Move tool to drag the image into your working file as a new layer. Choose Edit>Free-Transform from the menu and Shift-drag the corners of the bounding box to increase the size proportionately. Press Enter to apply the transformation.

2 Select the Pen tool. In the Tool Options bar, ensure that it is set to create paths and the Add to Path Area option is enabled. Carefully trace the head, shoulders, and hands of the figure. There is no need to include the area below his chest.

3 Once you've closed the path, ensure that the top layer is targeted and then choose Layer>Vector Mask>Current Path from the menu. The resulting mask will clip the contents of your layer. Use the Direct Selection tool to tweak the vector mask if necessary.

7 Right-click(PC)/Control-click(Mac) to the right of the layer thumbnail and layer mask thumbnail in the Layers palette. A pop-up menu will appear; choose the Duplicate Layer option from the pop-up menu. When prompted, specify the current document as the destination and click OK. Change the blending mode of the duplicate layer to screen and reduce the opacity to 51%. Duplicate this layer and then change the blending mode to overlay. Stacking up layers like this with varying blending modes really helps to enhance the overall contrast of the figure. Don't worry too much about overly saturated colors at this point, we'll address that next; this stacking method is to boost contrast while preserving image detail.

 Where to click

When you right-click(PC)/Control-click(Mac) on a layer in the Layers palette, a pop-up menu will appear. However, the options within the menu will be different depending upon exactly where it is that you click. For instance, the Duplicate Layer option is only available when you click to the right of the layer and layer mask thumbnails. Clicking on a layer thumbnail or a layer mask thumbnail will result in different menu options relative to that particular layer component.

8 Hold down the Control(PC)/Command(Mac) key and click on the vector mask thumbnail of your top layer in the Layers palette. This loads the vector mask as a selection. With the selection active, create a new hue/saturation adjustment layer by clicking on the Hue/Saturation button in the Adjustments palette. Reduce the saturation by 100% and click OK. Now, hold down the Control(PC)/Command(Mac) key and click on the adjustment layers mask in the Layers palette to load it as a selection. With this selection active, create a new selective color adjustment layer by clicking on the Selective Color button in the Adjustments palette. Choose neutrals from the Color menu and alter the individual color components as seen here.

PART THREE: The tearing effect

9 Open up the left.jpg file. You'll find a path included in the Paths palette. Control(PC)/Command(Mac)-click on the path thumbnail in the Paths palette to load it as a selection. Copy the contents of the selection and paste them into the working file as a new layer. Use Free-Transform to adjust the size and rotation of the layer contents. Holding down the Control(PC)/Command(Mac) key while you drag a corner point will allow you to freely distort the contents of the bounding box. Press Enter to apply the transformation when you're satisfied with the results.

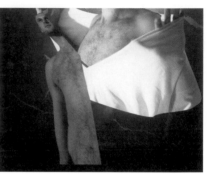

Using bits and pieces

Revise the shape of the left side of the figure by floating bits and pieces of his skin on a series of new layers.

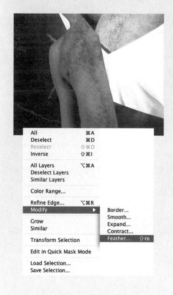

1 Use the Lasso to draw a very rough selection around an area of his chest on this layer. Feather the selection so that edges are soft via the Select menu, the Tool Options bar, or the Refine Edge command.

2 Choose Layer>New>Layer Via Copy from the menu to copy the selected area to a new layer. Move the new layer over to the right to widen his chest. Use this method to widen his neck as well.

3 Target all of the layers that make up the left side and then choose Merge Layers from the Layers Palette menu to merge them into a single layer. These layers are merged so that we can apply the liquify filter to his entire left side.

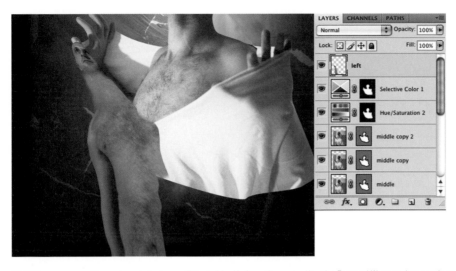

10 With your merged layer targeted, choose Filter>Liquify from the menu. Use the Forward Warp tool to gently push pixels around. The idea here is to reshape the left side so that it looks like it is being stretched or pushed. You'll want to warp his face so that it looks as if his hand is pushing through it. Also, remember to use the Reconstruct tool to undo anything that gets pushed too far and looks out of place. Take your time with this and press OK to apply the filter when you're satisfied.

Looking into the liquify effect

Here are some helpful hints for creating a convincing stretch effect within the liquify filter.

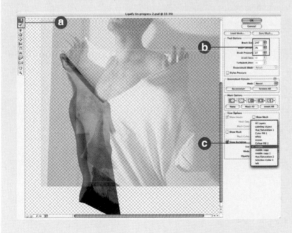

a You don't need to use any bloat or twirl functions to achieve a convincing effect. The Forward Warp tool is simple, yet it allows you a fair amount of control when pushing the pixels around so that you can get things looking exactly the way you want them to. The Reconstruct tool is there to remove anything you do that appears too drastic. A good method of working is to toggle back and forth between these tools as you go.

b Less is often more when it comes to liquify. Try using a large brush size combined with a low density and pressure setting. When you set up the tool like this, it is possible to slowly build up the effect. You'll have to paint areas over and over before things go too far and the effects look unrealistic.

c Because we want the final result to look as if it belongs in the scene, it is useful to enable the Show Backdrop option. You can choose which layers to display and how opaque to make them. Try choosing one of the main figure layers as a background, rather than showing all layers, to reduce the onscreen clutter as you work.

11 Reduce the opacity of your layer so that
you can see the background through it. Select
the Pen tool and then draw a path that will
define the edge of the left side. Having the
background partially visible as you work will
aid you in making the shape of his left side
look as if it belongs within the scene. When your
path is closed, choose Layer>Vector Mask>
Current Path from the menu to clip the layer with
your path.

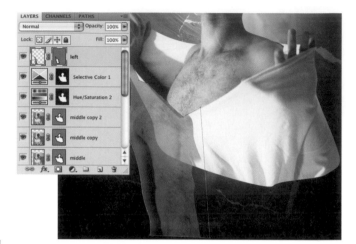

 **Why merge?**

Ideally, the best way to combine layers
is to convert them to a smart object.
That way, everything remains editable.
Although you can apply smart filters
like Gaussian Blur to a smart object,
the liquify filter cannot be applied
to smart object. That is why, in this
instance, we've merged all of the layers
that make up the left side before the
liquify filter was used. If you're worried
about making a mistake, duplicate your
layer before using the filter. Keep the
duplicate in the Layers palette with the
visibility disabled. That way, if you want
to revert the layer to its original state
at any point, you have a backup copy.

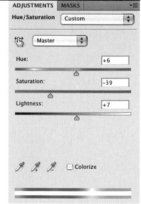

12 Return the opacity of your layer to 100% and then duplicate
it. Change the blending mode of the duplicate layer to overlay
and duplicate it too. Change the blending mode of your second
duplicate layer to screen and reduce the opacity to 38%. Hold
down the Control(PC)/Command(Mac) key and click on the
layer's vector mask to load it as a selection. With this selection
active, create a new hue/saturation adjustment layer. Set the hue
to +6, the saturation to −39, and increase the lightness to 7.

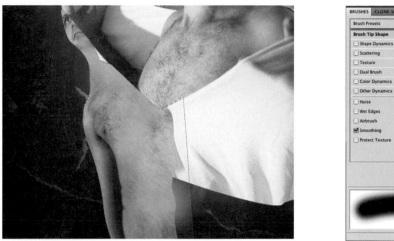

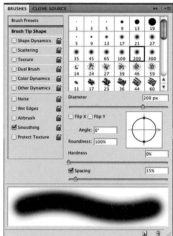

13 Generate a selection from one of the vector masks attached to any layer that is used to make up his left side. Create a new layer at the top of the Layers palette. Select the Brush tool. In the Brushes palette, choose a large, soft, round Brush Tip preset. Disable all dynamic functions except the Smoothness option. Sample a light skin color from an underlying layer and then paint, using a low opacity setting of around 15%, on this layer to smooth out the skin on the underlying layers. It is beneficial to have the appearance of smooth skin when combining two halves of the body.

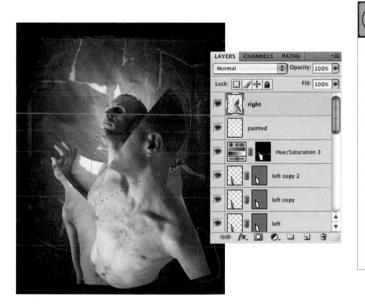

Use your discretion

No matter how closely you follow along, remember that things rarely look identical each time the same image is created. You'll need to follow along closely here, but you'll also need a willingness to improvise. For instance, on this page, it is unlikely that after transforming the right half of his body that it will be identical to what you see here. That is fine; just tailor the instructions to fit what is happening on your screen. Every transformation and hand-drawn selection border will differ slightly.

14 Open up the right.jpg file. In the Paths palette, load the existing path as a selection and then copy the contents of the selection. Return to your working file and paste the copied selection contents in as a new layer. Use Free-Transform to resize, reshape, and position the right half of his body where it belongs. Now his chest looks good, but other parts of the layer do not. To remedy this, use the Lasso to draw a rough selection around his head. Hold down the Shift key and draw another selection around the right side of his arm.

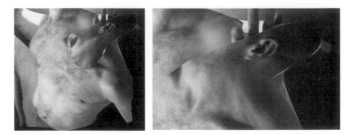

15 Choose Layer>Layer Mask>Hide Selection from the menu. Now, although these parts of the layer are masked and no longer visible, they are still there. Target the layer instead of the mask in the Layers palette. Use the Lasso tool to draw a selection around the head and neck on this layer. Then choose Layer>New>Layer Via Copy from the menu to create a new layer that contains the contents of the selection. Use Free-Transform to reshape and reposition the contents of the new layer. Add a layer mask and then use a soft brush or a series of gradients within the layer mask to hide any hard edges.

Here we go again

To construct the right side of his body, you simply need to repeat a few familiar procedures over and over again.

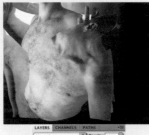

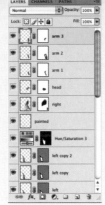

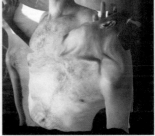

1 Use the previous method of making a selection, creating a new layer via copy, and then transforming and masking to build up a series of layers for the right side of his body. Use sections of his arm and chest as you see fit.

2 Target all of the layers that make up his right side in the Layers palette and then choose Merge Layers from the Layers Palette menu to merge them into a single layer. With the new merged layer targeted, launch the liquify filter.

3 As you did with the other side, use the Forward Warp tool to gently move the pixels around. Enable the Show Backdrop option to ensure that what you're doing will work within the scene. Press OK to apply the filter.

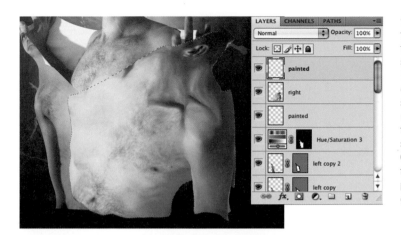

16 Create a new layer at the top of the Layers palette. Select the Brush tool. And then, as you did with the left side, use a soft, round brush tip with a low opacity setting to paint over areas of his skin. Use the Eyedropper tool to sample light areas of the skin on the underlying layer and then paint it onto this area using a very low opacity setting. When you're finished painting, Control(PC)/Command(Mac)-click on the merged layer underneath the new paint layer in the Layers palette to generate a selection from it.

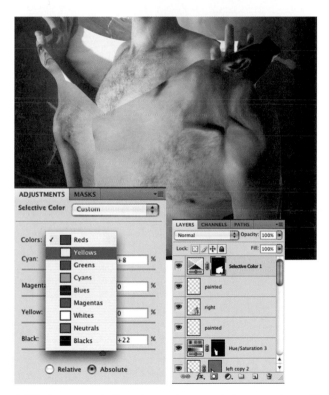

 Seeing through layers

When you are creating one side of his body from a number of copied components on a series of layers, it is good practice to get used to temporarily reducing the opacity of various layers as you work. This will allow you to see through certain layers and know how your positioning is working in relation to underlying layers. Reduce the opacity of the layer you're working with, transform it, position it, and then when you're satisfied that it works with the underlying layers, return it to full opacity. This method is very effective, use it often.

17 With the current selection active, create a new selective color adjustment layer. From the Colors menu, one at a time, choose the reds, yellows, neutrals, and blacks. Each time you choose a color, edit the cyan, magenta, yellow, and black sliders to make that particular color component match the left side. You can return to previous colors as you go. This is a very visual and intuitive adjustment, so be certain to pay attention to what is happening in the image window as you go.

18 Target all of the layers that comprise his right side: the liquified layer, the painted layer, and the adjustment layer. Add them to a new group. Target the new group in the Layers palette. Choose the Pen tool and draw a closed path that will define the area of his right side. When you've closed the path, choose Layer>Vector Mask>Current Path from the menu to convert your path to a vector mask that clips the contents of the group.

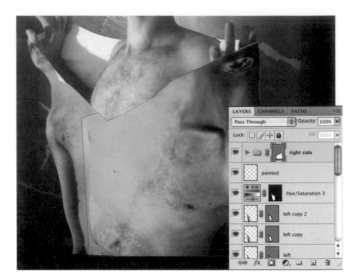

ⓘ Hiding vector masks

If you wish to edit a vector mask, you can do so at any point by using the Direct Selection tool. However, there will be times when editing a vector mask that it would be beneficial to see what layer content lies hidden outside the boundaries of the mask. To hide the effects of a vector mask, Shift-click on it in the Layers palette or click in the Disable/Enable Mask button at the bottom of the Masks palette. A red "x" will appear over the mask thumbnail and it will be disabled in the image window. To reactivate the mask, Shift-click on it in the Layers palette or click on the Disable/Enable Mask button at the bottom of the Masks palette again.

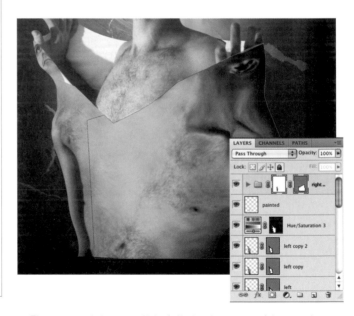

19 The vector mask does a good job of clipping the contents of the group; however, the area at the left where the right side meets the left side needs something smoother. Click the Create Layer Mask button at the bottom of the Layers palette to add a layer mask to the group in addition to the existing vector mask. Select the Gradient tool. Use a black foreground color, the Radial option, and the Foreground to Transparent preset to create a series of gradients within the new mask. Soften the area where the two sides of his chest overlap.

PART FOUR: Enhancing the central figure

20 Target all of the layers that make up his left side and add them to a new group as well. This will help to keep things in a logical order within the Layers palette. Control(PC)/Command(Mac)-click on an adjustment layer mask or vector mask thumbnail attached to any of your middle-figure layers in the Layers palette. This will generate a selection from the contents of the mask. Create a new layer and move it below the left- and right-side groups in the Layers palette. Choose lighten from the list of blending modes in the Layer palette's blending mode pop-up menu.

 Hiding selection borders

When painting over dark areas like this, working within a selection border is essential in ensuring that you don't stray onto the background. However, staring at the marching ants while you work can get distracting. Typing Control(PC)/Command(Mac)-h will hide your selection border. When the selection border is hidden, the same keyboard command will reveal it again.

21 Select the Brush tool. Choose a large, soft, round Brush Tip preset. Disable any dynamic functions but be certain to leave the Smoothness option enabled. Set the opacity very low to around 15–20%. With the new layer targeted, sample a light color from the middle figure's skin by holding down the Alt(PC)/Option(Mac) key to temporarily access the Eyedropper, and then clicking. Let go of the key and begin to paint over a darker area within the selection. Use this method to sample a variety of light colors and paint over dark regions, primarily the head and right arm, within the selection. Vary brush size and opacity as needed.

22 Create a new layer and select the Blur tool. Ensure that the new layer is targeted and set the strength of the Blur tool to 100%. In the Tool Options bar, enable the Sample All Layers option. Use a soft, round Brush Tip preset and paint over areas within the currently active selection on the new layer that, although already smoothed somewhat by paint on the underlying layer, still shows some of the grain from the original photograph. Now switch to the Smudge tool, set the strength to around 25%, and enable the Sample All Layers option. Use a similar Brush Tip preset to gently smudge areas within the active selection. Use numerous small strokes to resemble oil painting techniques.

 Smudge painting

When you are painting over areas of his face, neck, and shoulders with the Smudge tool, you must be willing to vary the tool options as you go. Reduce the size of your brush in areas like those around his eyes, so that you don't paint over areas that provide essential details. Also, if things are looking too fluid, try reducing the strength of the tool. You want to gently build up the effect by using multiple, gentle strokes. Working in this manner is what will allow you to simulate the blended quality of oil painting.

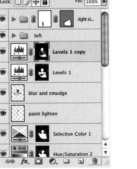

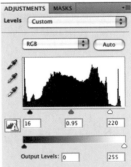

23 With the current selection active, create a new levels adjustment layer by clicking on the Levels button in the Adjustments palette. Leave the channel set to RGB and then drag the left and right input levels sliders toward the center of the histogram to increase the contrast. Now target the adjustment layer's mask and use the Radial Gradient tool to draw black to transparent gradients within the mask to soften the effect in areas where the contrast is too drastic. Duplicate the layer to intensify the adjustment, and continue to mask even more areas of this adjustment layer with similar gradients.

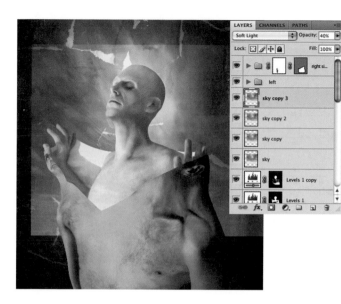

24 Open up the sky.jpg file, select all, and copy. Paste the copied sky image into your working file as a new layer. Position the sky layer on the canvas so that it overlaps his head and shoulders entirely. Reduce the opacity of the layer to 40% and change the blending mode to overlay. Duplicate the layer, return the blending mode to normal, and reduce the opacity of the duplicate layer to 11%. Now duplicate this layer, and then change the blending mode to luminosity. Again, duplicate this layer and then change the blending mode to soft light and increase the layer opacity to 40%.

 Duplicating and altering

As you create the effect of the sky overlapping his head and shoulders, it may seem like an awful lot of duplicate layers. However, working in this manner is a very intuitive and artistic way to get the results you're after. It really is as simple as trying different modes and opacity settings, one at a time, until you've found the combination of layers that works best. Also, remember that by keeping all of the layers separate, you can tweak individual layers at any point later on.

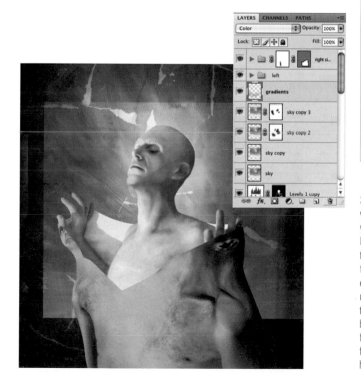

25 This may seem like a lot of duplication, but you'll certainly see the results take shape as you follow along. Finally, duplicate the top sky layer one last time. Change the blending mode to color and reduce the opacity to 27%. Feel free to add masks to individual sky layers and edit them as you've edited previous layer masks, using the Gradient tool to remove areas that are too prominent. Create a new layer with a color blending mode, and sample a light yellow color from within the image. Create a series of radial, foreground to transparent gradients overlapping his chest area.

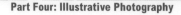

26 Create a new selective color adjustment layer. Increase the amount of cyan and black in both the neutral and black color components. Create a new layer and change the blending mode to multiply. Use the Brush tool to paint a soft, black brush stroke on this layer in the area where his stretched skin overlaps his chest, creating a shadow effect. Use an extremely low opacity setting so that the result is very slight. If your shadow still appears too prominent, reduce the layer opacity.

Add some internal texture

Use the first source image as your resource to make the inside of his skin look at home within this highly textured scene.

1 Use the Pen tool, set to create paths, with the Add to Path Area option enabled, to create a series of closed path components within a single path. Carefully trace all of the areas where you can see the inside of his skin.

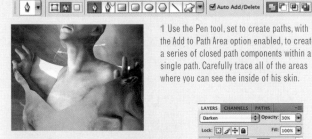

2 Load the path as a selection and then open up the background.psd file again. Use the Rectangular Marquee to select a section of the painting and copy it. Return to your working file and choose Edit>Paste Into to paste it into your selection.

3 Change your layer blending mode to darken and reduce the opacity to 30%. Duplicate the layer and change the blending mode to color. Increase the opacity to 35% and Control(PC)/Command(Mac)-click the layer mask thumbnail to generate a selection from the mask contents.

27 With your current selection active, create a new layer. Target this layer, set the foreground color to black, and select the Brush tool. Paint some very faint black shadows inside of the selection border where it needs to be darker to look realistic. Use a similar Brush Tip preset and opacity setting as you did when you created the previous shadow against his chest. With your current layer targeted, hold down the Shift key and also target the bottom sky layer. This also targets all of the layers in-between. Choose Layer>New>Group From Layers from the menu.

 Grouping layers

When you have a number of layers targeted within the Layers palette, a quick way to add them to a group is to type Control(PC)/Command(Mac)-g on the keyboard.

PART FIVE: Creating secondary elements

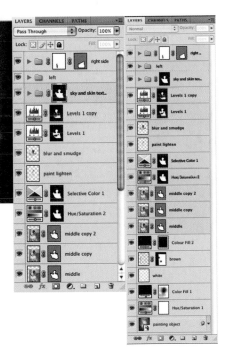

28 Hold down the Control(PC)/Command(Mac) key and click on an adjustment layer mask or vector mask thumbnail belonging to any of the middle-figure layers in the Layers palette. This will generate a selection from the contents of the mask. With the current selection active, target your new group in the Layers palette and then click on the Create Layer Mask button at the bottom of the Layers palette. This will mask the group so that nothing extends onto the background. Target this group as well as all of the other groups and layers that work together to create the main figure.

29 When you've targeted the layers and groups within the Layers palette, right-click(PC)/Control-click(Mac) on the area to the right of any targeted layer's thumbnails. A pop-up menu will appear. Choose Convert to Smart Object from the pop-up menu. Ensure that you are not clicking on a layer thumbnail or a layer mask thumbnail, or you will access a different pop-up menu that does not offer this function.

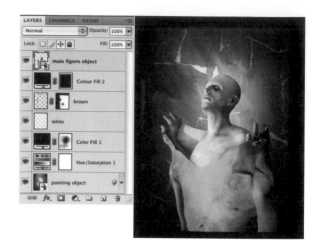

Adding texture

Paste imagery into alpha channels and channel-based selections to build up textured areas within the background of the image.

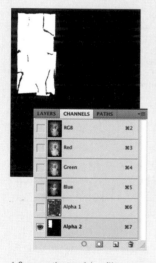

1 Open up the torn1.jpg file. Copy the contents of the file and then create a new alpha channel in the Channels palette of your working file. Paste the copied image into your new channel and load it as a selection.

2 Keep this selection active and then open up the texture.jpg file. Copy the contents of this file and return to the working file. With the current selection active, choose Paste Into from the Edit menu. Use the Move tool to reposition the layer within the mask.

3 Change the layer blending mode to multiply and drag it beneath the main figure smart object in the Layers palette. Duplicate the layer and change the blending mode to overlay. Duplicate this duplicated layer and change the blending mode to color.

30 Add these three texture layers to a new group. Add a mask to the group and then edit the mask by adding radial, black to transparent gradients into the mask. Create the gradients in the area where the texture falls behind his hand to blend it into the background. Now open up the man.psd file. Use the Move tool to drag the layer into your working file as a new layer and place it over your new textured background on the canvas. Position him close to the main figure's hand.

31 Enable the transparency lock for this layer in the Layers palette and then select the Smudge tool. Use the Smudge tool to paint over the figure on this layer, smoothing him and giving him a painted appearance. Use similar methods and tool options as you did when you painted over the main figure's head and shoulders earlier. Drag this layer into the textured layers group so that this layer is masked by the group's mask as well.

Smart objects

Onc of the main advantages to using smart objects is that they always remain editable. Right now, there are two smart objects in this file. One is the background object and the other is the main figure object. A quick way to edit either object is to simply double-click on the smart object thumbnail in the Layers palette. This will open a new document window containing the layered version of the smart object. Make any changes and then save. Close the file and you'll see the smart object in your working file is updated automatically.

32 Open up the sky.jpg file, use the Rectangular Marquee to select a small section of the sky, and copy it. Paste the copied section of sky into your working file as a new layer. Drag it into the texture group, beneath the figure layer in the Layers palette. Position it so that it shows through the hole in the figure. If there are any areas that extend beyond the edge of the figure, erase them, or select and delete them. Use the Pen tool to draw a path that indicates thickness, defining the inner sides of the opening.

Adding dimension

Create visible, inner sides of the opening, giving the figure a sense of thickness and depth.

1 Load your path as a selection and create a new layer. Drag the new layer above the man layer within the group. Sample a gray color from the figure via the Eyedropper tool and then type Alt(PC)/Option(Mac)-Delete to fill the selection.

2 Enable the transparency lock for the layer and use the Polygonal Lasso to draw a selection border around the inner side wall, isolating it from the inner bottom wall. Use the Brush tool to paint black into areas that require shading.

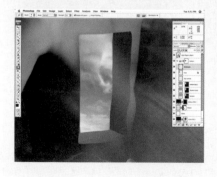

3 Choose Select>Inverse from the menu. Now paint some black shading onto the bottom area within the inverted selection. Deselect and then use the Smudge tool on this layer to smudge the painted areas so they look similar to the figure in terms of style.

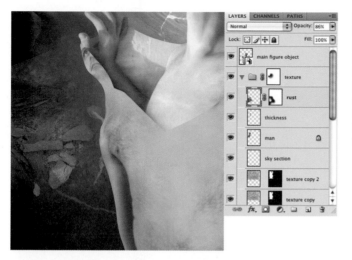

33 Open up the rust.psd file. Use the Move tool to drag the rusty image into the working file as a new layer. Because the layer currently targeted in your working file is within the texture group, the new layer will be placed on top of it within the group. Position the contents of the layer to the left side of the canvas. Add a mask to the layer and create a series of black to transparent radial gradients within the mask to hide any hard edges.

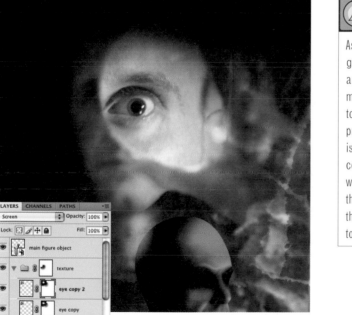

Unmasking layer content

As you add black to transparent gradients within your layer masks, there are bound to be occasions when you mask more of a layer than you want to. A quick way to unmask areas is to press the "d" key. When a layer mask is targeted, this will set the foreground color to white. Click and drag to create white to transparent gradients within the mask to gently reveal masked areas that were accidentally hidden by black to transparent gradients.

34 Open up the eye.psd file. Drag the layer into your working file and position it on the canvas in the upper left-hand corner. Add a mask to the layer and create a number of black to transparent radial gradients within the mask to hide the hard edges of the image. Change the layer blending mode to hard light and reduce the opacity to 61%. Duplicate the layer, change the blending mode to luminosity, and increase the opacity a little. Duplicate this layer too, and then change the blending mode to screen. Increase the opacity to 100%.

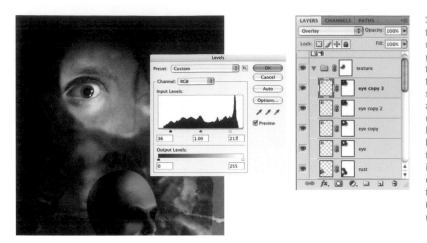

35 Target the layer's mask in the Layers palette and create more black to transparent radial gradients within the mask until the only visible part of the layer is the eye and the area immediately surrounding it. Duplicate this layer and change the blending mode to overlay. Target your new duplicate layer (not the mask) and choose Image>Adjustments>Levels from the menu. Drag the left and right input levels sliders toward the center of the histogram to increase the contrast. Then drag the left (black) output levels slider to the right to lighten the darkest areas.

PART SIX: Finishing touches

Paste in a painting
Create a custom alpha channel to use as the basis for a selection, which will mask a previously completed painting.

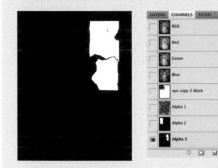

1 Open up the torn2.jpg file. Select and copy the contents of this file, then create a new alpha channel in your working file. Paste the copied image into your channel and then load the channel as a selection. Return to the Layers palette.

2 Open up the painting.jpg file, select all, and copy. Return to your working file. Ensure that your selection is still active and then choose Edit>Paste Into from the menu to paste the image into your file as a masked layer.

3 Target your new layer (not the mask) in the Layers palette and use the Move tool to reposition the layer content within the mask on the canvas area. Target the mask and add gradients, producing a soft blending effect.

36 In the Layers palette, Control(PC)/Command(Mac)-click on the main figure smart object to generate a selection from its contents. Choose Select>Inverse from the menu and target the aforementioned smart object. Open up the fence.jpg file and copy it. Return to the working file. With the inverted selection still active, and the figure smart object targeted in the Layers palette, choose Edit>Paste Into from the menu. After pasting, move the new layer's contents down within the layer mask. Target the new layer's mask in the Layers palette and then draw a linear, black to transparent gradient within the mask, from the middle of the canvas downward, to create a soft fade effect.

Adding final surface textures

Create an aged and tactile feeling by adding some hand-written text alongside scanned, distressed paper texture.

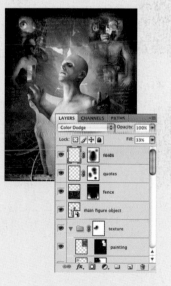

1 Open up the quotes.jpg file. Select all and copy. Return to your working file. Create a new alpha channel and paste the copied contents into it. Load the new channel as a selection. Create a new layer in the Layers palette.

2 Fill the active selection on your new layer with white. Change the blending mode to hard light and reduce the opacity considerably. Deselect, add a layer mask, and create a number of radial, black to transparent gradients within the mask to fade certain areas.

3 Open up the folds.jpg file and repeat the same process. Paste it into a new channel and load it as a selection. Fill the selection with white on a new layer. Mask it and then edit the mask, to mask out where folds overlap key images. Change the blending mode to color dodge.

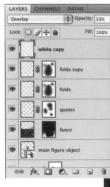

37 Duplicate this layer and change the blending mode of the duplicate layer to hard light. Reduce the opacity of the layer to 33%. Now, navigate down to the bottom layers in the Layers palette. Sitting above the bottom smart object, an adjustment layer, and a solid color layer is the white torn paper texture layer you created earlier in this chapter. You previously loaded a channel as a selection and filled it with white on this layer. Duplicate this layer and drag it to the top of the stack in the Layers palette. Reduce the opacity of the layer to 33%.

Removing sharp edges

If you find that the edges of your figure look too sharp, there is a way to soften them. Create a new layer above your head layer, but beneath the top four texture layers in the Layers palette. Target your new layer and disable the visibility of the four texture layers above it. Use the Blur tool, with the Sample All Layers option enabled, to paint over any sharp areas on your new layer. When you're finished, enable the visibility of the texture layers once again.

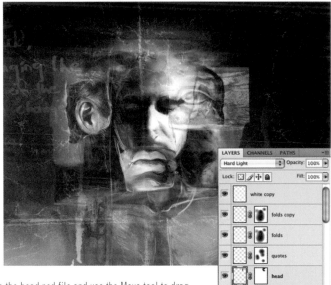

38 Now, add one last element to the image. Open up the head.psd file and use the Move tool to drag it into your working file as a new layer. Position it over the face of the painting at the upper right and change the blending mode to hard light. Add a layer mask and use the Gradient tool to edit the mask, gently blending the layer contents into the imagery beneath it. Move this head layer below the top four layers in the Layers palette so that the surface texture and quotes reside above it.

Now that you're finished, take a moment and look at some of the photographs that were used. These really are quite amateurish in terms of lighting, exposure, and focus. But what makes them valuable resources is that they provide excellent gesture, overall detail, contrast, and, in the case of the fence, texture. As a Photoshop artist, you need to be able to see beyond the traditional photographer's approach to capturing things. You need to plan and be able to spot the potential within your images, bearing in mind that each photo is a valuable starting point rather than an end in itself. Less than perfect images can be excellent resources when used as building blocks for photographic illustrations.

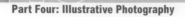
Try substituting other materials

Here, you can see that the head photograph was painted over using the same methods used to smooth the main figure on the previous pages. The bursting head effect was created in a similar manner to the tearing body effect, except instead of a torn T-shirt, a torn piece of paper was used.

A mainstream approach

Sometimes the practical, everyday use of certain techniques is not immediately evident. Especially when the subject matter created is so surreal. However, here is a fine example of these techniques employed for a real-world purpose. This image was originally commissioned for the cover of a Canadian health magazine. After that, it was used on posters and promotional material for a symposium on skin care held at a Toronto teaching hospital.

Chapter 20

The Cover Challenge

Here we are at the end of the book. Although it is not necessary to read this book in a linear manner, I think that this is a logical place to wrap it all up with a contest. Chances are you've had a good look at the cover image by now and if you've read through some of the chapters in this book, especially those in the final section, you've likely gained some insight into how it was created. So here's your chance to exercise what you've learned so far; show off a little and win a prize.

The cover challenge is simple: do your best at re-creating what I've done on the cover of this book. All of the files used are available for download in the contest section of the Web site. The cover illustration is a photography-based image, and all of the info contained in the chapters in the final section of this book will prove helpful as you approach the task of re-creating it. For details like prize info, deadlines, submission guidelines, as well as the resource files, please visit the contest section of www.creativephotoshopthebook.com.

I am looking forward to seeing what you will come up with. Good luck!

Here is a glimpse at the resource files that are available for download. The featured image is the culmination of all of these photographic resources. Everything I used to create it is right here.

Index